Global Youth?

This innovative collection of studies by international youth researchers critically addresses questions of 'global' youth, incorporating material from diverse regions such as Sydney, Tehran, Dakar, Paris and Bogotá. These studies showcase previously unpublished research on youth cultures beyond the English-speaking world and advance our knowledge about young people in different countries by exploring specific local youth cultures while mediating global mass media and consumption trends. By tracing some subaltern 'youth landscapes', telling some subaltern 'youth stories' previously invisible in predominantly western cultural studies and theorizing about youth, the chapters here serve as a refutation of the colonialist discourse of cultural globalization.

Bringing together an internationally diverse group of researchers in the field, this volume presents the first comprehensive review of global youth cultures, practices and identities.

Global Youth? will be a valuable addition for those interested in youth studies, cultural studies and sociology.

Pam Nilan is Senior Lecturer in the School of Humanities and Social Sciences at the University of Newcastle, Australia. She is currently writing a book on Australian youth and is conducting research with youth in Indonesia and Fiji.

Carles Feixa is Professor of Anthropology at the University of Lleida, Spain. His recent books include *Culturas Juveniles en España* (Madrid, 2004) and *Jovens na America Latina* (São Paulo, 2004). He is Vice-President of ISA Research Committee 34 – Sociology of Youth.

Global Youth?
Hybrid identities, plural worlds

**Edited by Pam Nilan and
Carles Feixa**

LONDON AND NEW YORK

First published 2006
by Routledge
2 Park Square, Milton Park, Abingdon, Oxon OX14 4RN

Simultaneously published in the USA and Canada
by Routledge
270 Madison Ave, New York, NY 10016

Routledge is an imprint of the Taylor & Francis Group, an informa business

© 2006 Pam Nilan and Carles Feixa for selection and editorial matter; the contributors for individual chapters

Typeset in Bembo by The Running Head Limited, Cambridge
Printed and bound in Great Britain by MPG Books Ltd, Bodmin

All rights reserved. No part of this book may be reprinted or reproduced or utilized in any form or by any electronic, mechanical, or other means, now known or hereafter invented, including photocopying and recording, or in any information storage or retrieval system, without permission in writing from the publishers.

British Library Cataloguing in Publication Data
A catalogue record for this book is available from the British Library

Library of Congress Cataloging in Publication Data
Global youth?: hybrid identities, plural worlds / Pam Nilan and Carles Feixa.
   p. cm.
   Includes bibliographical references and index.
Youth—Social conditions. 2. Youth—Social life and customs.
3. Globalization—Social aspects. 4. Popular culture. 5. Subculture.
I. Nilan, Pam. II. Feixa, Carles.
   HQ796.G5493 2006
   305.23509'0511—dc22
                                                 2006003787

ISBN10: 0–415–37070–1 (hbk)
ISBN10: 0–415–37071–X (pbk)
ISBN10: 0–203–03052–4 (ebk)

ISBN13: 978–0–415–37070–7 (hbk)
ISBN13: 978–0–415–37071–4 (pbk)
ISBN13: 978–0–203–03052–3 (ebk)

Contents

List of illustrations vii
List of contributors ix
Preface xi

Introduction: youth hybridity and plural worlds 1
PAM NILAN AND CARLES FEIXA

1 European youth cultures in a post-colonial world: British Asian underground and French hip-hop music scenes 14
RUPA HUQ

2 'I am English too': Francophone youth hybridities in Canada 32
CHRISTINE DALLAIRE

3 Ingenious: emerging hybrid youth cultures in western Sydney 53
MELISSA BUTCHER AND MANDY THOMAS

4 The social life of Japan's adolechnic 72
TODD JOSPEH MILES HOLDEN

5 The reflexive youth culture of devout Muslim youth in Indonesia 91
PAM NILAN

6 Youth subcultures in post-Revolution Iran: an alternative reading 111
MAHMOOD SHAHABI

7 **Music is the connection: youth cultures in Colombia**   130
GERMÁN MUÑOZ AND MARTHA MARÍN

8 *Tribus urbanas* and *chavos banda*: **being a punk in Catalonia and Mexico**   149
CARLES FEIXA

9 **Bboys: hip-hop culture in Dakar, Sénégal**   167
ABDOULAYE NIANG

10 **Global? local? multi-level identifications among contemporary skinheads in France**   186
YOURA PETROVA

Postscript: global youth and transnationalism: the next generation   205
CARLES FEIXA AND PAM NILAN

Index   213

Illustrations

Figures

2.1 Acadian Games drawing representing Acadian identity with a focus on family and friends, pride in speaking another language, a representative flag, deportation, a territory and traditional music — 42
2.2 Franco-Ontarian Games drawing about the francophone community — 43
2.3 Alberta Francophone Games drawing representing the inclusion of French mother tongue speakers and speakers of French as a second language in the francophone community, while excluding people who 'are completely English' — 45
8.1 Punks in *el Chopo* street market, Mexico City, 1991 — 163
9.1 Docta's graffiti at Maurice Delafosse High School — 173
9.2 Map of Dakar showing zones of study — 174

Tables

2.1 Linguistic characteristics of participants at selected francophone games — 47
5.1 Favourite television shows of 17- to 18-year-old Indonesian youth, 2004 — 99
5.2 Favourite films of 17- to 18-year-old Indonesian youth, 2004 — 100
5.3 Favourite music groups or performers of 17- to 18-year-old Indonesian youth, 2004 — 101
9.1 Language resources of posse members — 177
9.2 Means by which posse members met each other — 178

Contributors

Melissa Butcher has worked with young people in the formal and non-formal education sectors in Europe, India and Australia. She researches and publishes in the areas of globalization, migration, culture and identity. She is currently an Honorary Research Fellow at the Research Institute for Asia and the Pacific, University of Sydney, Australia.

Christine Dallaire is Assistant Professor in the School of Human Kinetics at the University of Ottawa. Her research focuses on the discursive production of minority identities through sport and games. She also works on health, and risks associated with physical activities.

Carles Feixa holds a PhD from the University of Barcelona and is Professor of Anthropology at Lleida University, Spain. His most recent books are *Culturas Juveniles en España* (Institut de Juventud, Madrid, 2004) and *Jovens na America Latina* (Escrituras/CEBRIJ, São Paulo, 2004) as co-author. He is Vice-President of ISA Research Commitee 34 – Sociology of Youth.

Todd Joseph Miles Holden is Professor of Mediated Sociology in the Department of Multi-Cultural Societies, Graduate School of International Cultural Studies at Tohoku University, Japan. He is currently completing books on media in the Asian context, and gender in Japanese advertising.

Rupa Huq lectures in sociology at Kingston University, UK. Her book *Beyond Subculture* came out in August 2005. Her extra curricular life includes politics – she has stood in both European and UK general elections – and motherhood – her son Rafi was born in 2004.

Martha Marín is an independent Colombian researcher and documentarist. Her research interests are in youth cultures seen from the aesthetic dimension, and in urban dance. She is co-author of the book *Secretos de Mutantes* (Central University Bogotá-DIUC Press, 2002).

Germán Muñoz lectures in the doctoral programme in Childhood and Youth at the University of Manizales, Colombia. He is currently conducting research on youth policy in communication at the Central University in Bogotá. He is co-author of the book *Secretos de Mutantes* (2002).

Abdoulaye Niang is Lecturer at Université Gaston Berger, Sénégal. He is a Junior Researcher in the National Working Group on the Music Industry, affiliated with the Council for the Development of Social Science Research in Africa, which publishes his research.

Pam Nilan is Senior Lecturer in the School of Humanities and Social Sciences at the University of Newcastle, Australia. She is currently writing a book on Australian youth and is conducting research with youth in Indonesia and Fiji.

Youra Petrova lectures in sociology at Paris XII – Créteil University, and is a Researcher at INSEP (National Institute of Sports), working principally on youth subcultural groups such as punks and skinheads. She completed her sociological studies at École des Hautes Études en Sciences Sociales/CADIS in Paris and has worked with CNRS-IRESCO/GSRL.

Mahmood Shahabi is Assistant Professor of Sociology at the University of Allameh Tabatabaei, Tehran, Iran. His doctoral research was completed at Essex University in 1998. His research and teaching areas are sociology of youth, sociology of mass communication, and cultural studies. He is currently conducting research on personal beauty cultures and industries in Iran.

Mandy Thomas, an anthropologist, has undertaken extensive research on popular culture, social and political change, and hybrid identities in urban culturally diverse Australia and in Vietnam. She is presently Executive Director, Humanities and Creative Arts, Australian Research Council.

Preface

The book *Global Youth? Hybrid identities, plural worlds* is based on the 2002 International Sociological Association (ISA) Conference in Brisbane, Australia. This volume is organized in collaboration with the ISA Research Committee 34 – Sociology of Youth. The RC34 consists of an international, loosely connected community of researchers that communicates by way of diverse professional meetings, the RC34 website and the electronic International Bulletin of Youth Research (IBYR).

This book is intended to enhance awareness of the global youth research community and thereby to foster and further the exchange of knowledge and ideas related to youth research. The production of the book is also evidence of the global participation of youth researchers, many of whom are members of RC34. The previous president, Lynne Chisholm, with the executive board, put shape and form around the programme at the ISA 2002 World Congress. The intensive pre-planning of the sessions produced a sequence of papers which were of a good quality and commanded interest and attention. The diversity of papers cemented the intellectual benefits of the Congress, as people grappled with the divergent conditions of young people in different parts of the world and the theoretical and empirical traditions invoked to describe and explain them. 'Hybrid identities, plural worlds', organized by Pam Nilan and Carles Feixa was one of the 14 RC34 thematic sessions. All but two authors of the book are drawn from this session. The papers were developed and edited by Nilan and Feixa to produce this timely and important collection of articles.

The book gives an overview with interest lying in the social construction of young people's identities. The focus is on young people as creative social actors and on cultural consumption and social movements. The individual chapters provide more in-depth analysis of the 'performative practices' of cultural hybridity by young people as they negotiate forms of personal and group identity during the contemporary period of rapid social transformation that is of concern and interest across the world. The book will convince the reader that in youth culture the global eclipses the local. The representation of the hybrid cultures and plural worlds of contemporary youth is challenging. Young people create their own cultures distinct from, embedded in, or in opposition to, the dominant cultures. This book contributes to the evolution of distinctive forms of youth culture, in both global and local contexts. It gives youth workers, researchers and policy-makers a history and context for contemporary youth issues. Looking at issues in a global, international perspective deepens our understanding as well as gives us new ideas for how to approach and understand young people's interests.

This timely book supports the ISA RC34 work which attempts to establish youth studies as a distinct discipline within the social sciences. It is not only highly relevant to social scientists around the world, especially youth researchers, but also for practitioners and students in youth and community work, and for those responsible for developing youth policy.

Helena Helve
President 2002–6 of the International Sociological Association Research Committee 34 – Sociology of Youth

Introduction

Youth hybridity and plural worlds

Pam Nilan and Carles Feixa

Defining our terms

To introduce the reader to this edited collection, we define how the terms 'youth', 'hybridity' and 'plural worlds' are used here by the range of authors. By 'youth' we refer collectively to a wide chronological scale – young people of both sexes in the age range 12 to 35 (or even 10 to 30 in some countries). This age range indicates the extent to which the cultural age category of 'youth' has expanded to include some who are legally recognized elsewhere in society as children, and some who are legally recognized elsewhere in society as adults. In this book we are less concerned with official status, and more concerned with social and cultural practices in the life trajectories of young people. Our interest lies in the social construction of identity, in young people as creative social actors, in cultural consumption and social movements – the distinctiveness of local youth cultures in a globalized world.

'Hybridity' has been variously defined in social sciences and cultural studies, especially in post-colonial theorizing. Our use of the term in this volume – cultural creativity, the making of something new through the combination of existing things and patterns – can perhaps be expressed as follows:

> Terms of cultural engagement, whether antagonistic or affiliative, are produced performatively. The representation of difference must not be hastily read as the reflection of pre-given ethnic or cultural traits set in the fixed tablet of tradition. The social articulation of difference, from the minority perspective, is a complex, on-going negotiation that seeks to authorize cultural hybridities that emerge in moments of historical transformation.
>
> (Bhabha 1994: 2)

Another author who has explored the theoretical possibilities of the concept for analysing postmodern worlds is the Latin American scholar Néstor García Canclini in his essay *Culturas Híbridas* (1989). In contrast with other terms in the same semantic field, like mixture (related to racial exchanges), syncretism (related to religious exchanges) and creolization (related to linguistic exchanges), hybridity has less to say about cultural connotations, and more about power relationships.

> We are conscious that in this time of *postmodern dissemination* and democratic decentralization, we are still confronted by the growth of the most concentrated forms of power accumulation and *transnational centralization of culture* that humankind has ever seen. The study of the *hybrid cultural basis* of such power can allow us to understand the *oblique* paths, the abundance of *transactions*, where these forces act.
>
> (García Canclini 1995: 25; our emphasis)

On the one hand, hybridization is a process of cultural interactions between the local and the global, the hegemonic and the subaltern, the centre and the periphery. On the other hand, hybridization is a process of cultural transactions that reflects how global cultures are assimilated in the locality, and how non-western cultures impact upon the West. It is significant that García Canclini's work points to youth cultures as laboratories for hybrid cultures. He refers to graffiti and musical fusions, using ethnographies by Latin American youth researchers to illustrate the 'fragmented' visual and virtual cultures of young people (Reguillo 2001).

The chapters in this book describe the performative practices of cultural hybridity by young people as they negotiate forms of personal and group identity during the contemporary period of rapid social transformation sometimes described as globalization. The notion of hybridity here is also informed by Bannerji's inference that it involves, at least potentially, an 'emancipatory' use of culture (2000) in the face of globalizing power relations. Further illumination of the term is provided by Stuart Hall's 'recognition of a necessary heterogeneity and diversity; by a conception of "identity" which lives with and through, not despite, difference; by hybridity' (1993: 401–2).

Hybridity often connotes border-crossing, 'in between-ness', mobility, uncertainty and multiplicity. It thereby resonates with our term – 'plural worlds' – the constitution of youth subjectivity within a number of salient discourses. Perhaps the most interesting thing about the widespread academic perception that contemporary young people inhabit *plural* worlds is, that as far as most youth are concerned, they only inhabit one, highly complex, 'world'. What may seem even contradictory identity discourses to an older generation often do not seem so to youth, who pull upon a pastiche of sources in their local creative practices (Willis 1990). For example, urban middle-class Islamic youth in the chapters by Nilan and Shahabi can be interpreted as having a foot in two opposing camps – western consumerism and devout Islamic faith – but this can only be sustained as an interpretation from an outsider position. Drawing upon Bourdieu's notion of habitus, which theorizes the 'relationship between the conscious self and the unthought' (Lash 1994: 154), the notion of plural worlds here implies the late modern 'reflexive habitus' identified by Sweetman (2003; see also Adams 2003). Young middle-class

Islamic people in the example above negotiate between the apparently competing identity discourses on offer by filtering, synthesizing, judicious choice – generative dispositions which encode habitually reflective and reflexive processes. This emergent 'reflexive habitus' of youth was originally framed around class distinctions, so that if there are those who 'win' in the reflexivity stakes, there are also 'reflexivity losers' (Lash 1994: 120). However, it is also possible that the new emphasis on reflexivity – self-conscious invention and reinvention in the shaping of youth identities – is a much wider feature of global culture now, and all youth engage in it to a greater or lesser degree.

This brings us to our final definition – 'global'. The book title asks a question: 'global youth?' We are not convinced that as far as youth culture is concerned the global eclipses the local in the end. This book sets out to confirm that. By global of course, we refer to globalization, a term so overused as to exhaust definition. For our purposes, we refer to those aspects of cultural and economic globalization emanating from the cultural 'cores' that threaten to sweep away distinctive local practices and identity frames in favour of a homogenized set of consumption practices and ways to think about identity. We agree with many post-colonial theorists who point out that the 'globalization thesis' itself is just another colonial discourse, thinly disguising the idea of 'vanishing' cultures, implicitly incapable of competing with the cultural products of European civilization (Abou-El-Haj 1991). The chapters in this book serve as further refutation of the colonialist discourse of cultural globalization. Our purpose has been not only to trace some subaltern 'youth landscapes', but also to relate them to some subaltern 'youth histories' – and 'youth stories' – previously invisible in predominantly western cultural studies and theorizing about youth. Finally, the connection between 'hybridity', 'plural worlds' and 'globalization' reminds us that, in the information age, generational identities are de-localized. As cool-hunters know very well, and as all the studies included in this book imply, cultural innovation can emerge with similar force from the centre *and* from the periphery (Featherstone 1990; Nilan 2004).

About this book

The contributors to this book describe and analyse youth and youth cultures in 11 countries of the five continents: Europe (Spain, France, Britain), America (Canada, Mexico, Colombia), Asia (Iran, Indonesia, Japan), Africa (Sénégal) and Oceania (Australia). Some of these writers have not previously published their research in English. Yet while we find much that is predictably different in these culturally varied research findings, we also find much common ground. How can this be so? What have Muslim youth in Tehran got in common with second-generation migrant youth in Sydney and youth in Mexico City? Does this constitute proof of the so-called 'global teenager' – the colonialist discursive object of cultural globalization – identified above?

We think not. Common ground is constituted both in youth membership of an identifiable generation (Mannheim 1927), and in the vital hybridity of distinctive youth cultures. The form and content of global youth products, trends and social movements are certainly discernible in their collective cultural preferences and practices, yet these are synthesized extensively, and realized variously, at the local level. For example, the chapters by Huq, Shahabi, Niang, and Muñoz and Marín address, among other things, the global trend of rap or hip-hop music, and its local meanings for youth in Britain, France, Iran, Sénégal and Colombia. The significant global youth music/protest movement symbolized in punk is explored in the accounts of Feixa (Spain and Mexico), Petrova (France) and Shahabi (Iran). All three of the latter authors draw our attention to the emphatically *local* meanings of punk in geographically distant urban youth cultures. It has been claimed that cross-cultural popular music forms operate as a form of distinctive youth communication. As Chuck D of Public Enemy once famously quipped – 'rap is the CNN for young people all over the world' (1997: 256) – but this does not mean that young people all over the world have culturally become the same.

Each young person described in these largely ethnographic accounts positions him or herself in 'plural worlds' to a greater or lesser degree – reflexively constituting his or her subjectivity in a range of local, regional and global contemporary identity discourses. In some accounts these are ethnically or linguistically distinct groupings. Dallaire's research focuses on the bicultural/bilingual identity and leisure practices of French Canadian youth, while Butcher and Thomas investigate the bicultural/bilingual identity and socio-cultural practices of second-generation Australian migrant youth. In his chapter on adolechnics in Japan, Holden draws our attention to the engagement of young urban peer groups with the 'virtual' world of technologically-mediated youth culture practices. Shahabi's chapter on Tehran youth culture and Nilan's chapter on Islamist youth culture in Indonesia describe how the consumption practices of ostensibly devout youth look towards both the traditional and modern worlds of Asia. The chapters by Feixa and Petrova find the sometimes violent world of youth gangs in Spain, Mexico and France to be intertwined with global popular music forms and local politics at the same time.

Global youth and cross-cultural studies

As youth researchers or scholars with an interest in youth, we must be careful not to listen only to theories and modes of analysis that emanate from the metropolitan 'cores' of northern countries (Amin 1990; Connell 2005). If social science investigation of youth phenomena is to be rich and challenging, we need to pay attention to how specific youth cultures are described and analysed by social scientists from academies in the 'south', from what Wallerstein somewhat problematically refers to as the 'periphery'. Indeed, this has been an important aim of this book. At the same time though, all those writing about youth in this book have one important demographic fact in common. Even though we write about youth, we ourselves are no longer young. We do not share as age peers in the experiences and practices of the youth we write about, even though the contributors here all understand their subjects very well, often from years of intense ethnographic study, and often from prior active participation in youth cultures when they themselves were young. However, inevitably when we listen to, and try to interpret, the voices of young people now, we filter what they tell us and show us through first, an academic research lens, and secondly, through the lens of our own historical youth experiences, whatever they were. Acknowledging that 'even ethnographic research struggles to breach the representational world and deliver a truly embodied knowledge of young lives' (Nayak 2003: 3), we agree that representing the hybrid cultures and plural worlds of contemporary youth is challenging. Yet the contributors to this volume have done their best to 'hear' what some contemporary global youth are saying so that this book can convey those messages and meanings to a readership that, for the most part, will not be 'young' either. Another feature of this book is that most of the authors are natives of the country they study. They focus on their own societies.

In an edited collection such as this, certain decisions had to made about focus. In choosing to look intensively at socio-cultural hybridity, creative synthesis and pluralistic identities, we have not foregrounded important youth issues like gender and class, simply because there was no room to do so. Furthermore, in our analytical pre-occupation with urban youth phenomena we have tended to leave out rural youth, even though modernizing transformations are equally significant in the construction of rural youth as social actors (Feixa and González 2005). What the book does achieve though, is a polyphonic showcasing of analyses of youth culture written from a variety of positions in the academy, many of which access 'non-Anglo' theorists and writers. In that sense we believe that this book transcends the accepted canon of western interpretive paradigms. With some important exceptions, most social science literature about youth continues to be produced according to white western perceptions of reality, and western traditions of social and cultural analysis, which in the past have given an ethnocentric inflection to global youth studies. For example, perhaps the most serious misguided assumption about non-élite youth in developing countries is that, without exception, they make a very early entry to adult life in labour and sexual activities. This represents an analytical position rife with significant socio-historical omissions and theoretical shortcomings (Reguillo 2001; Caccia-Bava, Feixa and González 2004). In fact, their stories strongly illuminate the phenomena of accelerated modernization and cultural hybridization no less than the lives of youth in more privileged situations.

We consciously avoid the terminological debate about youth cultural dynamics following the seminal work of the Birmingham School. The concept of *subculture* has been replaced by other theoretically-informed concepts such as *clubcultures* (Thornton 1995), *neotribes* (Bennett 1999), *lifestyles* (Miles 2000), *post-subcultures* (Muggleton and Weinzierl 2003), *scenes* (Hesmondhalgh 2005), *networking* (Juris 2005), *cybercultures* and so on. Each new label illuminates some specific area of youth global trends (consumerism, embodiment, de-classing, de-territorialization, performance, transnationalism, digitalism, and so on). The idea has been to replace the original 'heroic' notion of resistant subcultures with less romantic approaches, originally inspired in part by Bourdieu's concepts of habitus and distinction, by Maffesoli's tribalism, by McRobbie's feminist critique and by Castells' informational theories. These latter-day approaches certainly better reflect the fluidity, variety and hybridity present in contemporary youth cultures (Amit-Talai and Wulff 1995). Nevertheless, most of these new terms for youth cultures are based on ethnographic data and theorizing taking place in only a few western capital cities. In contrast, the chapters in this book propose some medium-level concepts, based on local and national knowledges, most of them non-western, that can be used in cross-cultural investigations. The seemingly infinite expansion of youth as a concept (the end of bounded age cohorts, the end of *rites de passage*), combined with the simultaneous extermination of young people as subjects (the end of a linear model of 'work', the end of the corporeality of youth – anyone rich enough can be 'young'), produces 'fragmented, hybrid and transcultural (youth) cultures' (Canevacci 2000: 29). Youth cultures without youth?

Global youth and global culture

Although, as indicated above, we refute any notion that homogenized global youth cultural practices are slavishly followed at the local level, that the primary youth 'world' is one of commodified, largely western (English language) culture, we do assume that as a generation, all youth are caught up to some extent in the 'network society' (Castells 1996, 1997). The young people studied here obtain their information, often their inspiration, from global sources. Castells maintains that this encodes a 'systematic disjunction between the local and the global for most individuals and social groups', creating a kind of crisis in 'identity politics' (1997: 11). The resulting 'ontological' insecurity (Giddens 1991: 185) encourages young people towards forms of group self-invention in lifestyle and consumption practices, using whatever cultural and linguistic materials are available.

In the era of 'manufactured' risks (Beck 1992; Giddens 2002: 31) the emerging entrepreneurial self finds 'meaning in existence by shaping its life through acts of choice' (Rose 1992: 142). Chisholm implies Touraine's terminology when she claims that 'the social actor, individually and collectively, returns to centre stage' (2003; Touraine 2003). Agreeing with Giddens (2002), she proposes that 'individuals come to experience social life as more contingent, fragile and uncertain. The construction of subjectivities and identities, too, becomes attuned to greater openness and hybridity'

(Chisholm 2003: 2). The modern process of 'individualization' means having few options but to live a highly reflexive life which opens towards a number of future possibilities. To do this requires the active creation of a self-identity, a very different process to taking self-identity from the social and cultural certainties of the traditional past. In the proliferation of apparent consumer choices and popular culture practices, mediated by global technology, 'both pluralisation and individualisation processes have exerted pressures on the standardised patterns of people's lives and have increased the range of socially acceptable and desirable identities and lifestyles' (Chisholm 2003: 3). If one effect of the intensification of the discourse of individualism is to undermine the usual collective mechanisms for managing risk (Beck 1992), then the constitution of local youth cultures can be seen as a strategy which consciously turns back to collectivism for managing both ontological and 'manufactured' risk. It is in this context that youth everywhere carve out identities and life trajectories for themselves, although as Marx points out 'they do not make it as they please; they do not make it under self-selected circumstances, but under circumstances existing already, given and transmitted from the past' (1978: 595).

In support of Marx's claim, some chapters in this book, especially those by Feixa, Muñoz and Marín, and Niang, focus on the youth culture of the poorest young people in non-western cities. Disadvantaged urban youth suffer greatly from the historical and increasing gap between rich and poor in all countries of the world. Martin and Schumann (1997) argue that we are moving towards a '20:80' society, where only 20 per cent of the world's population will be needed to continue production, leaving the other 80 per cent on the periphery – poor and unemployed (see also Stiglitz 2002: 248). Economic changes deriving from the globalization of the world economy in the late twentieth century have radically altered the life trajectory of young people as far as work is concerned (Sennett 1999: 17). No matter where in the world they are, the lives of young people fit less and less within a linear model of transition. Skelton lists some defining features of a traditional transition to adulthood: completing education, entering the labour market, leaving home to set up a new household, entering marriage or cohabitation, and becoming a parent (2002: 101). However, 'we are witnessing increasingly prolonged, decoupled transitions between education and work, dating and mating, and childhood and adulthood' (Côté 2003: 2). Similarly, participation in youth cultures can no longer be characterized as a brief period of 'gang' or 'peer group' activity restricted to a certain limited period in the teens and early twenties. The late modern extension of youth culture practices in two chronological directions, downwards towards late childhood, and upwards towards the mid- to late-thirties, means that participation in youth culture practices – in general – may last more than 20 years, even carry on towards middle age, while taking into account the kinds of dynamic shifts between subcultures described by Muñoz and Marín in their chapter on Colombia. Their account, and those of Niang and Feixa in this book, demonstrate that long-term participation in youth cultures and youth social movements is not just a feature of western, middle-class, urban life.

Finally, as indicated above, most of the chapters in this book are concerned with urban youth phenomena. Megacities are a characteristic feature of the era of globalization and most people in the world now live in one of them. The greatest movement from the rural to the urban milieu in any country is by young people looking for education and work. So the vast multi-ethnic cities of the planet are overwhelmingly where young people live and where they engage in representations of identity, both individually and in groups. Representations of spectacular youth culture identities, such as the French skinheads described by Petrova, or the Mexican punks described by Feixa, frequently occur in public urban space, stirring up feelings of fear and revulsion (moral panic) in the wider population. The slums of the inner cities, and the rows of subsidized low-income earner apartment blocks on the peripheries of cities, are often dangerous, liminal spaces, where youth seek sanctuary in gangs and lifestyle identity groupings. The megacities of the new millennium thereby provide new spaces for the clashing of cultures (Featherstone and Lash 1999: 1), as Petrova's chapter shows most eloquently.

Global youth and consumerism

On the conservative side, youth are certainly avid consumers of global cultural industry products and services. This forms such an important part of the cultural practice of young people everywhere that, worldwide, youth is a market 'potentially twice the size of China' (Erasmus 2003: 1). Through the 'new' media, youth (seemingly regardless of actual age) are central to the global leisure market, not just the 'marketing focus' for cultural industry innovations, but the source of their inspiration. CEOs (chief executive officers) send 'cool-hunters' down to the street, and to public places where young people gather to find the 'new' look and sound, the avant-garde trend, which global cultural industries can then commodify, regularize and market (Hebdige 1988) in the process Ritzer (1993) describes as McDonaldization.

The chapters by Nilan and Holden in this volume address this process specifically, but even those that deal with marginalized youth understand the local music-oriented cultures of hip-hop or punk as articulated in relation to global cultural 'products'. Yet this fact does not 'prove' at all the totalizing globalization thesis described above. It is possible for young people in developing countries to look and sound 'western' – as Niang says – yet objectively not be so at all. Youth cultures are always emphatically local, despite globally-derived details, since youth are embedded in immediate and embodied economic and political relations. Their reflexive engagement – choosing or rejecting, transforming or synthesizing – with global youth cultural products and practices – music, subcultures, fashion, slang – is shaped by their habitus: income, religion, language, class, gender and ethnicity, to create almost inevitably something which has not existed before.

All the chapters in this book implicitly recognize the creative, even often artistic processes, of young people in the constitution of identities and subcultural groupings. These creative processes work with whatever resources are most immediately available – both local and global. They are what Butcher and Thomas, referring to 'ingenious' Australian second-generation migrant youth, call 'merchants of style'.

Global youth and resistance

The classic 'youth culture as resistance' position of the Birmingham Centre for Contemporary Cultural Studies, based on Antonio Gramsci's theory of hegemony, proposes that dominant groups in society, who possess the most valued forms of cultural capital, create and define hegemonic culture which serves to support and enhance their powerful social position (Hall and Jefferson 1976). In implicit resistance to this hegemony, 'common' culture (Willis 1990) arises from the lives of other, subordinate groups and classes – 'in those cultural places which hegemonic culture is unable to completely penetrate' (Epstein 1998: 9). Youth cultures, especially those which challenge conservative ideas, can therefore be characterized as a form of 'resistance'. This position has been criticized from all sides in the field of youth studies and beyond, especially the concept of subculture as a form of resistance. Nonetheless, (sub)cultures as defined more recently by Muggleton (2000) offer young people a place to construct an alternative identity to the largely adult-defined subject positions offered to them by school, work, gender and status/class. The internal meanings and values of these (sub)cultures are articulated in relation to a variety of discourses – socializing, music, fashion (or the absence of it), prior youth subcultures and political activism. In many countries we should add religion to this list (Helve 1999: 3), conceptualized in both traditional and 'new-age' forms. Furthermore, since 'young people's lives actively reflect their relationship to dominant power structures' (Miles 2000: 6), the extent to which this relationship is in any way resentful and oppositional will be reflected in the expressive culture of youth groups and trends. Many of the youth culture groupings and practices described in this volume fit that description very well, whether we are talking about gothic white extremist skinheads in suburban Paris, or the proudly Canadian francophone youth studied by Dallaire who insist on using both English and French. In other words, most youth cultural practices at the group level are driven at the same time both by impulses of resistance and challenge, and impulses of conformity and legitimacy.

In several chapters, the relationship of local youth culture to political activism and subversive social movements is considered. Generally speaking, this relationship is difficult to find 'across the board' as it were. Using Maffesoli's (1996) metaphor, there is often a 'submerged' link between youth subcultural practice and wider subversive social and political movements, but this is most frequently an affinity link rather than the impetus for planned formal expressions of political resistance. So it is usually more in youth culture lifestyles that we find symbolic identity repertoires (Melucci 1989) which echo specific political movements, such as the anti-immigration violence of some French skinheads.

We can take as a current example of many global, decentralized and digital movements, the international anti-globalization network that flourished after the breaking down of the Berlin wall. As a movement with powerful appeal for young people it signifies a reaction to multinational corporations like the World Bank and the International Monetary Fund, to unsustainable development, and to franchises like McDonalds. But these kinds of largely youthful mass social movements also prefigure a constellation of new social actors – constituted in the emergence of highly nomadic subjectivities. We can find intriguing ethnographies about these new 'web-based' movements that demonstrate the significance of 'nomadic' young people moving across national frontiers and continents – both actually and virtually – in their support for global resistance movements: the *hacktivists* (Juris 2005). Juris' example demonstrates that it is not possible to conceive of a world divided between global hegemony and local resistances. Most contemporary social movements, especially youthful ones, are as globalized as the institutions they fight against.

Dedications . . .

In closing, we wish to acknowledge that this book took shape initially during the 2002 International Sociology Association (ISA) Conference in Brisbane, Australia. RC34 is the title by which the youth section of ISA is identified. Carles Feixa and Pam Nilan were asked by the then president of RC34, Professor Lynne Chisholm, to co-convene a thematic session called 'Hybrid identities, plural worlds'. Present RC34 president, Professor Helena Helve, also encouraged this publication as an example for world youth research networks.

All but two of the chapters in this book were developed from that thematic session after the co-convenors decided that it would be worth creating an edited collection from the wealth of international research material implied in the submitted abstracts. Additional chapters by Holden and Huq were by invitation of the editors. Communication with authors, and some translation and editing of the book was carried out in three languages – English and French (Nilan and Feixa) and Spanish (Feixa).

The resulting book builds conceptually upon the admirable edited collection of cross-cultural youth studies by Amit-Talai and Wulff, published by Routledge in 1995. A great deal has happened in that ten years. *Global Youth? Hybrid identities, plural worlds* owes a heartfelt debt not only to the actual contributors of chapters, but also to the pioneers of youth culture ethnography in all the continents represented here. Furthermore, although the authors in this volume come from a variety of academic discipline backgrounds – sociology, anthropology, cultural studies, communications, education – it was found in the editing process that most authors referred to some common (or perhaps not so common) theorists and earlier researchers. These can be identified in the bibliographies of each chapter, and our collective debt to their insights and findings is also recognized.

Finally, it is important to acknowledge the young people whose cultural experiences and voices we have tried to represent in this book. Despite their evident energy and creativity, the world of which they are taking possession is beset with seemingly intractable problems. As youth, they construct their individual and collective biographies without the assurances of the past, and in an atmosphere of heightened risk. The youth cultures they create are an important tool for dealing with these experiences and processes all over the world. In fact, all of the global order transformations which affect people at the local level affect young people most strongly, since they will be the inheritors of the outcomes. It is to young people everywhere that this book is dedicated.

Bibliography

Abou-El-Haj, B. (1991) 'Languages and models for cultural exchange', in J. Eade (ed.) *Living the Global City: globalization as a local process*, London and New York: Routledge.

Adams, M. (2003) 'The reflexive self and culture: a critique', *British Journal of Sociology*, 54(2): 221–38.

Amin, S. (1990) *Eurocentrism*, New York: Monthly Review Press.

Amit-Talai, V. and Wulff, H. (eds) (1995) *Youth Cultures: a cross-cultural perspective*, London: Routledge.

Bannerji, H. (2000) *The Dark Side of the Nation: essays on multiculturalism, nationalism and gender*, Toronto: Canadian Scholars Press Inc.

Beck, U. (1992) *Risk Society: towards a new modernity*, London: Sage.

Bennett, A. (1999) 'Subcultures or neo-tribes? Rethinking the relationship between youth, style and musical taste', *Sociology*, 33(3): 599–617.

Bhabha, H. (1994) *The Location of Culture*, London and New York: Routledge.

Caccia-Bava, A., Feixa, C. and González, Y. (eds) (2004) *Jovens na America Latina*, São Paulo: Escrituras.

Canevacci, M. (2000) *Culture Extreme: mutazione giovanili tra i corpi delle metropoli*, Rome: Meltemi.

Castells, M. (1996) *The Rise of the Network Society, The Information Age: economy, society and culture*, vol. 1, Oxford: Blackwell.

—— (1997) *The Power of Identity, The Information Age: economy, society and culture*, vol. 2, Oxford: Blackwell.

Chisholm, L. (2003) 'Youth in knowledge societies: challenges for research and policy', proceedings of *Making Braking Borders* (NYRIS) 7th Nordic Youth Research Symposium 2000, 7–10 June, Helsinki, Finland. Online. Available: <www.alli.fi/nyri/nyris/nyris7/papers/chisholm.html> (accessed 10 April 2005).

Chuck D (1997) *Rap, Race and Reality: fight the power*, New York: Bantam Doubleday Books.

Connell, R.W. (2005) 'Southern theory: writing sociology outside the metropole', The Australian Sociology Association Lecture, Ourimbah: University of Newcastle, 28.
Côté, J.E. (2003) 'Late modernity, individualization, and identity capital: some longitudinal findings with a middle-class sample', proceedings of *Making Braking Borders* (NYRIS) 7th Nordic Youth Research Symposium 2000, 7–10 June, Helsinki, Finland. Online. Available: <www.alli.fi/nyri/nyris/nyris7/papers/cote.html> (accessed 10 April 2005).
Epstein, J. (1998) 'Introduction: generation X, youth culture and identity', in J. Epstein (ed.) *Youth Culture: identity in a postmodern world*, Malden and Oxford: Blackwell.
Erasmus, D. (2003) 'Global teenager', Development Technology Network. Online. Available: <www.dtn.net/content/yesterday/5globalteen.html> (accessed 3 April 2003).
Featherstone, M. (ed.) (1990) *Global Culture*, London: Sage.
—— and Lash, S. (1999) 'Introduction', in M. Featherstone and S. Lash (eds) *Spaces of Culture: city, nation, world*, London: Sage.
Feixa, C. and González, Y. (2005) 'The Socio-Cultural Construction of Youth in Latin America: achievements and failures', in H. Helve and G. Holm (eds) *Contemporary Youth Research: local expressions and global connections*, Burlington and Aldershot: Ashgate.
García Canclini, N. (1989) *Culturas Híbridas*, Mexico: Grijalbo.
—— (1995) *Hybrid Cultures*, Minneapolis, MN: University of Minnesota Press.
Giddens, A. (1991) *Modernity and Self-Identity: self and society in the late modern age*, Cambridge: Polity Press.
—— (2002) *Runaway World: how globalisation is reshaping our lives*, revised edition, London: Routledge.
Hall, S. (1993) 'Cultural identity and diaspora', in P. Williams and L. Chrisman (eds) *Colonial Discourse and Postcolonial Theory: a reader*, London: Harvester Wheatsheaf.
—— and Jefferson, T. (eds) (1976) *Resistance Through Rituals: youth subcultures in postwar Britain*, London: Harper Collins Academic.
Hebdige, D. (1988) *Hiding in the Light*, London: Routledge – Comedia Series.
Helve, H. (1999) 'Multiculturalism and values of young people', *DISKUS* 5. Online. Available: <www.uni-marburg.de/religionsgewissenschaft/journal/diskus (accessed 7 July 2005).
Hesmondhalgh, D. (2005) 'Subcultures, scenes or tribes?', *Journal of Youth Studies* 8(1): 21–40.
Juris, J. (2005) 'Youth and the World Social Forum', *Youth Activism*, Social Science Research Centre. Online. Available: <www.ya.ssrc.org> (accessed 15 July 2005).
Lash, S. (1994) 'Reflexivity and its doubles: structure, aesthetics, community', in U. Beck, A. Giddens and S. Lash (eds) *Reflexive Modernization: politics, tradition and aesthetics in the modern social order*, Cambridge: Polity Press.
Maffesoli, M. (1996) *The Time of the Tribes: the decline of individualism in mass society*, London: Sage.
Mannheim, K. (1927) 'Das Problem der Generationen', *Kölner Vierteljahrshefte für Soziologie*, 2–3(7).
Martin, H.-P. and Schumann, H. (1997) *The Global Trap: globalization and the assault on democracy and prosperity*, London: Pluto Press.
Marx, Karl (1978) [1852] 'The eighteenth brumaire of Louis Bonaparte', in

R.C. Tucker (ed.) *The Marx–Engels Reader*, 2nd edition, New York and London: W.W. Norton.
Melucci, A. (1989) *Nomads of the Present*, Philadelphia, PA: Temple University Press.
Miles, S. (2000) *Youth Lifestyles in a Changing World*, Buckingham and Philadelphia, PA: Open University Press.
Muggleton, D. (2000) *Inside Subculture: the postmodern meaning of style*, Oxford: Berg.
—— and Weinzierl, R. (eds) (2003) *The Post-Subcultures Reader*, London: Berg.
Nayak, A. (2003) *Race, Place and Globalization: youth cultures in a changing world*, Oxford and New York: Berg.
Nilan, P. (2004) 'Culturas juveniles globales', *Revista de Estudios de Juventud*, 64: 38–48.
Reguillo, R. (2001) *Emergencia de Culturas Juveniles*, Buenos Aires: Norma.
Ritzer, G. (1993) *The McDonaldization of Society*, Thousand Oaks, CA: Pine Forge Press.
Rose, N. (1992) 'Governing the enterprising self', in P. Heelas and P. Morris (eds) *The Values of Enterprise Culture*, London: Routledge.
Sennett, R. (1999) 'Growth and failure: the new political economy and its culture', in M. Featherstone and S. Lash (eds) *Spaces of Culture: city, nation, world,* London: Sage.
Skelton, T. (2002) 'Research on youth transitions: some critical interventions', in M. Cieslik and G. Pollock (eds) *Young People in Risk Society: the restructuring of youth identities and transitions in late modernity*, Aldershot: Ashgate.
Stiglitz, J. (2002) *Globalization and Its Discontents*, London: Allen Lane/Penguin Press.
Sweetman, P. (2003) 'Twenty-first century dis-ease? Habitual reflexivity or the reflexive habitus', *The Sociological Review*, 51(4): 528–49.
Thornton, S. (1995) *Club Cultures*, Cambridge, MA: Wesleyan University Press.
Touraine, A. (2003) 'Equality and/or difference: real problems, false dilemmas', *Canadian Journal of Sociology*, 28(4): 543–50.
Willis, P. (1990) *Common Culture*, Boulder, CO: Westview.

1 European youth cultures in a post-colonial world
British Asian underground and French hip-hop music scenes

Rupa Huq

This chapter examines the productive engagement of second-generation ethnic minority youth in the UK and France with popular culture – specifically music. In the discussion below of British Asian underground and French hip-hop, it is argued that in both countries the shaping context includes not only global youth music forms and traditional cultural sources, but also marginalized urban city contexts, and national policies that address the alignment of ethnic minority groups with state interests. Below I use the term 'hip-hop' interchangeably with 'rap'. The former encompasses street-slang, graffiti, fashion and music while the latter is a musical form based on spoken vocal delivery where the lyrics are central.

Frith (1996: 269) writes that 'music is the cultural form best able to cross borders – sounds carry across fences and walls and oceans, across classes, races and nations'. These properties make music an ideal medium of articulation for the experience of migration and alterity in a new country. However, the young creators of contemporary British Asian underground and French hip-hop are second-generation minority youth. They have known no other home. They are not migrants but a settled population of young people participating in all aspects of local youth culture, while expressing their minority status and ethnic identity. Given the socio-spatial properties of popular music (Bennett 2000, 2001; Connell and Gibson 2003) in minority youth identity processes of location and relocation, it 'evokes and organizes collective memories and present experiences of place with an intensity, power and simplicity unmatched by any other social activity' (Stokes 1994: 3).

This chapter attempts to situate minority youth with their multiple identity sources in the new European cultural equation. British Asian underground music and French hip-hop are expressive youth cultural forms inflected within different national policies for the cultural management of ethnic difference. France employs a policy of assimilation/integration, while Britain practises an ethic of tolerance and multiculturalism. Below I consider the impact of post-colonial popular culture on national culture through analysing how some initially marginal forms of popular music have moved from the margins, to mainstream culture industries and consumption. The substantive part of the chapter presents case studies of these two musical forms and their popularity with young people in the contemporary urban metropolis.

Methodology

This chapter draws on interviews with practitioners and consumers of Asian underground music in London and Manchester, and of French hip-hop in Strasbourg. It is argued that in the new century, second-generation immigrant youth synthesize diverse cultural influences to create new musical forms reflecting the duality/multiplicity of their roots. This argument constitutes a rebuttal to late last century claims that we were seeing the end of youth culture/innovation in popular music, advanced in response to revivalist tendencies in music, for example the Britpop phenomenon, and the proliferation of re-releases and remixes. Underpinning all the discussion below are implicit themes of globalization and Europeanization, both likely to be of continuing importance in the UK and France as the new century advances.

Context of research

My doctoral research on youth culture in London began in the mid-1990s. Later studies took me to Strasbourg, France. I was studying youth culture – first, to address glaring omissions in the established canon of British youth studies, for example Hall and Jefferson (1976) and Hebdige (1979). Consequently, the two case studies reported in this chapter are located within a new 'canon' of research and theorizing that seeks to re-orient British youth studies within a more inclusive universe of specifically located urban cultural meanings (Muggleton 2000; Chatterton and Hollands 2003). The original Centre for Contemporary Cultural Studies (CCCS) analyses of youth contain many omissions: conformist youth of no fixed strict subcultural affiliations, young women and gay youth. Furthermore, aside from Jones' (1988) post-1970s valiant, if somewhat isolated, account, ethnic minority youth were either entirely absent from 1970s British youth studies with their limiting notions of subcultures, or present only in a partial way that bore very little resemblance to what was happening two decades on (see Hebdige's 1979 treatment of 'rude boys'). Writing at the time Brake (1980: 128) went so far as to state 'Asians are rarely found in youth culture'. These kinds of statements effectively precluded any possibility of acknowledging Asian youth as a creative or dynamic force in popular culture. Essentially negative portrayals prevailed. For instance 'Pakibashing' – white skinhead violence towards Pakistani male youths – was the most frequently mentioned phenomenon in relation to young Asians (Hebdige 1979). A major limitation of CCCS theorizing was reliance on class theory – an increasingly tenuous set of claims in the era of globalization:

> The conditions of post-Fordist Society have simply engendered new cultural forms and practices and revealed hybrid constellations and identities which the battery of concepts forged under classical Marxism is incapable of capturing.
>
> (Rojek 1995: 55)

Second, when my study of youth cultures commenced, contemporaneous British media discourse was making a case for the supposed dearth of original pop music. Journalists claimed this was symptomatic of the death of youth culture – imploded in an age of music revivalism (band covers) and computer games. It was a running academic joke that my project had been funded for three years to study something that quite simply no longer existed. However, a little over three years later I was able to state conclusively that youth culture did still exist, although perhaps not as previously conceived. Two of the most striking transnational examples of expressive youth cultures in the new Europe were the British Asian underground music scene and the French hip-hop scene.

An important and growing body of literature has recently been devoted to post-colonial theory (for example Said 1979; Gilroy 1993; Hall 1993; Spivak 1999). It is intended that the discursive treatment of the two cases of expressive youth culture that follows will serve as examples of much of this post-colonial theorizing. In particular I refute early analyses of second-generation ethnic minority youth cultures with their highly questionable 'between two cultures' understanding (for example Anwar 1976; Watson 1977) of the diasporic experience. Instead I argue for the duality or multiplicity of cultural points of identification of youth who are products of post-colonial diasporic flows. My interpretation draws on Gilroy's (1993) concept of 'double consciousness' in an increasingly 'globalized' world. Each respective musical form will be described in terms of why it has risen to prominence. This will be followed by a discussion of the social and political dimensions of each. The conclusion centres on the global implications of these diasporic popular music styles as urban expressions of youth culture in the new Europe.

Just as popular music reflects its times, so do research results. The research informing this chapter was conducted almost a decade ago. In the early twenty-first century the diversity of musical practices and outlets for pop fans has opened up new avenues for investigation. Internet chatrooms are supplementing, if not supplanting, print fanzines of old. Many 'record shops' only stock CDs, videos, DVDs and computer games. The interconnectedness of technology means that there is no need to set foot in any shop again with the advent of MP3 downloads, ebay and the latest 3G mobile phones. The choice of ring tone becomes an identity definer. All these 'new forms' impact on French hip-hop and Asian underground as the producers and consumers of these musics utilize technological and cultural resources.

Defining and contextualizing Asian underground and French hip-hop

In Britain the term 'Asian' (replete with past colonial meanings) refers specifically to people from the Indian subcontinent – India, Pakistan, Bangladesh and Sri Lanka. It effectively reduces the world's largest continent to nothing more than ex-British India. In France, the terms '*les noirs*' (blacks – West Africans) and '*les Africains du nord*' (North Africans) encode similar post-colonial meanings. It is important to recognize that British Asian underground and French hip-hop are umbrella terms that cover a range of musical styles and sub-genres popular with young people generally, but especially with immigrant youth from past colonies in the two countries.

Asian underground in Britain

The new musical label 'Asian underground' first entered common usage in Britain around 1997, heralded through newspaper reports. The year – 1997 – was seen as auspicious or even ironic depending on the media source. Certainly there was some significance in the fact that 1997 marked the fiftieth anniversary of Indian Independence from British rule. Despite the 1997 fanfare though, a number of bands linked with the Asian underground music scene had existed long before this date, as indeed had various precursor musical styles – *bhangra* music, 'the New Asian Kool' and 'the new Asian dance music'. Around 1997 these terms entered the common music vocabulary for the first time, rather than being invented then.

The aphorism 'Asian underground', used here for reasons of convenience, spans both a club scene with DJs as well as live music. It emerged when immigrant musicians combined western pop styles with traditional Indian influences, but does not describe a unique phenomenon. For example, there is a wealth of sonic difference between Nitin Sawhney's jazz-funk and the militant Muslim hip-hop of Fun-Da-Mental. Asian underground enjoyed a brief wave of intense popularity. At its height, Indian instrumentation and fashion were being used by mainstream pop performers such Madonna and Boy George. The instigators and innovators of the scene however, remain second-generation British-born youth from India, Pakistan and Bangladesh.

Hip-hop in France

Like the British Asian underground youth culture phenomenon, hip-hop in France is a popular music form and cultural scene reflecting France's colonial past and post-colonial present. It enjoys approximately the same significance for second-generation Franco-Arab and West African youth in France as Asian underground music does for young Britons of the Indian-subcontinent diaspora. French hip-hop is most often practised by young people whose parents or even grandparents came from the former French colonies of West and North Africa, although its fan base includes mainstream white youth. French rap is at the centre of the much wider French hip-hop cultural scene that also includes performative practices such as breakdance and graffiti. French hip-hop as a diasporic cultural expression of youth is unique for a number of reasons. Rap performed in the French language is extraordinarily popular. French hip-hop is at the forefront of campaigns to export French popular music worldwide. French industries in conjunction with the French government have financed promotions by the French Music Bureau which has branches in several European capital cities, including London.

As with British Asian underground, there are various subsets of French rap. Lapassade (1996) distinguishes between the music culture scene of 1983–90 when French rap was still an underground, underpublicized genre popular in only a limited number of outlying working class suburbs of Paris (*banlieues*), with the years 1990 onwards. After 1990, French hip-hop became a fully-fledged overground youth culture with much broader popular appeal to young people. During this period, two distinct forms of hip-hop emerged. Firstly, we can identify the 'hardcore' material of bands such as NTM (Nique Ta Mère – Motherfucker) and Ministère AMER (Ministry of Bitterness – where AMER is simultaneously both an acronym of *action, musique et rap* and a word meaning bitter). Secondly, there was 'cool' rap, such as MC Solaar. Bazin (1995: 214) calls this a two-pronged model since both belong within the French rap genre. Although both convey what Toop (1990) calls 'message rap', NTM issues a call to revolution, whereas MC Solaar aims to win over those who don't like rap (Bazin 1995: 254). However, as a typical binary, this demarcation is somewhat simplistic. For example, outfits such as the Marseilles mixed race band IAM are somewhere between the 'cool' and 'hardcore' camps and others have also crossed boundaries. French hip-hop bands can also change over time. NTM was long seen as a confrontational 'hardcore' act. However, their most recent album sees a shift in style to more peace-seeking lyrics.

The post-colonial context

Historically youth culture trends are frequently started off by an avant-garde élite of young people (Hebdige 1988). Following media exposure and marketing, a new trend subsequently moves towards general public tastes. This pattern can be identified in both French hip-hop and Asian underground, although officialdom was slow to catch on. It took until 1996 for the appropriately named Alliance Ethnik (Ethnic Alliance) to become the first French rappers to be bestowed with the best group award at France's Victoires de la Musique awards. A similar honour was bestowed on Asian underground in Britain in 1999 when Talvin Singh's album *OK* won the prestigious Mercury Music Prize for best British album of the year. In considering why it is that these forms of music have risen to prominence only relatively recently, we should note that recognition by, and backing from, major record labels has been important.

In Britain *bhangra* music, a style produced and consumed by Asian youth (Banerji and Baumann 1990), predated Asian underground by at least a decade. However, *bhangra* failed to dent the official sales charts. *Bhangra* music was distributed among Asian youth on cheap, illegally copied cassettes sold in specialist non-chart registered shops undetected by the wider music industry. Subsequent dedicated Asian underground labels have often featured tie-ins with larger record labels to ensure that they have better distribution to a wide youth market, for example, Talvin Singh's Ovni records, an imprint of Island. French hip-hop has even more crossed over into the mainstream recording business. For example, MC Solaar is currently signed with Warner Brothers, having previously been a Polydor artist, NTM is signed with Sony and IAM with Delabel/Virgin. This happened in the space of a decade. The 1990 compilation *Rapattitude* issued on Virgin records is seen as marking the beginning of French hip-hop's commercial recognition.

As well as greater commercial accessibility, another reason for the successful crossover of these formerly marginal ethnic musical genres is a new rhythmic accessibility which earlier 'purer' forms like *bhangra* lacked (Huq 1996). Furthermore, growing confidence in musical innovation among second-generation ethnic youth can be attributed to the fact that they are the second generation. Their growing visibility in the mainstream media reflects changing perceptions of minority populations as they shift in the popular imagination from 'immigrants' to a 'settled population'. A second-generation British Asian writer acknowledges her debt to the parent generation: 'Our parents would have loved to get into artistic practice but they had to come over to a new country and get jobs' (Meera Syal, telephone interview, London 1999).

Perhaps the most noteworthy aspect of British Asian underground and French hip-hop music respectively is their development from different circumstances of production in terms of national policies regarding the accommodation of ethnic difference. France and Britain both have significant minority populations as a result of their former colonial interests. Britain prides itself on following a broad ethic of 'multiculturalism' which has the tolerance of ethnic difference as its cornerstone. In France '*intégration*' is both the theory and practice of national policy. It is expected that minorities will assimilate into mainstream French society, taking on 'French' characteristics. Eventually, following a sufficiently long period of stay, French nationality will be achieved. In France there are no such things as 'ethnic minorities' or 'non-whites'. Instead, in keeping with citizenship and nationality requirements, there are French and non-French. Integration, if practised in its strictest form, suppresses ethnic and cultural differences. For example, the integration-allied notion of secularism in the French classroom made headlines concerning the Islamic headscarf in schools (Brulard 1997).

By contrast, in British non-denominational schools the celebration of all religious ceremonies is now normal; including Islamic *Eid ul Fitr*, Hindu *Diwali* and Jewish *Hannukah* as well as Christmas. However, the idea of multicultural 'tolerance' itself can be seen as a rather patronizing notion, implying that minorities and their superficial differences are there to be 'put up with, but only on limited terms – as long as they do not get too powerful and have any real influence in society'. In Britain there is not the same tradition as in France of attaching high value to citizenship, perhaps because of the (constitutional) monarchy. British nationals have more traditionally been conceived of as subjects rather than through the civic concept of citizen.

Defining national identities in France or Britain is not easy (Storry and Childs 1997). Conservative political discourses reference nostalgic cultural identity tropes which implicitly marginalize the younger generation. Conservative discourses in recent years include the Thatcher/Major emphasis on traditional Victorian values/'back-to-basics' Britishness, and various pronouncements by right-wing politicians in France from Front Nationale leader Jean-Marie Le Pen to Jacques Chirac. The subtext in discursive yearning for 'the good old days' references an apparently homogenous pre-twentieth century society sharply at odds with the multi-ethnic nature of contemporary Britain and France. French and British cultural policy, in attempting to assert national identity, has at times appeared defensive in nature; responding to a perceived threat of Americanization. Ironically, French rap and British Asian underground have been beneficiaries of certain recent initiatives in this vein, although probably in unintended ways. For example, French government-imposed quotas of French language output on national and local radio in 1994 proved a key factor in assisting the growth of French rap. In a similar vein, following the launch of 'Cool Britannia' by Tony Blair's government – aimed at projecting a tolerant, open, multicultural national image – Talvin Singh was invited to play at the annual Labour Party Conference. Entwined with recent attempts to manufacture national cultural identity, the invention and production of both British Asian underground and French hip-hop are strongly characteristic of the nations that they hail from. Their distinctiveness emphasizes that national identity is not static but forever shifting. In their very existence as second-generation youth popular cultural music forms they are redefining Britishness, Frenchness and Europeanness.

Hybridity of these new musical forms

Referring to France, Poulet writes (1993: 312) 'from the multiple ethnic communities of big cities in France are emerging new musical hybrids reflecting both their ancestral musical heritage and their French content'. As in the United States, the text is inseparable from its (sub)urban context (Bazin 1995). For example, an alternative explanation of NTM's acronym (Lapassade 1996: 54) is '*Le nord transmet le message* (message transmitted from the north)', referring to the band's origins in the lower socio-economic north Parisian *banlieue*. The implication is that these are humble beginnings to be proud of. Rather than just creative second-generation minority youth 'making good' though, remaining in touch with 'tough origin' roots is an integral part of how these bands promote themselves. The group Ministère AMER produced the album *95 200* after the postal code of Sarcelles, yet another tough north Parisian *banlieue*.

This is similar to the British group E17 who play on a 'hard' Walthamstow image. Academic accounts of French rap all note that it is rooted in lived urban second-generation ethnic youth expression. Dance is the corporeal expression of French rap and hip-hop and its visual art – graffiti – is practised on such urban canvas as public transport (Bazin 1995: 237). For Cross (1993: 64) American hip-hop evokes 'new soundtracks for urban survival'. For Cathus (1994: 205) 'it is the power of street experience that gives hip hop its aesthetic power'. The term 'street credibility' is not meaningless. If the tough urban street is rap's stage, it can be worked into a cartography of contemporary youth social relations.

In Britain, Asian underground is intrinsically urban. Asian underground and *bhangra* nights are now fixtures of the club scene for young people in London, Manchester and Birmingham. Day-time gigs are held too (Huq 2005). These happen between midday and 6 pm to combat strict parental restrictions on going out at night. They contradict received notions of youth culture as part of the night-time economy. They truly reflect the meaning of the oft-used term '24 hour city' (Bianchi 1995; Lovatt 1995; Hobbs, Hall, Winlow and Lister 2000; Chatterton and Hollands 2003). At the same time a residential microdiaspora seems to be evolving where British Asian communities disperse further and further out from what were seen as traditionally ethnic areas of inner cities by following suburbanized patterns of settlement. Their distinctive youth popular musical forms follow them. Accordingly *bhangra* nights are now a feature of suburbs like Watford and Ilford to the north and east of London's core. At the same time, many dislike the implied narrowness and exclusivity of the term 'Asian underground'. A large proportion of its contemporary fanbase are white trendies. David Bowie and Björk were among those spotted in Asian underground club audiences in 1997. *Bhangra* artist Punjabi MC from Birmingham recently commented publicly, 'to me Asian underground is just what's happening in East London'.

British Asian underground and French hip-hop as political pop

At a time when young people and their preferred music – contemporary pop – are both being accused of lacking radicalism, French hip-hop and British Asian underground have not only demonstrated political awareness in their output, but have been utilized by officialdom, which has attempted to use the popularity of these musical forms for its own ends.

In France, French hip-hop has been co-opted by both the French left and right for political purposes. The 'Université du Hip Hop' festival of summer 1996 organized by Été Jeune, the Strasbourg local council youth arts and cultural service, serves as an example. The week-long festival included daily debates with speakers in conference format – subjects included women in hip-hop, and commercialization. There were workshops on graffiti, rap, and fanzine writing, with seven nightly concerts in different venues across the city. The event was all free entry. However, its freedom from institutionalization was more debatable. The local transport authority donated a bus for graffiti art. An entire housing estate in the *banlieue* of Illkirch was set aside as a graffiti-permitted zone for the week with spray cans provided by the city council.

Such artificial attempts to modulate and control the culture sit somewhat incongruously with the dispossessed/protest aspect of both graffiti and hip-hop (Cross 1993; Rose 1994). The Strasbourg Université du Hip Hop can either be seen as responding to young people's needs, or alternatively conceptualized as a patronizing attempt to pacify youth. This kind of official, top-down, artificial organization of youth culture is contrary to the concept of 'underground' on which authentic avant garde youth cultures are predicated. Some youth see it as lifestyle policing:

> France is a police state. It's centralized, everything is controlled: the administration, the papers, everything is had [recorded]. Pirate radio gets very quickly fucked up by the state for example. Hip-hop's been on the French scene since the early eighties. The media didn't believe it or push it [at first]. Regular people couldn't get to it. In 1996 it's getting popular, so they want everything under control.
> (Mr E, 23-year-old graffiti writer and DJ, Strasbourg, 1996)

We may note that the relative benevolence of Strasbourg's socialist regime contrasts with local government attitudes to rap in municipalities controlled by the Front Nationale. When the Front Nationale gains local government it often drives prohibitive and extreme decisions about youth culture. One example was the Chateauvallon theatre in Toulon, known for imaginative multi-cultural programming. It was closed down soon after the Front Nationale accession to power. The Sous-Marin alternative music café in Vitrolles (bordering Toulon) was also closed down on the pretext of drugs and noise. The four Front Nationale-run municipalities in France in 1996 had a reputation for withdrawing books on ethnic populations from their libraries, and renaming streets after right-wing luminaries.

In regard to the suppression of second-generation ethnic youth culture, the most notable example of Front Nationale censure was a criminal charge against hip-hop group NTM. In November 1996 the band was sentenced to a six-month prison sentence, a fine of 50,000 francs and an additional six-month ban on all French performances by a local judiciary. NTM was found guilty of the antiquated and little used offence of *outrages par paroles*, referring to anti-police remarks made by NTM at a festival in Toulon during summer 1995. The legal decision raised questions of morality, far right cultural policy, the situation of youth in the *banlieues*, and the sanctity of artistic creation. It was much debated. *Le Monde* (16 November 1996), the leftist daily paper *Libération*

(16 November 1996) and the weekly *Télérama* (27 November 1996) all ran editorials attacking the decision, later partially overturned by the national justice department. Front Nationale leader Jean-Maric Le Pen declared his party's position as follows: '*Rap, tag [graffiti] sont des modes passagères des excroissances pathogènes*' ('rap and tag are passing fads of pathogenic outbursts'), *Le Monde*, 23–4 June 1996. The NTM affair made a public example of two young men whose immigrant origins were ceaselessly stressed: 'Kool Shen' (Bruno Lopez) of Portuguese stock, and 'Joey Star' (Didier Morville) from the Caribbean Antilles. Supporters of the NTM decision constantly referred to the group's full name on television, 'Nique Ta Mère', to reinforce the shock factor of swear words and anti-family sentiments.

However, while the adoption of the black American ghetto 'motherfucker' term can be seen as a genuinely sexist assertion of virility (Badache 1995), the implicit objection of older generation conservatives to the term had the opposite effect on youth. NTM music sales skyrocketed. Young people wanted to tap into this forbidden, outlawed underworld. In this way circumstances forced a political dimension onto NTM which complemented the social commentary of their lyrics, for example, the words of their song, *Police*, which partly fuelled the original controversy. Other French rappers, anti-racist organizations, student unions, pressure groups and trade unions were among those who demonstrated in support of NTM against the censure.

In Britain, new Asian dance music has also been celebrated for its political content (Hutnyk, Sharma and Sharma 1996). We may note that Fun-Da-Mental played at the Socialist Workers Party (SWP) summer school and donated tracks to compilation albums for both criminal justice and anti-racist charities. However, not everyone was thrilled with the band's political affiliations. *Time Out*'s review of their album *Erotic Terrorism* (25 March 1998) criticizes it for being message over music, 'it's a dour, shouty, funkless, tuneless, unfocussed, alienated, *depressing* din . . . in Fun-Da-Mental's case, good intentions + no tunes = no challenge to anyone'. Here we see a tension between entertainment and political value. Band leader Aki Nawaz has rejected claims that the group rams its politics down listeners' throats:

> *A:* We've got a lot of energy. Everybody sees us as controversial – all that stuff. I think it's laziness, the usual things what a lot of white people will put against you because they're not used to you speaking out. I think that we could easily be a thorn in the backside of a lot of liberal people, or people that think that they're liberal. I think as Asian people we're kind of throwing back at them. They'll come up with their terms, what they've thought up but its all bullshit.
> *I:* What exactly are your politics?
> *A:* It does go beyond racism, to global issues – politics, religion, tradition, culture, roots. We're humanists, that's all we are. It's all human rights. We're all equal.
> (Aki Nawaz of Fun-Da-Mental, LA2 venue, London, 1994)

ADF, a band which grew out of a London community music project, has also played numerous anti-racist benefits. ADF championed the case of a young Asian waiter jailed for self-defence following a racist attack through releasing the single *Free Satpal Ram* and allowing petitions at their concerts urging the same. ADF support the ethnic women's pressure group the Southall Black Sisters and commemorate past struggles like the Amritsar massacre. DJ John Pandit, the band's 'political strategist' in the early days of ADF's career maintained a day job as a youth worker for a civil rights advice and support group in Tower Hamlets, East London. He rejected accusations of the band as a political rent-a-cause outfit. He told me at the time:

> We find it difficult to be just entertainment. A lot of groups will have a radical sound and attach themselves to these campaigns because it's flavour of the month . . . [but] we've been through this, seen it all, Ani [Dr Das] from his educational point as a tutor and me being involved in anti-racist work for 10 years now. There's no problem working with all of these people but they need education as well. They're front groups, sure, but then all groups are a front for something.
> (DJ John Pandit of ADF, Community Music Centre, Farringdon, London 1994)

In France, Marseilles hip-hoppers IAM also share the same 're-investing in our own community' ethos, having established recording studios for local youth in their home town.

Another *prima facie* connection that can be made between British Asian underground and French hip-hop in regard to anti-racist politics, is 'black' identity assertion, a significant political claim for second-generation ethnic youth in both countries. Lapassade notes '*noirceur*' (blackness) as critical to rap in general (1996: 52–65). However, a number of 'white' parishioners have been active in French hip-hop, for example, MC Solaar's producer Jimmy Jay, Kool Shen (Bruno Lopez) of NTM, and IAM's Akenaton. Interestingly, while research has previously shown that Asians dislike applying the term 'black' to themselves (Baumann 1996), it has been shown more recently (Ghelani 2001) that British Asian youth are 'reconfiguring what it means to be Asian' by adopting urban black stylistic codes such as American hip-hop derived fashion and language, often ironically.

Humour and linguistic practice

In regard to youth 'subcultures', the agenda of cultural practitioners 'in the field' and academic conceptualizations of them do not always follow a neat homological fit. Critics of the CCCS have not been slow to point this out. The same could also be said of those who analyse and write about British Asian underground music. Hutnyk, Sharma and Sharma's (1996) volume carries the declaration 'For [sic] a Black politics . . . for everyone engaged in anti-imperialist, anti-racist struggles' on the book jacket. However, painting British Asian underground and French hip-hop as meaningful only in terms of radical politics neglects a great deal about these bands and performers, and the understandings young people have of them. Some artists have even gone some way to distance themselves from political posturing – openly rejecting a political stance. Bally Sagoo's breakthrough Sony album consisted of old Asian film-score classics remixed with throbbing western baselines and traditional sitar and string section instrumentation. Subsequent Asian underground chart successes have continued the formula of fusion, for example Punjabi MC's *Mundian To Bach Ke*, a rap track which sampled the theme tune from 1980s children's television show *Knightrider*, proved to be a European chart smash in 2003 some five years after its initial release in the *bhangra* clubs. More recently Rishi Rich and Jay Sean from the London districts of Southall and Hounslow respectively have also peddled a mixture of Asian hip-hop, as has Raghav – of Canadian descent. None of these artists makes any secret of the fact that they wish for commercial, mainstream success rather than being consigned to the underground.

Like Sagoo, Talvin Singh sees himself essentially as a musician and not a vehicle for post-colonial vengeance:

> I don't really want to be political all the time. I don't fit into that and I don't want to. I wanna enjoy things which I like whether they have an Asian value or not . . . rather than going 'you fucked us up. I'm gonna fuck you up'. Fuck *who* up? Are these people any part of that? Let's move our shit on.
> (Talvin Singh, musician, the Vibe Bar, London, 1998)

The utilization of humour which connects with mainstream youth culture is a common feature of both French hip-hop and British second-generation Asian pop. In France, one of MC Solaar's trademark features is his use of word-play in songs. He has, for example, satirized boy bands on the track *Boys Bandent*. IAM's lead singer Akenaton on his solo effort *J'ai pas de Face* (*Faceless*) poked fun at this same target. The *bhangra* genre too has inverted earlier moments in mainstream pop history with titles like *Bomb the Tumbi* which played on the classic *Bomb the Bass* and *Never Mind the Dholaks* which played on the Sex Pistols' *Never Mind the Bollocks*. Replacing the third word in each case with an Indian musical instrument name speaks to the second-generation Asian audience while evoking earlier moments of rock history. These wordplays reflect a 'playful', postmodern side to British Asian pop in subverting convention and tweaking received orthodoxies. Indeed the high degree of intertextuality in second-generation ethnic music scenes in both France and Britain indicates hybridity – popular cultural forms combining humour and music which appeal to the biculturalism of their youth audiences. In France we can see the same phenomenon in *banlieue* films like *La Haine* and *100% Arabica*.

Breaking with linguistic convention is one of the most noteworthy features of French rap. A culturally defensive French policy of recent years was the 1991 *Loi Toubon* (Law of Toubon) which sought to replace Anglicisms which had crept into the French language by defined French words sometimes created for this purpose, for example, '*le balladeur*' in place of '*le walkman*'. Needless to say, youth culture was seen as the chief offender in the linguistic phenomenon of borrowing from English which the law tried to address. The polyglot *patois* of French rap, however, goes wider than simply the inclusion of English words in ordinary French slang. The slang form *verlan* (backslang composed by reversing consonants and changing around vowels in words) is often used. Moreover, other variations of *le Français branché* (cutting edge French), combining African, Arab, Gypsy and American sources, are among key features of French rap. There is accordingly a burgeoning literature (Ball 1990; Verdelhan-Bourgade 1990; Pruvost and Sablayrolles 2003) on the French rap *patois* paralleling the work of Hewitt (1986) on the lexicon of Black British youth. New times – hybrid times – also demand neologisms. Kaur and Kalra (1996) for example, have come up with the term 'BrAsian' to define the British Asian who inhabits both of these cultures as opposed to earlier ideas that ethnic youth were caught between them.

Conclusion: the global implications of British Asian underground and French hip-hop in the new Europe

Comparing apparently similar phenomena across two different countries is not always straightforward. Basic conceptual differences go wider than the obvious linguistic ones. For example, the term 'post-colonial' is not used in France. Nonetheless we can draw out a number of similarities between these two nation states. At the same time as negative youth discourses on 'generation X' and 'slackers' were circulating in Britain and the United States, in France the term *'generation bof'* (from the idiomatic expression '*bof*' to convey indifference) was common currency among French journalists describing youth culture. Yet this kind of facile stereotyping was contradicted by the emergence of vibrant youth cultural scenes such as hip-hop in France and Asian underground in Britain. Negative race stereotypes were also challenged by the emergence of these forms.

Applying the terminology, both British Asian underground and French hip-hop are the product of 'post-colonial' circumstances of production – the period after 1945 which saw the formal independence of former French and British colonies. This period has meant a serious rethinking in both Britain and France, with the realization that their sovereignty is in sharp decline. The cultural hegemony of these two colonizing nations is no longer unassailable. The significant argument advanced here is that, to some extent, the hybridized musical forms described above demonstrate a new internationalism in youth culture and a move away from the old 'American dream' of white teen culture. These are not borrowed musical forms. For example, French hip-hop is commonly understood to be 'street' music but it has not simply evolved from its American 'street' equivalent. It is incontestably French in the same way that Asian underground music is inherently British.

In short, British Asian underground music and French hip-hop are multi-faceted, ethno-European popular musical forms fraught with contradictions. Authenticity and cultural empowerment are complicated issues in both as they face the paradox of juggling grassroots credibility with mass acceptance. For example, even the term 'Asian underground' is disliked by some of those involved, as 'underground' suggests 'unsuccessful'. This highlights an identifiable cultural and political tension for second-generation Asian youth. While British Asian underground practitioners want to be part of the overground so they can obtain mainstream success, any such move would necessarily entail a loss of the 'cool' cachet that the music has hitherto enjoyed with fans.

While globalization for some suggests greater freedoms and mobility, Bauman (1998) reminds us that it has had the opposite consequence on economic and political refugees who have found it limiting in terms of border controls and immigration clampdowns. The impact, in purely economic terms, of globalization on popular culture is clear to see in its co-option by multi-national commerce. Major record company involvement in both previously marginal music scenes shows the extent to which the market is now involved. Moreover, there has been some crossover interaction between the two countries which addresses the ever-growing fan base. In France, UK Asian underground group ADF's album *RAFI* sold 20,000 copies on the independent French label Delabel before they signed their major deal with London Records. Similarly, several British Asian underground acts have toured France. French hip-hop has a wider constituency than just French ghetto youth – it is extremely popular with middle-class youth without whom it could never attain its current sales figures.

In addition to this, French hip-hop sells to youth in Francophone Switzerland, Belgium, Canada, West Africa and the French Pacific. Virgin Records in Britain recently issued two compilations of French rap for non-French audiences: *Le Flow* and *Le Flow 2*. Furthermore, a decade after his discovery in France, Sénégal-born French rapper MC Solaar now receives British press coverage, although somewhat muted. For example, he was the subject of a cover story in the British *Financial Times* Weekend Magazine (22 September 2001). A trawl through Google reveals that his 2004 album *Mach 6* received its most fulsome web review on the site of the leftist British magazine *The Socialist Review*, which rated it among the year's best. The tracks *Au Pays de Gandhi* and *Guérrilla* were venerated as 'political'. Record sales indicate that both French hip-hop and British Asian underground also appeal to a post-youth fanbase in their thirties, as well as to younger second-generation minority youth, and the wider teen cohort.

There are challenging and creative visions of France and Britain respectively constituted by French hip-hop and British Asian underground music. If we look through the lens of these hybrid musical forms, through the eyes of a diasporic youth generation, these two states are not monocultural and fixed entities but multicultural and dynamic, each characterized by diversity. With ethnic minority youth at their centre, they contradict the received wisdom of national identity in two countries that are normally imagined as white-faced. State policy about the treatment of immigrants and minority ethnic groups in both countries differs, and this affects the terminology that people use, but these youth cultural forms continue on regardless, as autonomous forms of self-expression.

This youth culture phenomenon is repeated throughout post-colonial Europe. Standard classifications of hip-hop as essentially American are contradicted by the second-generation German Turkish rap scene (Kaya 2001), and by Italian rap (Wright 2000) among others. Mainstream accounts of the phenomenon, however, tend to slide back into the ideology of formal state policies. So, while French academic theorists of rap note its connections with immigrant youth culture they tend to see it as a triumph of integration (Lapassade 1996: 13). Furthermore, studies of French hip-hop (see Bazin 1995; Lapassade 1996) frequently imply it as essentially derivative. These studies pay homage to, and copiously reference, the contents and accounts of American hip-hop as a cultural phenomenon; a compliment unsurprisingly not returned in similar American academic endeavours (Cross 1993; Rose 1994). There are a growing number of academic accounts which address British Asian youth – much welcome after the previous deafening period of silence on the topic – but some accounts slide into a neo-liberal exhortation on the virtues of multiculturalism. What is often missed in mainstream academic accounts of both French hip-hop and British Asian underground is their iconoclastic constitution of a non-western – yet globally distributed – youth culture. The mainstream emergence of these two musical styles is occurring at a time when many fear globalization. Outside the United States, globalization is often taken as a synonym for 'Americanization', particularly the global hegemony of cultural industries like commodified youth culture. In this situation the success of French hip-hop and British Asian underground seem to suggest a decentring of the West.

This chapter has tried to challenge some of our traditional assumptions when dealing with youth cultures – in particular the long-established CCCS, rather narrow British focus on class. The two European hybrid musical forms of the new century discussed above would be difficult to fit into the old CCCS class-centred frameworks of understanding. Crucially both British Asian underground and French hip-hop operate in undeniably globalized conditions of youth culture where ideas, music, technology and people can circulate on a scale unseen before. This is fundamentally alien to the CCCS paradigm of fixed predetermined life-cycles and cultures rooted in territorialized physical space and played out on street corners. The socio-spatial map of youth culture in Europe and the world has been dramatically reconfigured in recent times. This chapter constitutes an argument for acknowledging the duality or multiplicity of cultural points of identification for European youth who are products of post-colonial diasporic flows. They do indeed seem to have a 'double consciousness' which informs the production of new musical forms, but this is not expressed as a simple binary.

In conclusion, the strength of British Asian underground music and Francophone hip-hop are testimony to the enduring power of popular music and its centrality in generating new cultural forms – allowing young people to express their multiply-constituted identities – drawing on local, ethnic, social and other resources. Today's musical youth have a wide-ranging, eclectic choice of listening at their disposal spanning electronic dance music, hip-hop, Indie, rock and numerous permeations of the above, which can only be understood in the context of dynamic cultural processes in an age of globalization. Such new global youth cultures complicate the assumed simplistic correlation between culture and geography. There is a growing literature on the consequences of globalization in creating hybridized diasporic youth cultures (Krims 2000; Mitchell 2001; Connell and Gibson 2003; Nayak 2003). However, further, more finely-nuanced research is urgently needed, including a consideration of gender relations, for example.

The story of post-colonial popular musical youth cultural forms in the new Europe of the twenty-first century does not stop with Britain and France. If anything, these multiple phenomena are likely to mushroom, and fracture further into even more dynamic and complex forms as the third-generation ethnic minority children of the third millennium grow up. The parallel transnational and post-colonial musical forms of British Asian underground and French hip-hop are a powerful counter-balance to outmoded national government policies that seek to impose centrally determined uniform national identities. They are also, importantly, the ideal soundtracks to accompany the life trajectories of young Europeans in the post-millennial, post-subcultural, postmodern, post-industrial, post-Fordist and post-colonial times that we inhabit.

Bibliography

Anwar, M. (1976) *Between Two Cultures*, London: Community Relations Council.
Badache, R. (1995) 'Le monde du NTM! Le sense caché de l'injure rituelle', in *Agora: debats jeunesses*, 3eme Trimestre, Paris: L'Harmattan.
Ball, R. (1990) 'Lexical innovation in present-day French: "le Français branché"', *French Cultural Studies*, 1(1): 21–35.
Banerji, S. and Baumann, G. (1990) 'Bhangra 1984–8: fusion and professionalization in a genre of South Asian dance music', in P. Oliver (ed.) *Black Music in Britain: essays on the Afro-Asian contribution to popular music*, London: Open University Press.
Bauman, Z. (1998) *Globalization: the human consequences*, New York: Columbia University Press.
Baumann, G. (1996) *Contesting Culture: discourses of identity in multi-ethnic London*, Cambridge: Cambridge University Press.
Bazin, H. (1995) *La Culture Hip Hop*, Paris: Desclée de Brouwer.

Bennett, A. (2000) *Popular Music and Youth Culture: music, identity and place*, Basingstoke: Macmillan.

—— (2001) *Cultures of Popular Music*, Buckingham: Open University Press.

Bianchi, F. (1995) 'Night cultures, night economies', *Planning Practice and Research*, 10: 121–6.

Brake, M. (1980) *The Sociology of Youth Culture and Youth Subcultures*, London: Routledge and Kegan Paul.

Brulard, I. (1997) 'Laïcité and Islam', in S. Perry (ed.) *Aspects of Contemporary France*, London: Routledge.

Cathus, O. (1994) 'Funk et effervescence', *Le Gredin*, Paris. Online. Available: <www.gredin.free.fr/sociologie/o.cathus/funketeffervescence.html> (accessed 17 June 2005).

Chatterton, P. and Hollands. R. (2003) *Urban Nightscapes: youth cultures, pleasure spaces and corporate power*, London: Routledge.

Connell, J. and Gibson, C. (2003) *Soundtracks: popular music, identity and place*, London: Routledge.

Cross, B. (1993) *It's Not About a Salary: rap, race and resistance in Los Angeles*, London: Verso.

Frith, S. (1996) *Performing Rites: on the value of popular music*, Oxford: Oxford University Press.

Ghelani, T. (2001) 'Asian young people's use of African American commodified cultures', paper presented at Beyond hip-hop: youth cultures and globalization, ESRC Interdisciplinary Youth Studies seminar, Sheffield University, 26 November.

Gilroy, P. (1993) *The Black Atlantic: modernity and double consciousness*, Cambridge, MA: Harvard University Press.

Hall, S. (1993) 'Cultural identity and diaspora', in P. Williams and L. Chrisman (eds) *Colonial Discourse and Postcolonial Theory*, New York: Harvester Wheatsheaf.

—— and Jefferson, T. (1976) (eds) *Resistance through Rituals: youth subcultures in post-war Britain*, London: Harper Collins Academic.

Hebdige, D. (1979) *Subculture: the meaning of style*, London: Routledge.

—— (1988) *Hiding in the Light*, London: Routledge – Comedia Series.

Hewitt, R. (1986) *White Talk Black Talk: inter-racial friendship and communication amongst adults*, Cambridge: Cambridge University Press.

Hobbs, D., Hall, S., Winlow, S. and Lister S. (2000) 'Receiving shadows: governance and liminality in the night time economy', *British Journal of Sociology*, 51(4): 701–17.

Huq, R. (1996) 'Asian kool? Bhangra and beyond', in J. Hutnyk, A. Sharma and S. Sharma (eds) *Disorienting Rhythms: the politics of the new Asian dance music*, London: Zed Books.

—— (2005) *Beyond Subculture*, London: Routledge.

Hutnyk, J., Sharma, A. and Sharma, S. (eds) (1996) *Disorienting Rhythms: the politics of the new Asian dance music*, London: Zed Books.

Jones, S. (1988) *Black Culture, White Youth: the reggae tradition from JA to UK*, Basingstoke: Macmillan Education.

Kaur, R. and Kalra, V. (1996) 'New paths for South Asian identity and musical creativity', in J. Hutnyk, A. Sharma and S. Sharma (eds) *Disorienting Rhythms: the politics of the new Asian dance music*, London: Zed Books.

Kaya, A. (2001) *'Sicher in Kreuzberg' – Constructing Diasporas: Turkish hip-hop youth in Berlin*, Bielefeld: transcript.

Krims, A. (2000) *Rap Music and the Poetics of Identity*, Cambridge: Cambridge University Press.

Lapassade, G. (1996) *Le Rap ou la Fureur de Dire*, Paris: Loris Talmart.

Lovatt, A. (1995) 'The ecstasy of urban regeneration: regulation of the night-time economy in the post-Fordist city', in J. O'Connor and D. Wynne (eds) *From the Margins to the Centre*, Aldershot: Ashgate.

Mitchell, T. (2001) (ed.) *Global Noise: rap and hip-hop outside the USA*, Middletown, CT: Wesleyan University Press.

Muggleton, D. (2000) *Inside Subculture: the postmodern meaning of style*, Oxford: Berg.

Nayak, A. (2003) *Race, Place and Globalization: youth cultures in a changing world*, Oxford: Berg.

Poulet, G. (1993) 'Popular music', in M. Cook (ed.) *French Culture since 1945*, Harlow: Longman.

Pruvost, J. and Sablayrolles, J.F. (2003) *Les Néologismes*, Paris: Que Sais-Je?

Rojek, C. (1995) *Decentring Leisure: rethinking leisure theory*, London: Sage.

Rose, T. (1994) *Black Noise: rap music and black culture in contemporary America*, Middletown, CT: Wesleyan University Press.

Said, E. (1979) *Orientalism*, New York: Vintage Books.

Spivak, G. (1999) *A Critique of Postcolonial Reason: towards a history of the vanishing present*, Cambridge, MA: Harvard University Press.

Stokes, M. (1994) *Ethnicity, Identity and Music: the musical construction of place*, Oxford: Berg.

Storry, M. and Childs, P. (1997) (eds) *British Cultural Identities*, London: Routledge.

Toop, D. (1995) *Ocean of Sound: aether talk, ambient sound and imaginary worlds*, London: Serpent's Tail.

Verdelhan-Bourgade, M. (1990) 'Communiquer en Français contemporain: quelque part ça m'interpelle, phénomènes syntaxiques en Français branché', *La Linguistique*, 26(1): 53–69.

Watson, J. (1977) (ed.) *Between Two Cultures: migrants and minorities in Britain*, Oxford: Blackwell.

Wright, S. (2000) '"A love born of hate": autonomist rap in Italy', *Theory, Culture and Society*, 17: 117–35.

2 'I am English too'
Francophone youth hybridities in Canada

Christine Dallaire

> I speak French, but I also equally speak English, it seems. And, I don't know, my family is French, both sides of my family, their grandparents and all that. I am of French descent, but I would not say that I am only French, because I am not . . . I am English too. I am a bilingual Canadian.
>
> (youth at the 2001 Franco-Ontarian Games)

This chapter looks at the phenomenon of hybridity of youth identities in the situation of local, linguistic/cultural minorities struggling to retain francophone identity within the discursive context of global hegemony of the English language. Many francophone minority youth in Canada refuse a singular francophone identity and instead reproduce themselves as hybrids, claiming both francophone and anglophone subjectivities. In explaining that they are 'English too', these young people situate themselves within the larger anglophone majority and portray themselves as 'true' Canadians. They not only *speak* both official languages but also *identify* with both French and English language communities. They even insist on this dual affiliation when discussing their sense of self in the context of youth games meant to foster francophone pride. To examine the hybridity of these minority youth and the discursive contexts in which they make sense of who and what they are, this chapter summarizes the findings of a comparative ethnography of three francophone youth games.

The Acadian Games (Jeux de l'Acadie), the Alberta Francophone Games (Jeux Francophones de l'Alberta) and the Franco-Ontarian Games (Jeux Franco-Ontariens) offer a germane empirical context to study minority youth identity construction because they were instituted to encourage youth to speak French and reinforce their francophoneness. However, despite the francophone mandate of the games, youthful participants nonetheless claimed hybrid identities, where hybridity refers to the mixing of two contradictory linguistic and cultural subjectivities. This chapter focuses on these hybridities and uncovers their configurations. The discursive and performative character of francophoneness in Canada is outlined in the first section below. The second section outlines the study of the three games. A synthesis of the findings illustrates the particular complexities of francophone youth hybridities.

Whereas the manifestations of these hybridities are similar among young people at the three games, the characteristics of their francophoneness vary. Furthermore, their asymmetrical character complicates these hybrid identities since youths' francophone and anglophone subjectivities are rarely performed equally. The chapter concludes with the impact of hybridity on the identity construction of minority francophone youth.

The discursive construction of francophoneness and youth hybridities

While French and English are Canada's two official languages, Canadians for whom French is a first language represent less than one-quarter of the total population (Statistics Canada 2002). Most reside in Quebec where they represent the majority of the provincial population. This chapter focuses on the remaining million francophones who live as linguistic minorities in other provinces. In a context where their younger generation is incessantly subject to the homogenizing influence of North American English language popular culture and media, these francophone minorities must work to ensure the reproduction of francophoneness.

Francophoneness is an effect of discourses that produce francophone identities by ascribing meaning to the distinctive features of the practice of French language, and of the cultures associated with French language in Canada. While the Canadian census defines 'francophone' on the basis of mother tongue, the concept is understood here to refer to all types of identities linked to francophoneness as well as affiliations individuals may develop towards French-speaking minorities, for example: Acadian, French Canadian, Franco-Ontarian and Franco-Albertan identities. Foucault's (1976, 1983) discourse analysis is useful to understand how certain cultural characteristics, linguistic behaviours and other practices are associated with what it means to be a francophone. Butler's (1990, 1993) feminist adaptation of Foucault's work is also helpful to appreciate the performative character of francophone identity as it is constituted through the practices regulated by francophone discourses. In fact, discourses producing francophoneness provide the 'truths' that not only become the definitions through which French speakers recognize themselves as francophones, but also govern the actions that repeatedly reproduce them as francophones.

We find one such francophone identity discourse in Acadia. The 1604 French settlement in Canada occupied a territory – l'Acadie – the region today known as the Maritime Provinces (Arsenault 1999). Acadians were deported between 1755 and 1762 because of their refusal to pledge allegiance to the British crown, insisting instead on neutral status in conflict between the French and British empires (LeBlanc 1999). This event had devastating consequences on Acadians and their descendants. It still influences the discursive construction of today's Acadian identity and distinguishes it from other Canadian francophone identities. Emphasis on history and culture, combined with a focus on ancestry – families that survived deportation – and founding myths, has fostered the construction of an identity based on ethnicity (Johnson and McKee-Allain 1999). The old Acadie nation is today divided into provincialized minorities in the three Maritime Provinces (Thériault 1994): the Acadian minority of New Brunswick which accounts for 85 per cent of Maritime Acadians of French mother tongue (Statistics Canada 2002), and the Acadian minorities of Nova Scotia and Prince Edward Island.

French Canadian ethnicity originally united the descendants of Nouvelle-France settlers, but the discursive fragmentation of French Canada and birth of the Québécois nation led to the emergence in the 1960s of provincially-based minority identities, such as Franco-Ontarian in Ontario and Franco-Albertan in Alberta (Juteau-Lee and Lapointe 1983). These new minorities developed, to varying degrees, more politically- and contractually-oriented collective identities rather than general French Canadian ethnicity as a result of their changing relationships with provincial and federal governments (Thériault 1994). In fact, the *Official Languages Act* of 1988, in the context of Canadian multiculturalism, reshaped provincial francophone identities into new French language minorities (Bernard 1998). The legal protection of French language combined with immigration from French-speaking countries contributed to the discursive transformation of former French Canadian and Acadian ethnic groups into linguistic minorities. Nonetheless, the once dominant francophone ethnic discourses still have wide currency. Thus the discursive shift is far from complete for all francophone minorities.

Ethnic and linguistic francophone identity discourses do share an important characteristic in that they establish an opposition between francophoneness and anglophone identity. French mother tongue, and speaking in predominantly French, define francophones in contrast to anglophones who live their lives in English. Although over 80 per cent of Canadians who declare French as their first language can speak English (Statistics Canada 1997), these discourses position English as a second language – less meaningful to self-identification. It is this 'truth' that today's francophone youths resist, given that speaking and living in English is also significant to their sense of self. This chapter argues that while their identity practices are in part governed by francophone discourses, these young people constitute themselves as hybrids. They draw on pan-Canadian identity discourses to integrate a new combined francophone/anglophone identity that better reflects their view of themselves.

Like other studies of youth identities (Kraidy 1999; Noble, Poynting and Tabar 1999) and of ethnicity (Slabbert and Finlayson 2000; Meerwald 2001), the concept of hybridity proves valuable here to understand diverse ethnic and linguistic border-crossing experiences. If hybridity designates the transgression of socially constructed cultural boundaries (Pieterse 1995, 2001), then in this chapter, it signifies the mixing of two distinctive, but not fixed, cultural and linguistic identities, into a new dual identity. Hybridity does not merely refer to the sum of the constitutive parts of identity. Following Papastergiadis (2000) one could say that minority francophone youth hybridity is more than the addition of anglophoneness to a prior francophoneness, and more than the conflict between them. It is rather the conjunction and juxtaposition of these two dimensions of identity, their collision and impossible reconciliation. The focus here on identities related to French and English languages conveys the fact that young people in this study referred to linguistic practices as core dimensions of their self-definition. French versus English linguistic practices are really at the crux of francophone games, as they are in francophone minority identity discourses in Canada. They have consequently become the principal performance that produces youth as francophone, or not.

The arena: the games and methodological details

Faced with a 'crisis of assimilation' in the late 1980s, the national association of francophone minority youth recommended that leisure activities, particularly sport, be developed to provide youth with enjoyable opportunities 'in French'. Too often it seemed compulsory French language use, particularly in francophone schools, marked youth experiences of francophoneness. They consequently associated francophoneness with the constraints and sanctions they suffered if they did not speak French. Conversely, they were drawn to the social status of English, pervasive throughout their leisure activities, from media and popular culture, to organized activities such as sport. Hence, if the complete assimilation of youth into the anglophone majority was to be prevented, it was deemed crucial to promote activities associating francophoneness with fun and play.

The existing successful Acadian Games were proposed as a model solution for other francophone minorities. The Jeux de l'Acadie are the longest-running francophone minority games. Athletes are recruited among New Brunswick francophone schools and also from Nova Scotia and Prince Edward Island. This two-tiered, multi-sport event modelled on Olympic Games philosophy and structure annually draws over 1,000 10- to 17-year-old participants. Between 1979 and 2004, about 80,000 young people participated in regional contests and 19,000 competed in the finals. Allain (1996) observed that the games provide not only sport, economic, infrastructure and tangible political benefits for New Brunswick's Acadian minority, but also contribute non-tangible benefits such as the promotion of pride among youth, and stronger Acadian self-confidence. Impressed by such achievements, the Alberta francophone youth association created the Alberta Francophone Games in 1992 – to stimulate a comparable community synergy in the Franco-Albertan minority, and to promote French language and culture among 12- to 18-year-olds. Since its inception, this annual multi-sport attempt at replicating the Acadian Games gathers between about 150 to 300 young people for a 'francophone' weekend, where sport is meant to be the principal medium through which French language is lived. Since participants are selected on their propensity to speak French throughout the weekend rather than athletic abilities, the Alberta Games offer recreational activities, while the Acadian Games are closer to mainstream competitive sport. In contrast to both these games, the Franco-Ontarian Games constitute a successful multidisciplinary event – youth festival rather than sporting event. Established in 1994, the Jeux Franco-Ontariens draw about 800 14- to 18-year-old students from francophone schools. Organizers purposefully moved away from the competitive sport model so that the event attracts not only the school 'jocks' but also the school clowns, artists, musicians, singers and school council leaders for a celebration of youth and francophoneness.

This ethnographic analysis draws on a variety of data collection techniques to explore identity construction at the games. It includes data collected for a prior ethnography of the Alberta Francophone Games and more recent information gathered from all three games. Fieldwork was most useful for comparing the francophoneness of the games and the identity practices of both organizers and participants. The researcher's presence in the field is in fact the central feature of ethnography (Sands 2002). Participant observation at the Alberta Francophone Games in 1996, 1997 and 2002 and at the 2001 Acadian and Franco-Ontarian Games permitted direct experience of the setting and atmosphere and, more importantly, provided for interaction with youth. Concurrent document analysis of the various records and files of the organizations staging the three games, in conjunction with interviews with a large number of organizers, provided the background information to situate the history of the games, and to distinguish better their respective francophone characters. A total of 35 organizers and volunteers of the Alberta Francophone Games were interviewed between 1996 and 1997, and 2001 and 2003. Interviews were also conducted with 14 Franco-Ontarian Games organizers and 20 Acadian Games organizers in 2000 and 2001. Karine Henrie and Véronique Martin, graduate students, assisted in conducting interviews.

Questionnaires and interviews with youth, supplemented by drawings, significantly enhanced the investigation of youth identities. A questionnaire requiring both open and closed responses was administered to youth at the three games to collect demographic data as well as information about their identity, linguistic practices and involvement in francophone activities. Response rates were high: 140 of 150 questionnaires were returned at the 1996 Alberta Francophone Games, 164 of 180 at the 1997 event, and 31 of 35 at the 2002 event. At the 2001 Acadian Games finals, 815 of 1,047 questionnaires were returned and 588 of 759 at the Franco-Ontarian Games in 2001.

Questionnaire data was decidedly helpful in discerning the characteristics of participants, while 30-minute group interviews allowed youth to discuss their identity and how they conceive of francophone minorities. Thirty-nine boys and girls were interviewed at the 1997 Alberta Francophone Games, in addition to another 28 participants in 2002. At the 2001 Franco-Ontarian Games, interviews were conducted with 107 participants, and at the Acadian Games, with 175 boys and girls. Following interviews, respondents were asked to draw or write their conception or definition of francophone identity or 'francophone community'. Almost all focused on this latter concept. Twenty-six drawings were collected at the 1997 Alberta Francophone Games, and 27 in 2002, 113 drawings at the 2001 Franco-Ontarian Games, and 181 at the 2001 Acadian Games. The group interviews and drawings provide many insights as they allowed the young people to explain the meanings they attribute to their linguistic and identity practices, and to elaborate on how they make sense of who they are. Comparative analysis of the three games and their participants reveals the complexities, similarities and differences between francophone youth hybridities. All translations in this chapter were provided by the author.

Manifestations of francophone youth hybridities

> Because Canadian is not just francophone . . . It is francophone and anglophone. And I am not only a francophone, I am both.
> (participant at the 1997 Alberta Francophone Games)

Data reveals that hybridization unquestionably shapes the francophoneness of a sizeable proportion of participants at the games. The analysis below shows that participants manifestly produce mixed identities. They highlight in interviews that they are 'more than just francophones', and specify in questionnaires that English-French bilingualism is prominent in their sense of self (Dallaire 2003). Their hybridized subject positions are not constituted only in francophone discourses, but in anglophoneness – clearly demonstrated through their choice of 'bilingual' and 'Canadian' identities as best descriptions of their sense of self. These young people connote a specific *identity* quality to 'bilingual' rather than denoting linguistic attributes. This is the most obvious expression of francophone youth hybridity.

While previous studies of minority francophone youth have noted the emergence of a 'bilingual' identity, such as Gérin-Lajoie's recent ethnography (2003), this research clarifies that it encodes participation in both the French *and* English-speaking communities, asserting belonging beyond the francophone minority. Moreover, the claim of 'Canadian' identity adds a 'national' quality and definition to their bilingualism. Discourses depicting Canada as a bilingual nation where both French and English are official languages, and carry the same political weight, undeniably play a critical role in the construction of their hybrid identities. Such views appeal to francophone minority youth as they draw on them in assuming that a Canadian speaks both languages. However, in reality only 17.7 per cent of Canadians can conduct a conversation in both official languages (Statistics Canada 2002). Despite this fact, discourses of Canadian bilingualism allow these young French-speakers to situate themselves within an imagined hybrid majority rather than siding with either linguistic community.

Hybridity is however not as straightforward as just claiming bilingual or

Canadian identities. Interviews unexpectedly revealed that even when youth declare identities historically associated to monolithic francophoneness, they also indicate anglophoneness as well. For instance, when asked to explain why they identified as Franco-Albertans, two girls at the Alberta Francophone Games explained,

> *Ch*: Well, it is because . . . I live in Alberta, I speak French and English and both about equally.
> *I:* Then why not just say that you are Albertan? Why the need to add 'Franco'?
> *Ch*: Because you want to know that you are a francophone.
> *D:* I am Franco-Albertan too because I always lived in Alberta and I learned French before English.
> (participants at the 2002 Alberta Francophone Games)

For some, claiming Franco-Albertan, Franco-Ontarian or Acadian identities actually presumes bilingualism. Thus, to be a francophone in youth identity narratives no longer means that one speaks French and constructs one's identity primarily based on francophoneness, but rather that one speaks both French and English frequently. For these minority francophone youth, fluency in English is perhaps a given since it is omnipresent in Canadian society (outside Quebec of course) and in their day-to-day lives. Francophone identity markers then serve to specify francophoneness in addition to taken-for-granted anglophoneness.

Current francophone and Canadian identity discourses and related identifiers often do not, or at least not suitably, convey the meaning they wish to put forward. Francophone minority youth choose a range of different identity markers to emphasize their hybridity. As one participant at the Franco-Ontarian Games put it, 'I don't know how I would say it, but I am Franco-Ontarian and I am anglophone' (2001). While they all share an insistence on both francophoneness and anglophoneness, there is no consensus among young people participating at the same event on exactly how to express this hybridity, let alone at the three games. To complicate matters further, they articulate different rationales for dual affiliation, reflecting their varied relationships to francophoneness as such, and to various francophone identity discourses. For example, some chose a hybrid identity because, despite having learned French as a first language, they did not feel part of the ethnicities predominantly associated with francophoneness. In other cases, hybridity emphasizes the primacy of English for youth who learned French only in school as neither parent speaks French. Enunciating a bilingual or Canadian identity thus designates their affiliation with the French-speaking minority without claiming cultural or linguistic lineage. Yet the quote at the beginning of this chapter shows how other youth produce themselves as hybrid despite singular French Canadian or Acadian ancestry and French mother tongue. While francophoneness is important to them, so is participation in the larger English-speaking Canadian society:

> I think that it is also important to not only live in a francophone community. It is good to have it. But I would find . . . I know there are some people who are always only with people who are just francophones. And they do not really have friends outside the francophone community. I think that is really not good because it is a small francophone community and if we stay together and do not speak to other people it does no good at all.
>
> (participant at the 1997 Alberta Francophone Games)

Finally, hybridity is a strategy for some youth to emphasize their mixed cultural and linguistic heritage. 'And I, with a French mother and an English father, I am directly bilingual. And that is why I would first say that I am Canadian' (youth leader at 2001 Franco-Ontarian Games). As Phoenix and Owen (2000) found in their study of young Londoners of black and white parentage, youth from mixed families resist being strictly associated with either one ancestry or the other.

Some youth effectively produce integrated dual identities. For instance, some of the youth quoted above clearly state that they are both francophone and anglophone. Thus, like other minority youth (Noble, Poynting and Tabar 1999), they reproduce strategic and positional hybrid identities – generating agency and consciousness (Mujcinovic 2001), while some ambiguously shift between francophone and anglophone identities rather than consciously articulating a combination of both. In neither case though, do they reject francophoneness. Instead, they demonstrate that singular francophone identities do not adequately represent their sense of self. They refuse the 'either or' perspective of the hegemonic dichotomy that opposes what it means to be francophone or anglophone in Canada. This is what distinguishes hybrid youth from other francophones, such as the majority of (older) organizers of the three games, who draw only on francophone discourses to construct their sense of self even if they can speak English.

> It's weird. I don't know what it is, because there was a time, my generation, if you asked them if they were francophones, I think that the tendency was 'Yes, I am a francophone. And yes, I am bilingual but I am still a francophone in that.' Now, you ask a youth and he will say: 'I am bilingual.' Well, jeez, we don't understand that. How can your culture be bilingual? No, I am a francophone who has learned English.
>
> (organizer of the 1997 Alberta Francophone Games)

Like the organizers, some youth at the games certainly reproduce singular francophone identities – the games are where they reaffirm this exclusive francophoneness. Yet questionnaire results show that about 40 per cent of participants at the Acadian and Franco-Ontarian Games, and between a third to half of youth at the 1996, 1997 and 2002 Alberta Francophone Games, identify primarily as bilingual, Canadian or both – identity markers that clearly support the hybridity revealed by interviews.

However, a nuanced and tentative interpretation is preferred, as youth may be adding an anglophone dimension to historically monolithic francophone identities. Thus, the number of young people who conceive of themselves as *francophones-plus* is higher than the combined total of youth identifying as Canadian and bilingual. Whether evident or inconspicuous though, all expressions of hybridity that produce youth as both francophone and anglophone enunciate discourses that circulate beyond the borders of francophone minorities and their games. The next section focuses on the characteristics of the different forms of francophoneness emphasized at the three games and reproduced in youth identity narratives.

The games and their distinct francophoneness

As mentioned earlier, francophone discourse in Canada establishes French linguistic practice as the basic criterion for francophoneness. While the three games share this fundamental definition in their mandate to foster francophone pride and identification, each event promotes distinct notions of what it means to be francophone. The different francophone discourses circulating at the games correspond in large part to the particular discursive features of their respective local francophone minorities. As a result, francophone youth hybridities become more complex to describe, as their francophone component is far from uniform across the games.

The Acadian Games

The cultural discourse producing an ethnic Acadian identity is prevalent at the Acadian Games. In fact, ethnic 'Acadian' specificity is mostly taken for granted by the association staging the event. Organizers do acknowledge that not all francophones in the Maritimes identify with Acadianness and efforts have been made to accommodate such differences: by using the term 'francophone' in official documentation, and by underlining the French linguistic criterion shared by all involved. Yet the event celebrates Acadian folklore. The profusion of Acadian flags, symbols, colours, traditions, music and dance throughout the weekend exemplifies the strong sense of Acadian ethnicity. Organizers specify that ancestry is not required to claim Acadian identity. Maritime francophones who want to share in specific Acadian culture are welcome in the Acadian community. However, French must be one's first language or spoken by parents or grandparents. This is stipulated in the selection criteria for Nova Scotia and Prince Edward Island. Young participants usually reproduce a similar version of this ethnic discourse in talking about who they are, and in their representation of the Acadian community:

Acadian for me is the fiddle, step dancing and that kind of music. And to know a bit of history, the deportation and *stuff* [original word in English] like that. I think that is what it is to be Acadian.

(participant at the 2001 Acadian Games)

Thus, 82 per cent of the 181 youth drawings illustrate the 'Acadian' cultural character of the identity and/or community being reproduced at the games – for example, Figure 2.1.

The Franco-Ontarian Games

In contrast, the Franco-Ontarian Games are marked by the fervent articulation of a linguistic discourse producing a multicultural and inclusive francophone identity based on one's commitment to 'living in French'. Known for its expertise in francophone cultural development, the youth association staging the games strategically enunciates this uniform and coherent identity discourse throughout the games. In fact, all aspects of the event, from the content of ceremonies to the cultural and social activities, are tailored to deliver the same message. It is not surprising then that research participants reiterated the same definition of francophoneness, emphasizing its transcultural features and commitment to speak and 'live in French' in both drawings (see Figure 2.2) and interviews.

I think that you're a Franco-Ontarian . . . in your heart . . . If you live in Ontario, you are attached to French, Franco-Ontarian, culture, you fit with what I think is a Franco-Ontarian . . . You don't have to be white, to be here since the 1800-I-don't-know-what. You can be of another culture, from another country. You live in Ontario and you live our reality, you're a Franco-Ontarian in my mind.

(participant at the 2001 Franco-Ontarian Games)

As the most culturally diversified youth cohort of the three games, the multicultural quality of this discourse appeals to young francophones and they represented this in their responses. That approximately a quarter of them claimed a variety of ethnic heritages, sometimes more than one, is the most telling measure of participants' multicultural identity. Most of these ethnicities are not obviously associated with francophoneness – for example, Chinese, German, Greek, Italian, Finnish, Scottish, Mexican and Ukrainian. Other cultural ancestries do imply a colonial or other connection to French language, such as Congolese, Zaïrese, Algerian, Malagasy, Burundian, Lebanese and Moroccan. Yet all exemplify cultural features far from the historical French Canadian ethnicity of Ontario's francophone minority. The list of declared first languages and home languages is correspondingly varied.

The major unifying discourse is declared pride in being a francophone, and active commitment towards the French language and francophone institutions

42 *Christine Dallaire*

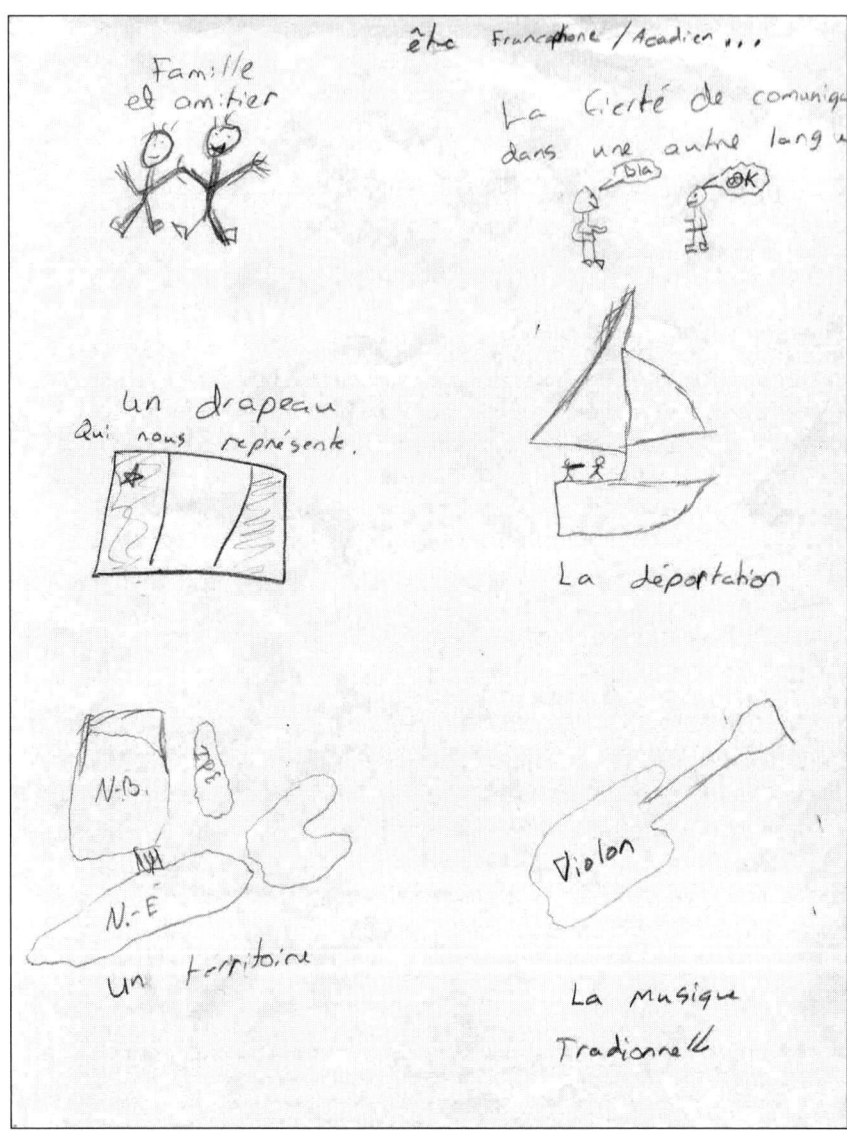

Figure 2.1 Acadian Games drawing representing Acadian identity with a focus on family and friends, pride in speaking another language, a representative flag, deportation, a territory and traditional music

despite living amid the anglophone majority. It is a discourse that youth reproduced in their discussion of francophoneness:

> S: For me, there is only one thing really: the need to be proud . . . Really, we have to be proud. If we are proud, we really get involved.

Figure 2.2 Franco-Ontarian Games drawing about the francophone community: 'We stick together despite our size, height or colour. We are proud of who we are . . . we are Francophones!'

If everyone, all francophones of Ontario are proud and show it, people will react to that and we will have, maybe, more activities in French, more things in French in the English-speaking community.

N: That's it. It's pride. That's what it takes to be francophone. Because if you're proud, you'll speak it. And if you speak it, French will live in Ontario. And will blossom. And that's it. You must be proud. And if you are proud, the rest will come. But at the heart, it's pride.

A: The moment you speak French in Ontario, you are considered a Franco-Ontarian. But to be a real Franco-Ontarian, you have to love, you have to be prepared to fight to have your language and participate in things.

(participants at the 2001 Franco-Ontarian Games)

Participants are aware that other versions of francophoneness exist, but they endorse Franco-Ontarian Games organizers' vision of transculturalism and inclusion that creates an intense, discursively stable, youthful and inviting francophone environment.

The Alberta Francophone Games

Just as the simultaneous circulation of the French Canadian ethnic discourse and the parallel linguistic discourse generates competing 'truths' about francophoneness in the Franco-Albertan minority, it also produces contested ideas about francophone identity at the Alberta Francophone Games (Dallaire and Denis 2000). Organizers vacillate between linguistic and cultural definitions of francophoneness, and inevitably produce a discursively unstable francophone subject. This uncertainty is then replicated by participants, who produce the same hierarchy of francophoneness where French speakers are considered francophones, but those who share French as a first language and presumably francophone culture, have a stronger claim to francophone identity. In questionnaire and interview data, respondents most commonly referred, at least on the face of it, to the performance of French language as the basis of francophoneness. Yet interviews and drawings illustrate the continued relevance of the *cultural* discourse, in that participants recognize it and pronounce it as a basis for francophoneness. Furthermore, they speak of French Canadian traditions as customs families might infrequently partake of, for instance at Christmas or at the winter carnival. In contrast to Acadian youth narratives of ancestral folklore recuperated in contemporary practices – updated and enjoyed at Acadian 'parties' and at the Acadian Games – participants at the Alberta Francophone Games tend to portray French Canadian customs as a thing of the past. They seem not to expect, nor want, the games to highlight French Canadian traditions such as music and food, unlike youth at the Acadian Games who take pleasure in the ethnic Acadian character of the event.

For some, there is no point of engagement between the French Canadian and the linguistic discourse. On the other hand, some participants enunciate both discourses and even shift from one discourse to another during the interview. However, the most frequent definition of francophoneness in youth narratives remains the performance of the French language and they particularly focus on the inclusion of all French speakers in this, regardless of mother tongue. Participants at the Alberta Francophone Games were all aware that first language potentially differentiates francophones from non-francophones but they implicitly rejected this definition. As one youth wrote:

> The francophone community is the francophones in the region who know and speak French. I think that it can be your first language, but it does not have to be your first language.
> (participant at the 1997 Alberta Francophone Games)

This view is not unexpected since the Alberta Francophone Games recruit not only in francophone schools, but also in French immersion schools to ensure a larger number of participants. French immersion schools teach French language to non-French-speaking students and eventually teach the entire curriculum in French. Consequently, about one-third of participants at the 1996 and 1997 games were recruited from French immersion schools, while youth without French as a first language represented 16 per cent of participants at the 2002 edition. Thus, in greater proportion than the other two games, the Alberta Francophone Games recruit youth whose relationship to French is associated with school. The recruitment of participants from French immersion schools creates heated debate among organizers on the quantity of participants versus the quality of participants – their propensity to speak French throughout the weekend – and its impact on the franco-

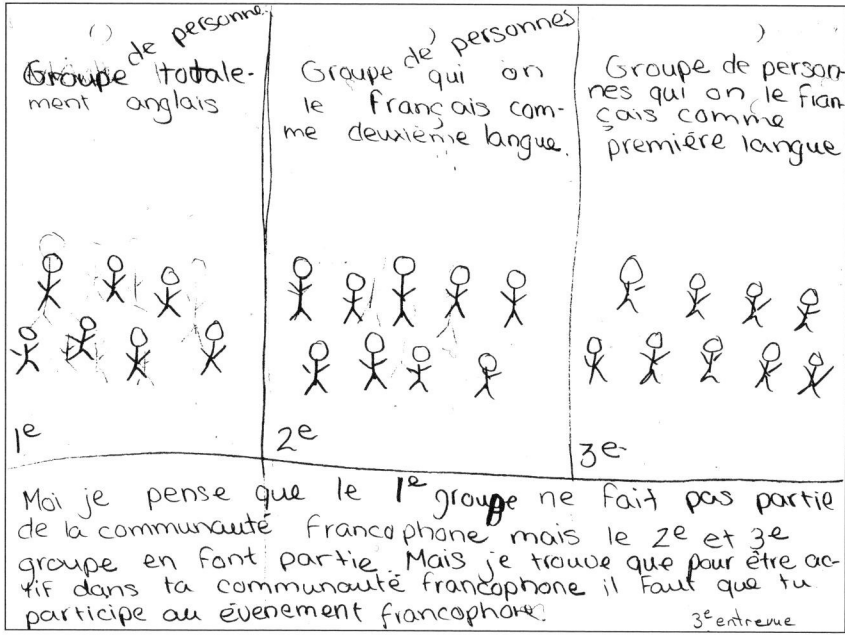

Figure 2.3 Alberta Francophone Games drawing representing the inclusion of French mother tongue speakers and speakers of French as a second language in the francophone community, while excluding people who 'are completely English' (first group on left). This participant also states that to be active in one's francophone community, one must participate in francophone events.

phoneness of the games. Youth who have French as a first language and who study in francophone schools seem to feel it is more important to stage a large event including participants who might inevitably speak English at some point, rather than holding a small event completely in French. As a result, they highlight this inclusiveness in interviews and drawings (see Figure 2.3).

To sum up, the discursive instability of francophoneness is most pronounced at the Alberta Francophone Games. Youth at the Acadian Games repeat the Acadian identity discourse, but their francophoneness is not homogeneous either. However, while not all youth at the Franco-Ontarian Games share the same cultural connections to the French language, they articulate the most consistent and uniform definition of francophoneness, a francophone identity discourse that rejects the ethnic criteria and instead stresses commitment to 'living' the French language as the defining feature of francophoneness. These divergent ideas of what it is to be 'francophone' at the three games point to the fragmentation of minority francophone identifications among young French-speakers, and the range of hybrid identities that integrate francophoneness and anglophoneness. As a result of the muddled and complex intersection of different francophone identity discourses across Canada, the francophone dimension of these hybridities changes from one provincial francophone minority to the other, and within these minorities as well.

Asymmetrical hybridities

In the context of the games, youth from the strongest francophone minority perform the strongest francophoneness and the weakest anglophoneness. The following section outlines the relationship between francophone minorities' social power and the configuration of youth hybridities (Dallaire and Denis 2005). Two dimensions of social power are most significant in this analysis: population size and institutionalization. The relative proportion of the francophone minority in the provincial population indicates that minority's social power within provincial boundaries. Such boundaries become significant in the transformation of francophone identities (Juteau-Lee and Lapointe 1983; Thériault 1994), and are the setting for political struggles to ensure survival of the French language. The degree of 'institutional completeness' (Breton 1964, 1991) of francophone minorities also influences the availability of opportunities for interaction among francophones and the extent to which French is 'lived'.

Asymmetrical hybridities in the Acadian Games

Table 2.1 shows that, of the three games, participants at the Acadian Games manifested the strongest and least varied relationships to the French language.

Acadian Games youth constitute three categories on the basis of francophoneness. Around 70 per cent (the majority) share French as their first language, come from francophone families, possess Acadian, French Canadian or French heritage, and communicate only or mostly in French at home and with friends. A further 15 to 20 per cent declare both French and English as first languages, come from linguistically mixed families and report speaking French and English equally. The remaining 10 to 15 per cent have English as a mother tongue, come from non-francophone or linguistically mixed families, and mainly use English. Of ten participants who declare having neither French nor English as a first language, seven of them identify *franglais*, *chiac* and *brayon* as their mother tongue – terms referring to a mix of French and English.

New Brunswick youth accounted for more than 75 per cent of games participants and constitute the majority of youth at the games who predominantly live in French. This is because the approximately 240,000 New Brunswick Acadians represent one-third of the provincial population and show the highest rate of linguistic continuity as 92 per cent of those with French as their first language communicate in French at home (Allaire 1999; Statistics Canada 2002). In relative terms, they are the strongest francophone minority at the provincial level. A second contributing factor to the stronger use of French by New Brunswick participants at the games is that recruitment

Table 2.1 Linguistic characteristics of participants at selected francophone games (%)

		AG total 2001 n = 815*	AG NB 2001 n = 615	AG NS 2001 n = 97	AG PEI 2001 n = 89	FO 200 n = 587	AFG 1996 n = 144	AFG 1997 n = 164	AFG 2002 n = 31
Youth first language	French	71.6	78.6	52.1	46.7	57.7	42.6	50.0	62.5
	English	8.8	4.2	24.0	21.7	14.7	34.0	28.7	12.5
	Fr. + Eng.	18.4	16.0	24.0	28.3	23.9	18.4	18.9	21.9
	Other	1.2	1.1	0	3.3	3.6	4.3	2.4	3.1
Parent first language	French both parents	74.0	80.7	53.1	52.8	57.0	49.3	52.1	46.7
	French one parent	23.0	17.8	39.6	39.3	31.7	22.1	20.9	40.0
	Other both parents	3.0	1.5	7.3	7.9	11.3	28.7	27.0	13.3
Home languages	French	74.8	80.6	54.5	58.8	52.3	24.8	28.2	48.4
	English	12.5	6.1	34.4	31.1	31.7	36.9	38.7	38.7
	Fr. + Eng.	10.1	10.3	10.1	8.9	13.3	34.8	31.3	12.9
	Other	2.5	3.0	1.0	1.1	2.7	3.5	1.8	0
Language with friends	French	68.0	76.6	43.9	37.6	32.2	5.9	8.1	13.0
	English	12.7	6.2	35.7	29.1	45.8	60.7	50.0	51.6
	Fr. + Eng.	16.6	14.1	20.4	30.1	21.3	32.6	42.0	35.5
	Other	2.7	3.0	0	3.2	0.7	0.7	0	0

Notes

* The total is higher since it includes six participants from a Newfoundland guest delegation and also because the respondents' province of residence was not available on the remaining questionnaires.

AG = Acadian Games, NB = New Brunswick Province, NS = Nova Scotia Province, PEI = Prince Edward Island Province. FO = Franco-Ontarian Games, AFG = Alberta Francophone Games.

The total number of answers within each category is sometimes less than the value of *n* since not all questionnaires were completed in full.

is restricted to francophone school students who are fluent enough to be educated exclusively in French. Finally, New Brunswick Acadians benefit from a network of well-developed institutions active in sectors of daily social life – education, religion and community – the press and electronic media, as well as arts and culture.

Acadian minorities in Nova Scotia and Prince Edward Island, with populations of about 35,000 and 6,000 of French mother tongue in each case, represent only about 4 per cent of their respective provincial populations (Statistics Canada 2002). Not only is their population size smaller, but the degree of institutional support is less. While francophone schools and school boards have been created and developed since the 1982 *Canadian Charter of Rights and Freedoms*, full education in French is not yet available to all Acadian French-speaking or French origin youth. So in these two provinces, youth from French immersion schools are recruited to the Acadian Games if French is the first language of one of their parents. These youth certainly benefit from the 'Acadian' and francophone games environment. Fieldwork reveals that while participants occasionally use an expression or word in English, French dominates practically all exchanges. For many, Acadian identity is an unquestioned 'essence'. Some even found it difficult to explain why they identify as Acadians, as if it was not a conscious decision, simply an indisputable fact. As one boy declared: 'I don't think I am Acadian, I am Acadian' (2001 Acadian Games field notes). There is a disparity between what youth say in interviews regarding their mixed linguistic practices, and what emerges from questionnaires, interviews and fieldwork in terms of the prevalence of French. They perceive themselves as hybrid, but at the games, they engage in practices that produce them predominantly as francophones.

Asymetrical hybridities in the Alberta-Francophone Games

Performance of francophoneness was different at the Alberta Francophone Games. Participants' spontaneous use of English to one another was a discursive practice that contributed to the construction of their distinct hybrid identity, where francophoneness was a weaker component than anglophoneness. They frequently used English, or a combination of French and English, when conversing with friends. The shift was automatic since they speak English with ease. Even participants with French mother tongue from francophone families seemed to find it difficult and 'unnatural' to communicate in French, let alone speak it spontaneously and constantly. Significantly, they explained their own francophoneness as a conscious and strategic project.

They expressed an emotional and/or a pragmatic attachment to the French language and/or French Canadian culture, but they have to make a conscious effort to maintain their French. Thus they frequently underline the importance of 'rehearsing' French language in order to preserve it or improve it. Whereas speaking French is a spontaneous practice for youth at the Acadian Games, it is an intentional undertaking for Alberta francophone youth, *whether they claim it as their first language or not.* Alberta Francophone Games youth have the highest rate of affiliation to anglophoneness and the lowest rate of francophone identification and practices. They do not all think of themselves as 'true' francophones, but they can all speak some French and, as a result of this, they at least partly identify with francophoneness.

This is consistent with the circumstances of the Franco-Albertan community. The size of this minority – 62,000 – means they are only 2 per cent of the provincial population (Statistics Canada 2002). While the community has achieved a certain degree of institutional completeness in education, community, culture and media, this is not as extensive as for Franco-Ontarian or New Brunswick Acadian minorities. At 34 per cent, its rate of linguistic continuity is one of the lowest in Canada (Allaire 1999). Thus, participants at the 1996 and 1997 Alberta Francophone Games had the weakest links to French language. Both parents of about half of the participants had French as a mother tongue, a fifth of the participants came from linguistically mixed families, and neither of the parents of the remaining third had French as a first language. Results from 2002 questionnaires show the participants with stronger connections to French language – more of them speak French at home and have French as their first language, but it must be noted that only 35 young people took part in these games because of exceptional circumstances which favoured this kind of selection.

Asymmetrical hybridities in the Franco-Ontarian Games

Outside Quebec, the Franco-Ontarian minority is the largest in Canada, with a population of half a million. However, although this means there is a long established institutional network, Ontario is Canada's most populous province, and francophones account for only 5 per cent (Statistics Canada 2002). Subsequently, youth at the Franco-Ontarian Games do not display the strong connections to French language of New Brunswick Acadian youth. Youth from francophone families, with French as a first language, who mainly communicate in French at home and with friends, account for approximately 60 per cent of games participants, which places them midway between youth at the previous two games discussed above. The rate of linguistic continuity of Ontario francophone youth, at 63 per cent (Allaire 1999), is also halfway between those of New Brunswick and Alberta youth. Like youth at the Alberta Francophone Games, they combine French and English in their conversations. Yet they converse in French with more ease. Another contrast is that youth at the Alberta Francophone Games use French to communicate with adults, but frequently switch to English when speaking to peers, whereas youth at the Franco-Ontarian Games mostly communicate in French among themselves. They expect that an effort shall be made to speak French most of the time, acknowledging that the point of the event is to celebrate francophoneness. Some even remind their peers to communicate in French if they overhear them speaking English.

Comparison of the affiliation and performance of francophoneness among participants at the three games illustrates that hybridity does not mean that francophoneness is equally smoothly blended with anglophoneness. The degree of specific francophone minority social power in provinces gives partial explanation of youths' different configurations of hybridity. Variations in stability and specificity of francophone discursive production, its impact on the performance of, and affiliation to, francophoneness, also merits closer examination. Indeed, analysis of the articulation of francophone discourses at the three games shows that the discursive production of francophoneness is more stable and distinct at the Acadian and Franco-Ontarian Games where youths highlight their explicit attachment to francophoneness by identifying most frequently as Acadian (38 per cent), or Franco-Ontarian (38 per cent). And it is in a more uncertain discursive context that youth at the Alberta Francophone Games manifest the weakest ties to francophoneness by more commonly identifying as Canadian (47 per cent in 1996 and 35 per cent in 1997).

Conclusion

The picture of hybrid francophone identities that emerges in this chapter provides evidence of the challenges for cultural/linguistic minority youth in creating a viable social identity in the discursive context of English language hegemony. This study of francophone minority youth in Canada demonstrates that hybrid identities are not only the prerogative of youth of mixed linguistic or ethnic ancestry. Hybrid cultural/linguistic identity may also be constituted by minority youth of singular cultural lineage, such as French Canadian or Acadian ethnicity. Moreover, minority youth with a strong enough affiliation to, and appreciation of, francophoneness, willingly take part in francophone events, even while constructing hybrid identities which make clear that they are 'not just francophone'. Hybridity here therefore connotes the desire of minority youth to claim belonging to the English majority without denying their cultural/linguistic specificity – in this study asserting affiliation to Canadian anglophone society without forsaking francophoneness. However, we must ask: if it was not for the official status of the French language in Canada, would youth still give it as much legitimacy and want to identify with it?

This research indicates that hybridity *per se* may not be the most important threat to the reproduction of francophone minorities. Youth may integrate other identities such as anglophoneness without undermining their francophoneness and perform a level of francophoneness that sustains a viable cultural identity in the communities they come from. Asymmetrical hybridities where the minority/francophone component is strongly subjugated to the majority/anglophone component are more effective indicators of potential menace to the survival of francophone minorities. Given the challenge of ensuring that youth will continue to effectively reproduce themselves as francophone, francophone games are an important unifying strategy. While youth at the three games participate primarily for the sport, cultural and social activities, the francophone character of the event remains an important part of why they come. Using sport, cultural and social activities to strengthen francophoneness among French-speaking and French origin youth is an attractive and workable strategy, but may not be sufficient in itself to prevent further shifts in francophone identities in subsequent generations.

Bibliography

Allain, G. (1996) 'Fragmentation ou vitalité? Les nouveaux réseaux associatifs dans l'Acadie du Nouveau-Brunswick', in B. Cazabon (ed.) *Pour un Espace de Recherche au Canada Français*, Ottawa: Les Presses de l'Université d'Ottawa.

Allaire, G. (1999) *La Francophonie Canadienne: portraits*, Quebec: AFI-CIDEF.

Arsenault, S. (1999) 'Aires géographiques en Acadie', in J.Y. Thériault (ed.) *Francophonies Minoritaires au Canada: l'état des lieux*, Moncton, New Brunswick: Éditions d'Acadie.

Bernard, R. (1998) *Le Canada Français: entre mythe et utopie*, Ottawa: Le Nordir.

Breton, R. (1964) 'Institutional completeness of ethnic communities and personal relations of immigrants', *American Journal of Sociology*, 70: 193–205.

—— (1991) *The Governance of Ethnic Communities: political structures and processes in Canada*, New York: Greenwood Press.

Butler, J. (1990) *Gender Trouble: feminism and the subversion of identity*, New York and London: Routledge.

—— (1993) *Bodies that Matter: on the discursive limits of 'sex'*, New York and London: Routledge.

Dallaire, C. (2003) '"Not just francophones": the hybridity of minority francophone youths in Canada', *International Journal of Canadian Studies*, 28: 167–204.

—— (2005) 'Asymmetrical hybridities: youths at francophone games in Canada', *Canadian Journal of Sociology*, 30(2): 143 68.

—— and Denis, C. (2000) '"If you don't speak French, you're out": Don Cherry, the Alberta Francophone Games, and the discursive construction of Canada's francophones', *Canadian Journal of Sociology*, 25(4): 415–40.

Foucault, M. (1976) *Histoire de la Sexualité I: la volonté de savoir*, Paris: Éditions Gallimard.

—— (1983) 'Afterword: the subject and power', in H. Dreyfus and P. Rabinow (eds) *Michel Foucault: beyond structuralism and hermeneutics*, Chicago, IL: University of Chicago Press.

Gérin-Lajoie, D. (2003) *Parcours Identitaires de Jeunes Francophones en Milieu Minoritaire*, Sudbury: Prise de Parole.

Johnson, M. and McKee-Allain, I. (1999) 'La société et l'identité de l'Acadie contemporaine', in J.Y. Thériault (ed.) *Francophonies Minoritaires au Canada: l'état des lieux*, Moncton, New Brunswick: Éditions d'Acadie.

Juteau-Lee, D. and Lapointe, J. (1983) 'From French Canadians to Franco-Ontarians and Ontarois: new boundaries, new identities', in J.L. Elliot (ed.) *Two Nations, Many Cultures: ethnic groups in Canada*, Scarborough: Prentice Hall.

Kraidy, M.M. (1999) 'The global, the local, and the hybrid: a native ethnography of glocalization', *Cultural Studies in Mass Communication*, 16: 456–76.

LeBlanc, P.E. (1999) 'Les grandes périodes de l'histoire de l'Acadie', in J.Y. Thériault (ed.) *Francophonies Minoritaires au Canada: l'état des lieux*, Moncton, New Brunswick: Éditions d'Acadie.

Meerwald, A.M.L. (2001) 'Chinese at the crossroads', *European Journal of Cultural Studies*, 4(4): 387–404.

Mujcinovic, F. (2001) 'Hybrid Latina identities: critical positioning in-between two cultures', *Centro Journal*, 13(1): 44–59.

Noble, G., Poynting, S. and Tabar, P. (1999) 'Youth, ethnicity and the mapping of identities: strategic essentialism and strategic hybridity among male Arabic-speaking youth in south-western Sydney', *Cultural/Plural*, 7(1): 29–44.

Papastergiadis, N. (2000) *The Turbulence of Migration: globalization, deterritorialization and hybridity*, Cambridge: Polity Press.

Phoenix, A. and Owen, C. (2000) 'From miscegenation to hybridity: mixed relationships and mixed parentage in profile', in A. Brah and A.E. Coombes (eds) *Hybridity and Its Discontents: politics, science, culture*, London and New York: Routledge.

Pieterse, J.N. (1995) 'Globalization as hybridization', in M. Featherstone, S. Lash and R. Robertson (eds) *Global Modernities*, London: Sage Publications.

—— (2001) 'Hybridity, so what? The anti-hybridity backlash and the riddles of recognition', *Theory, Culture and Society*, 18(2): 219–45.

Sands, R.S. (2002) *Sport Ethnography*, Champaign, IL: Human Kinetics.

Slabbert, S. and Finlayson, R. (2000) '"I'm a cleva!": the linguistic makeup of identity in a South African urban environment', *International Journal of the Sociology of Language*, 144: 119–35.

Statistics Canada (1997) '1996 Census: mother tongue, home language and knowledge of languages', *The Daily*, data released on 2 December 1997 from the Nation series, catalogue no. 93F0024XDB96000, Ottawa, Ontario: Ministry of Industry.

—— (2002) *2001 Census – Analysis Series. Profile of Languages in Canada: English, French and many others*. Data released on 10 December 2002, catalogue no. 96F0030-XIE2001005, Ottawa, Ontario: Ministry of Industry.

Thériault, J.Y. (1994) 'Entre la nation et l'ethnie: sociologie, société et communautés minoritaires francophones', *Sociologie et Sociétés*, 26(1): 15–32.

3 Ingenious

Emerging hybrid youth cultures in western Sydney

Melissa Butcher and Mandy Thomas

> There are people who belong to more than one world, speak more than one language (literally and metaphorically), inhabit more than one identity, have more than one home; who have learned to negotiate and translate *between* cultures, and who, because they are irrevocably the product of several interlocking histories and cultures, have learned to live with, and indeed to speak from, difference. They speak from the 'in-between' of different cultures.
>
> (Stuart Hall 1996: 206, original emphasis)

This chapter examines the generation of hybrid youth cultures by young people from migrant backgrounds in Sydney, Australia. The research, part of a project over several years, found that migrant youth are generating new forms of cultural expression: in their talk, music, fashion, cars, computers, media consumption and social lives, everything from getting dressed and making-up for a night on the town, to driving around and just hanging out. In synthesizing new hybrid forms of popular expression, these young people accessed not only readily available global youth culture, but also diasporic connections with their parents' homeland. They frequently drew on mainstream Australian culture as interpreted by peers and represented by media. They enacted and practised hybrid forms of culture and identity in their schools, in their local communities and further afield. This dynamic cultural production was affected by the socio-economic circumstances of their families and the local urban environment. Lack of economic and socio-cultural resources was found to restrict possibilities for the involvement of some in conspicuous youth culture, yet it was also evident that this drove the inventive (even ingenious) production of new cultural possibilities.

Australia is a nation of migrants. All but the indigenous people arrived since 1788, initially from Europe, but increasingly in recent decades from Asia, the Middle East and the Pacific. Australian government migration policy has moved from the ideology of assimilation, to integration, to multiculturalism, to the twenty-first century notion of cultural diversity which, while progressive in some respects, maintains elements similar to the integration agenda of the last century. The research documented here began in one of the most culturally diverse centres in Australia – the sprawling suburbs of western Sydney, stretching 50 kilometres inland. It was conducted at a time when the atmosphere of debate surrounding cultural diversity in Australia was very tense.

Spring 2001 was marked by a public outpouring of anger, from journalists, social commentators and politicians, following a spate of sexual assaults in western Sydney committed by young men from Lebanese backgrounds. It is a mark of Australian media coverage that the terms 'gang', 'crime' and/or 'drugs' are frequently paired firstly with 'youth' (Davis 1999), then with 'Middle Eastern', 'Asian' or 'ethnic' (Collins, Noble, Poynting and Tabar 2000; White and Wyn 2004: 46). The heightened emotions and tensions were compounded by two other significant events. The first was the *Tampa* incident: a Swedish cargo vessel, on the request of Australian coastal authorities, rescued 400 Middle Eastern refugees in the Indian Ocean when their boat sank. Labelling them 'illegal immigrants', the Australian government refused to allow the *Tampa* to disembark its passengers. Weeks later the Australian government announced its 'Pacific Solution'; funding neighbours Nauru and Papua New Guinea to house and process the refugees.

The other significant event was '9/11', its impact reverberating onto the streets of Sydney. Misconceptions of Islamic culture became the norm in debates that demanded the Arabic/Islamic community in Australia explain why 'their' young men were violent and irresponsible (see Poynting, Noble, Tabar and Collins 2004). Media and political leaders addressed these complex issues through an established lexicon of stereotypical images and rhetoric. This exacerbated tensions in the wider community, indicating that there was (and continues to be) a contestation of boundaries in redefining what it means to be Australian, and the stories that underpin the sense of who Australians are. This constituted a dramatic, but rich context in which to research youth cultures in western Sydney.

While the target of public outrage at the time was the 'gang' of young men involved in the sexual assaults, what also came under attack was cultural diversity itself. There was a reinforcing of the tenet that migrants must integrate and submit to overarching ideals of Australian values, without any definition of what exactly those values are. Multiculturalism remains a key phrase delineating ideal Australian life, but as an ideology it is scrutinized as constituting social risk. A negative focus on cultural diversity in western Sydney, often stereotyped as barren and dangerous in the collective perception of the city, combined with the perennial concern over law and order, fuelled a moral panic. We argue that this was exacerbated by the gnawing perception of irreversible cultural change in Australia, driven by globalization and flows of migration. These factors were perceived to threaten the myths underpinning the 'Australian story'. As Bhabha (1990a: 300) argues 'Counter-narratives of the nation that continually evoke and erase its totalising boundaries – both actual and conceptual – disturb those ideological manoeuvres through which 'imagined communities' are given essentialist identities'.

We began our research with youth from Middle Eastern and Asian backgrounds who lived in the suburbs of western Sydney. The purpose was to document their attitudes, identity referents and creative expressions to ascertain how they were redefining Australian culture and its associated representations. We found a diverse range of strategies by which these young people made sense of themselves and their world as they negotiated a place between and within home, their friendship networks, mainstream Australian society and global influences. The most vivid expression of this process was in the creation and consumption of popular culture. The focus here is on their 'ingenious' use of speech, food, music, fashion, leisure activities, media consumption, mobility, and technology, in everyday activities, social experiences and interactions, as a means of better understanding the complexity and diversity of young migrant identities and their contribution to Australian culture.

Methodology

This was a collaborative project between the Centre for Cultural Research (University of western Sydney) and the Migration Heritage Centre (State Government of New South Wales), in association with the Sydney Powerhouse Museum. From February to July 2001, six young research assistants from second-generation Asian, Middle Eastern and Pacific Islander backgrounds, began interviewing 16- to 22-year-olds in western Sydney who were also from second-generation migrant backgrounds – Australian born children of overseas born parents, or those who came to Australia at a young age. Over 50 in-depth interviews took place. Questions related to consumption patterns, leisure activities, use of public space, friendship groups and attitudes towards, and understandings of, identity and culture. Three focus groups, participatory activities such as shopping days with young women, interviewing young people in the city on Saturday night, and ethnographic observations and descriptions of malls and other popular youth 'hang outs', provided further data. Young people from migrant backgrounds also took part in the project's advisory committee.

The focus on second-generation Middle Eastern and Asian youth reflected the fact that as the most recently arrived migrants, their experiences are different from those of youth from more established migrant communities. Unlike previous generations, these young people grew up within the late twentieth century, publicly-promoted discourse of multiculturalism that advocated: cultural pluralism, pride in ethnic origins, keeping distinctive language and cultural norms through successive generations, and bicultural citizenship. Yet in some ways this was a troubling discourse for second-generation young people who struggled at times to balance the demands of two cultures and to find a distinctive, but comfortable identity. Many of those interviewed grappled with the term 'multiculturalism' in their definitions of Australianness. They also grappled with the negative stereotyping of migrants.

Results from this research could not be generalized, but from the wealth of data, the following themes relating to migration and identity were highlighted and will be elaborated upon. The first is the shifting meanings given to former identity referents, such as family, who pass on cultural values and points of continuity such as language but who were also a source of conflict. Friends reinforced ethnic identity referents but were also involved in the 'hybridization' of popular culture practices. Locality, the sense of belonging to a geographically-defined urban area, was a central identity referent. Being a 'westie' (slang for those living in western Sydney) and simultaneously a 'wog' (slang for non-Anglo migrants) were cited as integral constituents of identity. These terms are generally used pejoratively by those who are not westies or wogs but youth in this study often reappropriated them as defiant representations of their identity in opposition to a dominant Anglo Australia.

The second theme was tension between being 'in-between' and belonging. They must 'negotiate and translate *between* cultures', and speak 'from the "in-between" of different cultures, always unsettling the assumptions of one culture from the perspective of another' (Hall 1996: 206). They sometimes give the impression that they belong to both, yet neither, culture – 'the problem of outside/inside must always itself be a process of hybridity, incorporating new "people" in relation to the body politic' (Bhabha 1990b: 4). The third theme builds upon this notion of hybridity, identifying questions of choice in the process of acculturation.

Popular culture and redefining identity

Is there any 'typical' experience for young Australians? Even before ethnicity is added to the equation, Australian youth culture is already marked by diversity: whether the flamboyant 'street machine' (customized car with pounding music), or the less visible, creative, underground, online 'zine' (alternative magazine). Music tastes range from independent punk rock to global fusion, while youth lifestyles vary from the surfers of the northern beaches to the Goth community of the inner city. This diversity was reflected in this study. What was apparent in their stories also was their desire to make their mark in an independent and distinctive way, at the same time as wishing to foster the grounds of belonging to a specific social group, or to several specific social domains.

This activity of creative distinction yet social belonging was marked out in everyday practices of popular culture. Popular culture is by nature transitory, and youth culture even more so. According to Willis (1990) and Friedman (1994), what is consumed or created in popular culture is reflective of, part of, the conscious construction of identity. Popular culture practices circumscribe boundaries of belonging, creating insider/outsider distinctions. Youth styles are themselves 'significant boundary markers between groups' (Clarke 1983, cited in Wulff 1995a: 71). Transnational, national, regional and localized youth cultural practices are distinctive. Several youth workers commented on the microcosm of their localities; how they work with youth in Parramatta is not how they work with youth in Blacktown or Liverpool, even though all are part of greater western Sydney. Transnational, national, regional and localized popular cultures were all significant influences on the construction of subcultures and identities of these second-generation youth. More broadly, popular culture provides the repertoire of representations that underpin cultural identity. For example, dominant representations of Australian culture might once have included the masculine 'Bronzed Aussie Lifesaver' or the 'Man from Snowy River'. But as cultures shift and change over time, so too these images are challenged and new ones formed. Similarly, the use of elements of popular culture by the youth in this study challenged, sometimes defiantly, sometimes unconsciously, mainstream lexicons of identity, both 'Australianness' and 'ethnicity'.

A significant impulse in young people's production and use of popular culture is the social need to maintain a sense of belonging. The spectrum of understanding about belonging for young people from Australian migrant backgrounds was outlined in Guerra and White's (1995) earlier study. On the one hand, second-generation migrant youth can immerse themselves in their first language culture, maintaining the culture of their parents in Australia. On the other hand, they can reject their migration heritage and cultural background and attempt to assimilate into host country culture. Finally, there is the potential to reconcile their identity by selecting and adopting different aspects of the two cultures until they feel comfortable (Guerra and White 1995: 5). It is the last of these scenarios that was most favoured among young people in this study, but this was not static. Young people could pass through any of the phases identified above and shift to another (Elley and Inglis 1995), for example, rediscovering their cultural heritage (see Pyong and Kim 2000). Several who rejected their parents' language as children decided as young adults to relearn it, to mark out difference from mainstream Australian culture.

Furthermore, the notion of belonging is ruptured by their ever-present role as translator. In everyday life they translate not just for their parents, and not just language. They are engaged in translating the social, political and organizational structures of mainstream Australian society as they move between different cultural spaces – filtering messages from parents, peers, extended family, teachers, youth workers, media and institutions of authority such as police and local councils. In western Sydney, the different social worlds of young people from different backgrounds overlap, intermesh or remain separate, as negotiations between different realms of belonging take place.

Before embarking on an analysis of their narratives of belonging, we provide an overview of the use of elements of popular culture in carving out the cultural spaces of participants' identity strategies. Finding an outlet for cultural expression, including devising reflexive representations of the self, is an impulsive human need (Butcher 2003), and part of how multiple and diverse spaces of identity are defined.

Merchants of style

Fashion is a good example of the use of popular culture to construct and demarcate new identities. Participants frequently made distinctions between members of their subcultures based on whether they were recently arrived, and this was reflected in style. Being 'FOB' – fresh off the boat – was a disadvantage; it was seen as being out-of-fashion, 'not cool'. For example, Cuong, 21, who came from Vietnam when he was 12, was often told by his younger sister: 'Don't wear that! It looks too fobby'. While pride in cultural background was appealing for some, if a homeland association made one appear newly-arrived and therefore out of touch, attempts to appear more 'local' and long-term were made.

There were distinctive fashion styles ascribed to particular groups of young people, ostensibly based on ethnicity (see Tong 2003), although these were always changing relative to global youth culture. In terms of continuity and distinction, second-generation migrant youth expressed a sense of connection to their parents' cultural background through accessories such as jewellery or symbols on clothing, for example, the Turkish national symbol or gold Buddha as a pendant, the Cedar of Lebanon or Thai script on items of clothing. Expressive display through fashion was also prevalent in material extensions of identity such as cars and modified computer cases. But identity was strongly expressed through the body itself: moving in groups, carrying ornamental accessories such as colourful, customized mobile phones, gelled and shiny hair, layers of jewellery, and clothes with reflective surfaces. The sheen of these young men and women was eye-catching. For many, hair became their most individual expression of identity: rainbow colours, blonde tips on black hair, oiled and carefully maintained dreadlocks, elaborate buns, shaved sides with styling product above on longer coloured locks. One young woman stated explicitly, 'Straightening your hair is part of a wog girl's life' (Belinda, 18 years, Lebanese background).

For others, fashion sense was associated with distinguishing themselves not only from the culture of their first-generation migrant parents, but also from an economically disadvantaged background.

> I: Where do you do most of your shopping?
> A: Oxford. Esprit. Usually more Armani, that type – class. Because when I was young my parents never bought me anything so I told myself like when I grow up and I have money I'm going to buy myself really nice clothes and so yeah I usually buy a lot of dress up clothes . . . I like to look really high class.
> (Andrew, 21 years, Vietnamese background)

Dress also related to the external display of values. For example, a young Lebanese woman felt Lebanese girls 'cover up' more, wearing longer sleeved shirts rather than spaghetti straps or 'boob tubes', for the sake of 'comfort'.

Even so, the way these young people dressed was often viewed as transgressive by parents who spoke of wanting their daughters to wear looser and longer clothes, and their sons to wear tighter trousers, avoiding the baggy look they associated with 'gangsters'.

While some cultural practices, like music and clothing choices, car modifications, for example, have an air of history about them, that is, young people in previous generations were engaged in similar activities, the contemporary era provides a set of influences that ensure new meanings are given to these activities and their outcomes. Furthermore, the introduction and use of new technology has greatly impacted on communication and networking patterns. In particular, young people have translated their sociability into new formats – SMS and email, and into cyber-space with chat rooms and LAN gaming (Livingstone 2002; Gibian 2003; Lally 2003).

The reclamation of new spaces of activity – both physical and cyber – new everyday practices, innovative dress and music, even changing vocabularies (Butcher and Thomas 2003) marked out new boundaries of belonging, and in the process challenged old ones. However, this agency was not always oppositional, with existing attachments sometimes reinforced by the adoption of first-generation-defined 'correct' behaviour and modes of expression when in particular cultural spaces. For these young people there is a sense of belonging to a migrant background, to an Australianness, and importantly, to a third space (Bhabha 1994) delineated, in particular, by friendship groups. Second-generation migrant youth in western Sydney are capable of moving between these spaces of belonging at different times and places depending on the requirements of a given social situation. Along with this identity mobility was at times a sense of confusion, concomitant with feeling 'in-between'.

Belonging

Young people from migrant backgrounds demonstrated a necessary flexibility to deal with the multiple cultural spaces of belonging they operated within (White and Wyn 2004: 48). In this and other contemporary studies (Noble, Poynting and Tabar 1999) there are examples where it is no contradiction to come from one cultural background, for example, Lebanese, but use inclusive descriptors in networks of friends from similar cultures, for example, 'we are all *wogs* together'. Ethnicity at times became a convenient label demarcating networks of friends rather than a particular cultural group. Nor was it a contradiction to feel both strongly connected to one's parents' heritage, and to a sense of being Australian.

> When we're together as a family I feel very Filipino because it's something Filipinos are very proud of, their family bonds . . . I'm Australian because I take an interest in the running of Australia, I'm concerned with the issues that affect the people in Australia, that's what makes me

Australian. I listen to Australian music, I watch Australian movies, the Olympics, so I would say I am part of that culture.

(Marielle, 16 years, Filipino background)

Marielle's comments point to the most important source of belonging and reference point for the values and beliefs that underpinned their sense of identity: the family:

I: Tell me about when you most identify with your cultural background.
E: I guess it would be with family and friends. Like my family and friends, I'm not saying all Turkish is the same, but my family are really, really close. We get together. There's people you've known all your life that are just as close as a brother or sister. We have dinner, we go to dinner, we go out to movies together, we go to peoples' houses.

(Enver, 22 years, Turkish background)

The family was the point of orientation from which most took their bearings. For example, when asked to nominate role models the first name given was often a member of the immediate family, such as a mother or older sibling, rather than a public figure. Susan, below, also nominates a member of her peer group, which could at times be considered an extension of family. Cathy Freeman and Malcolm X were among the few 'icons' nominated as role models; interesting choices for young people who often expressed a feeling of being marginalized. 'Role models? My mum, my best friend, Cathy Freeman too because she's not ashamed of her culture and I admire that' (Susan, 18 years, Lebanese background).

However, the family was also a point of orientation by negation, that is, young people defined themselves in opposition to what they saw their family as representing; being 'traditional' or 'old fashioned'. Language use in particular became a marker of transition; of distinction (from families) and belonging (to English speaking Australia):

Q: How are you more Aussie than your parents?
Because I speak English to them [laughs]. Yeah the way I was brought up.

(Johnny, 23 years, Vietnamese background)

I'm very different in that I'm more free. I speak English so it makes me independent in Australia.

(Hiba, 18 years, Lebanese background)

I'm different [from my parents] because I was born here and I actually know how to talk English. I don't know what else.

(Manaya, 15 years, Lebanese background)

When young people were not fluent in their parents' language, which was not uncommon, the result was inevitably communication difficulties and a feeling of remoteness from close family ties.

> Language wise, even though I speak Chinese I'm not articulate in Chinese and they're not articulate in English, so how do you go between that and explain what you want? How can you talk to them about things they're probably not used to talking about? And another thing is I think my parents are really smart, but I can't have those conversations that I think kids who grow up just speaking English with their parents can. Because they can, like my dad talks about politics and things, he watches the world news and he knows more about politics than I do, I can say that honestly. But just imagine if I could talk to him about things like that or with my mother as well. Because my mother talks to me a lot, but it's the Chinese/English thing if only we could speak the same language. If we were both articulate in the same language then that would be so good.
> (Siv, 21 years, Chinese-Cambodian background)

In this way the family was also a point of tension, a liability and a factor that created new stresses, providing at times a negative sense of value in their cultural background.

> I: Are there moments when you feel strongly Vietnamese?
> L: Not really, no. Wait, hang on, except when I have to go out, in terms of social life and lifestyle it's a lot more strict and there's a lot more rules. I've been brought up that way. Because my parents always told me about how it was so rough for them coming over to Australia, and I get the lecture all the time about how I have to try really hard so I don't get stuck in factory work and things like that.
> (Linda, 18 years, Vietnamese background)

There is a dynamic tension between release and restraint on display here. Release from tradition and the restraints of former social mores was made available by changes in the conditions of possibility. There are therefore inevitable tensions between the individual and the collective. Most young people wanted to adopt values and a lifestyle different to some degree from their family's expectations. According to Wulff (1995b: 9), this is necessary as a result of social change; parent culture is not always useful as a survival tool for the second generation who must develop their own repertoire of resources. Some interviewees felt Anglo Australians were 'lucky' as they didn't have to juggle parental demands with the expectations of their peers, but this view also represents certain misconceptions about the Anglo community. While not always the case, some participants had a low level of contact with Anglo youth or youth from other migrant backgrounds, primarily owing to location within highly concentrated single community social and education networks.

Both the difficulties and pleasures of families were often centred on those valuing strong ties with parents and older relatives. The conflicts frequently revolved around personal freedoms and relationships, particularly for young women.

> Girls can't have boyfriends and you're not supposed to do things till you're married, you can't do things because other Turkish people are going to see you and it doesn't look good . . . I do have some of the traditions in me but being so strict, like my parents aren't that strict, but being so strict can be really frustrating. [*On following her parents' views?*] Some things I do but some things I don't, like being so strict on boyfriends. I think in these days and especially in Australia you should let your children go out with someone. If you don't go out with them, how are you supposed to know 'yes this is the right person for me' or know that he is not or she isn't? So you should be able to go out and experience life yourself. Whereas their parents were like 'Oh this is what you have to do' and they have always agreed to it but I think it's changed now. You don't have to do everything your parents say.
>
> (Refika, 21 years, Turkish background)

For young men, conflicts were more common in relation to careers, and the way they spent their time and money. Pressure to conform to expected gender roles was felt more intensely by young women, and several longed for a subjective notion of 'freedom'. As Vasta suggests (1994: 23), young women are more likely to be thought of as cultural custodians, responsible for maintaining tradition: 'I cook a mean pasta [*laughs*] and I help my mum when she cooks so when I get married I'll know how to cook all the Lebo food' (Adele, 19 years, Lebanese background).

Young women tended to have more private and personal aspects to their cultural expression, whereas young men were more public in their display, particularly those from Middle Eastern backgrounds. This is not to say that young women and Asian youth do not display cultural interests and sensibilities, but physical display by many young men of Middle Eastern origin makes them appear more visible. It is understandable at times that other people feel a sense of anxiety when confronted with these often striking male performances. While young people from culturally diverse backgrounds are out and about clubbing, performing karaoke, having picnics at beaches and parks, cyber-gaming and occupying public spaces for shopping or meeting friends in cafes, attention is invariably drawn more to larger groups who are noisier and more physically demonstrative. Young men from Middle Eastern backgrounds are often the focus of intense surveillance by police and security, as well as concerned people not privy to the codes of their cultural behaviour and informed only through media reports (Cuneen and White 2002: 189).

While groups of young men from Middle Eastern backgrounds may appear as threatening 'gangs', their activity in public space can be simply an expression of the culture of hanging out, away from spaces of constraint such as school and family (Pe-Pua 1996: 115). It can be seen as an attempt to subvert their perceived position of marginalization; marginal by virtue of being not only young, but young *and* from a non-Anglo background, *and* from western Sydney. They deliberately mark out their difference and publicly demonstrate it (see also Collins, Noble, Poynting and Tabar 2000: 168). The process of this revalorization is at the heart of much conflict between young people, the community and authorities, particularly over the use of public space increasingly encroached upon by commercial interests and public liability claims (Cuneen and White 2002: 194).

Many youth in this study had begun to shed or adapt aspects of their former heritage and to adopt as an added layer what they perceived as elements of being Australian. However, we found Australian culture was often described in a stereotypical manner: light hair, blue eyes, surfing, being 'laid-back', barbecues, beer-drinking and so on. Even some foods were considered more Australian than others.

> I: What do you eat at home?
> A: Lebanese food, unless my Dad decides he wants to be an Aussie and cook roast lamb or something.
>
> (Adele, 19 years, Lebanese background)

In general, participants used the term 'Australians' to refer to the Anglo community, thereby excluding themselves. Yet, at the same time they were often keen to stress that they were Australian, and strongly identified with being Australian, even when they did not match their own physical description of what 'Australians' were.

> I'm an Aussie. Well, I don't look like one but I've been born and raised here so that's what I am. . . . [*How do you define being Australian?*] Eating my meat pie, drinking my beer on the beach. I love that life. I think it's a changing concept that until maybe ten or twenty years from now we won't have a definition of. [*Why?*] Because Australia is only new and it needs more time to develop before it can reach a stable identity.
>
> (Mustafa, 20 years, Lebanese background)

However, rather than definitively rejecting a migrant background, these young people sought to reconcile the disjunctions of 'being in-between' by reworking relationships and everyday practices to create a new sense of belonging in a 'third space', predominantly defined by friendship networks.

Being and belonging 'in-between'

While many young people juggled their parent's heritage and mainstream Australian culture, the overriding sensibility of the need to belong created a state of 'being in-between'. This was expressed by interviewees as they negotiated life between their cultural backgrounds, friends and wider Australian society, juggling different expectations by adopting different behaviours, language, even values, in different spaces such as home, school, in public space, at work, and with friends. This was a more stressful process for some, indicated by a sense of confusion within their narratives:

> I: How would you describe your own cultural background?
> G: Well my sort of cultural background it's a mix, like I can't say I'm Turk because I'm Aussie sort of thing. You know what I mean? [*If she were asked?*] I'd say I was mixed. I fit in fine. My best friend is an Aussie. I don't feel like I don't belong.
> (Guliz, 20 years, Turkish background)

> Well I can't decide what I am. Sometimes I'm like 'what's up bro' and other times I'm like 'g'day mate'. Sometimes I eat woggy food and sometimes I eat meat pies.
> (Manaya, 15 years, Lebanese background)

Manaya highlights how many youth, particularly from Middle Eastern backgrounds, have taken hip-hop originating from black American youth culture as part of the expression of their own identity in contemporary Australia. The alienation embedded in the music and imagery of hip-hop resonates with their own sense of exclusion from mainstream Australian culture. This exclusion was particularly evident in their criticisms of Australian media representations of migrant youth, and lack of migrant characters on television, for example, in popular teen soaps like *Neighbours* and *Home and Away*.

We found that when they felt a sense of exclusion or alienation this was a driving motivation towards developing a strong sense of attachment to their cultural background, particularly when they felt that it was threatened (for example, maligned in public debates) or when they were in situations where they felt uncomfortably 'different'.

> I: Tell me about when you most identify with your cultural background?
> E: I think I most identified with my cultural background when I was in a position where I was like 'I'm so not like this'. I went to a friend's birthday party when I was – it was at Uni and she was graduating and she was English, like Australian and everyone was just drinking beer and it was so different. I went 'Oh my God!'. That's when I felt very Turkish.
> (Ebru, 22 years, Turkish background)

> I: Do you feel Chinese?
> V: Not really, sometimes when around other Chinese, because they

bring out the Chinese in you. Or when you are around no Chinese, because you are the only one there.

(Vivien, 18 years, Chinese background)

Vivien added 'I don't really think about it, it's not an issue', signalling comfort with being 'in-between'. For many, it was 'not an issue' to be identified as Chinese or not, Lebanese or not, or Turkish or not. This perhaps indicated a trend towards a feeling of comfort with the ambiguity of hybridity, of migrant status. For others this feeling was clearly unsettling and to banish the discomfort they took the path of identifying more with their parents' background than with what they perceived as mainstream Australian culture.

I: Would you describe yourself as being Australian?
S: I don't know. I find myself laid back and easy going but it doesn't mean that I'm necessarily Australian. I'd consider myself as Turkish even though I was born here, lived here and have the whole accent thing going. [*Do you feel in between?*] Not really, I consider myself to be Turkish. [*If somebody asked?*] I'd say Turkish. They always ask me. [*On the look of an Australian?*] Fair, white coloured hair, light eyes.

(Sarah, 17 years, Turkish background)

While some like Sarah felt grounded in their parents' cultural background, others could not shift the uncertainty of their in-betweenness. Some even expressed an identity 'crisis':

My identity shifts. Sometimes I think I'm too Leb to be Aussie, but sometimes I think I'm too Aussie to be Leb.

(Belinda, 18 years, Lebanese background)

I: How would you describe your own cultural background?
H: It's really hard to define myself in that way because I'm in Australia right now, I was born in France, my parents were both born in Cambodia, but their background is Chinese but they were in Vietnam and they spoke Chinese and Vietnamese. My mum speaks eight languages and my dad about six. So it's really hard to say 'Oh I have an Asian background, I was born in France and living in Australia', you know, I get this identity crisis, you know you've got people saying well what nationality are you? So I think, I'd say it's just an amalgam of everything put together . . . I do find that I am Asian, I do have that cultural thing because of family, from my parents and things like that. But I do have the Australian in me as well, but I think I have some of the French thing as well from growing up there.

(Haline, 20 years, Cambodian, Chinese, Vietnamese and French background)

Many young migrant people in Australia have similar remarkable personal trajectories making it difficult to label them with any particular identity.

Adaptive strategies

To overcome the sense of cultural dissonance, the feeling of 'not fitting in', young people adopted various strategies, including dividing space up into different zones of behaviour, and nominating other factors such as religion, gender and being from western Sydney as further parts of their identity. Being from western Sydney, in particular, was often appropriated as a defiant marker of pride rather than negation, especially when on excursions into the city itself.

> The way we dress, the way we act, it's so different. Like my friends and I will go to the city or Chatswood or something and everyone is dressed so proper. It was so funny, we went to the J-Lo concert, and the girls in front of us they were so proper, they just stood there calmly. And we were being loud and I distinctly heard one of them say 'Damn Westies' [*laughs*]. It was so funny that people could pick out that we were Westies. I can feel it in me. It's a place I can always come back to.

She continued on this theme:

> We were on the train back [from Darling Harbour] and we could see Penrith outside the train window, and I said 'Ah we're back here from being in the Harbour', and [my friend] said to me 'But it's a place I will always come back to' because we've got so many memories there, it's a great place.
>
> (Marielle, 16 years, Filipino background)

Another strategy was to adopt the hyphen as Haisam does below, perhaps indicative of a 'hyphenated' life; a metaphor that implies fusion, hybridity, creole or mestizo, terms commonly used to describe places like western Sydney where so many cultural backgrounds coexist and intermingle.

> H: I'm an Arab and I love being an Arab. Wouldn't wanna be anything else. How do I describe it? Proud, yeah, we're proud.
> I: How do you define being an Australian?
> H: Eating my meat pie and drinking my beer. Seriously.
> I: Would you describe yourself as an Australian?
> H: I'm a Lebo-Australian.
>
> (Haisam, 22 years, Lebanese background)

Friendship networks were a very important source of belonging and security as they enabled the sharing of common understandings of migrant experiences in the same generation (Collins, Noble, Poynting and Tabar 2000; White and Wyn 2004: 47). Most young people in this study expressed a deeper connection with people from other migrant backgrounds than with Anglo Australians. Many also felt that their diverse friendship networks delineated their lives from that of their first-generation parents, who had less mixed social networks. Many participants moved between friendship groups as they moved out of the local neighbourhood, to university or workplace.

> I have a whole heap of friends, like a different set for Uni, a different set from school, like that. Because when I started Uni I had to make a new set of friends because none of my friends are really like into art, so friends at Uni are totally different from the ones I had before. None of them are Filipino so I had to, not really conform, fit in, because none of them are Filipino. Back in school it was predominantly Filipino.
>
> (Marjay, 19 years, Filipino background)

Rather than simply harking back to homeland traditions, ritual and ceremony, memory and ancestry, these young people actively created new links, attachments and affinities between and across different cultures. The sense of cultural ambiguity felt by many led to new means of sharing, adapting and fusing spaces, languages and (life) styles in their quest for their own modes of cultural expression and social belonging.

> I: So what do you adopt?
> C: I take the things that I think will give me a positive effect on my life later on. I try to adopt things from either race that are good qualities and leave those that are bad. For example the generosity of Australians and the strong work ethic of the Chinese . . . I don't think racial identity would be a problem anymore because you have so many people who you can classify as Australian these days. It's the clichéd version of Australian lifestyle and thinking of giving everyone a fair go, being a lot more broad-minded than a lot of other nationalities. And being less opinionated than everyone else. [*Do you see yourself as Australian?*] I'm Australian because I've adopted those concepts in my identity but nothing else. I haven't accepted beach, booze and beer into my life.
>
> (Chi, 22 years, Chinese-Vietnamese background)

These adaptations were highlighted in their consumption and construction of popular culture. Young people claim open public spaces like shopping centres, car parks and railway stations for their social activities. These spaces are marked as territories for gatherings with friends. Fashion, music and leisure activities at these sites reveal a rich variety of influences and borrowings ranging from black American street culture (language and dress), to the influence of their own cultural backgrounds, to global and local mainstream youth cultures. These young people are both very localized – using 'global' technology like chat rooms and mobile phones to talk with friends who live just down the road – and highly mobile, often travelling from outer suburbs to the inner-city for leisure activities.

This creative appropriation of spaces and styles signified a social inventiveness in generating new forms of popular culture which were being incorporated into the city landscape in particular locales. In this way, young people from migrant backgrounds in western Sydney actively disrupted the available mainstream youth culture, and in doing so, whether consciously or not, asserted new ideas, meanings and practices of culture laced with significant borrowings and evocations of 'otherness'.

Conclusion

The young people from various migrant backgrounds in this study demonstrated strong strategic attachments to distinctive cultural identities. They were actively 'finding ways of being both the same as and at the same time different from the others amongst whom they live' (Hall 1996: 206). They employed a range of strategies to negotiate a hybrid place between, and within, their family home, their friendship networks, mainstream Australian society and global influences. Most striking was their 'ingenious' use of speech, food, music, fashion, leisure activities, media consumption, mobility, and technology, in everyday activities, social experiences and interactions.

They were both proud of their migrant backgrounds and able to adopt elements that they identified as 'being Australian'. They could move away from explicitly ethnically defined cultural identities, focusing on other categories such as religion, locality, occupation or gender to define their place in Australian society. They commonly defined themselves as contemporary Australians but had strong connections still to their parents' traditional cultural background. Moving between cultural spaces, between family and friends, and dealing with Australian institutions such as school and the workplace was, for some, a more stressful experience than for others, with conflict in particular between parental expectations and the desire to be accepted by peers. Their social mobility and their skill at accommodating different cultural settings, from Lebanese weddings to Chinese New Year celebrations, at times induced a feeling of being 'in-between'. This 'in-betweenness' was experienced as a sense of loss and confusion, but also constituted a varied set of skills to draw upon at different moments.

These young people invested migrant heritage with a new meaning, consciously or not, of hybridity, but even this had its complexities. They would express hybridity in some settings and specific or generic Australian and global youth culture practices in others. Identity display and performance was used as a strategic element in finding a sense of belonging, of place. This suggests that the construction and display of a cultural identity was a highly conscious decision for the most part, and was often related to how secure they felt in particular situations.

While some young people very consciously claimed their ethnicity, they also linked a more tolerant and open-minded attitude on their part to association with diverse friendship networks. Culturally diverse peer groups gave young people the ability to associate less problematically with a wider range of youth, making connections and establishing cross-cultural interests and activities. While many young people maintained a sense of exclusion and rejection from mainstream Australian society, for the most part they were not cynical about a commitment to values of tolerance, equality and diversity.

Their expressions of youth culture were invested with continual references to everyday experiences in Australia, but also incorporated a search for affinities and connections across cultures. These young people appropriated and created symbols and markers that were relevant to their own cross-cultural experiences, whether remixed *bhangra* music or a fashionable *hijab* (Muslim head scarf). It is apparent in their narratives that the heritage of migration is more than stories of settlement and memories of homeland, more than the distinctive cuisines, music and rituals of their parents' culture. The heritage of migration is transformative and inventive. It produces hybrid youth cultures which are continually being reinvested with new meaning from a range of sources, and which will impact on the cultural production of Australianness; the images, ideas and everyday practices that make up what it means to be Australian.

There are institutional restraints, issues of responsibility and structural influences that impact on the expressions of youth cultures in general. The operation of top-down power relations remains significant in contemporary Australian society; in the social hierarchies at play in the urban landscape, and in the nuances of social control which deem youth culture somehow of less worth than mainstream cultural production. It is however, clear that the neat borders of official multiculturalism are more apparent in the minds of policy-makers than real. Apparent transgressions of those boundaries, pronounced in media debates and political rhetoric, arouse widespread public anxiety, and highlight the need to reassess whether multiculturalism is only considered acceptable under certain conditions. Young people are drawn to cultural mixing and amalgamation, almost as a matter of necessity in a populous and complex urban environment. Their 'ingenious' intercultural skills strongly imply effective operation in future poly-ethnic cities, since many are successfully handling multiple cultural frameworks everyday (Amit-Talai 1995: 228). The challenge is to ensure that Australian social and political institutions create a positive environment for young people to develop a sense that they belong and have an identity that is valued and respected. If the cultural agency of young Australians is fostered and their contributions to urban life recognized, then a new space can be opened to reimagine migration as being at the vanguard of cultural production and expression.

Bibliography

Amit-Talai, V. (1995) 'Conclusion: the "multi" cultural of youth', in V. Amit-Talai and H. Wulff (eds) *Youth Cultures: a cross-cultural perspective*, London and New York: Routledge.

Bhabha, H. (1990a) 'DissemiNation', in H. Bhabha (ed.) *Nation and Narration*, London and New York: Routledge.

—— (1990b) 'Introduction: narrating the nation', in H. Bhabha (ed.) *Nation and Narration*, London and New York: Routledge.

—— (1994) *The Location of Culture*, New York: Routledge.

Butcher, M. (2003) *Transnational Television, Cultural Identity and Change: when STAR came to India*, New Delhi: Sage.

—— and Thomas, M. (2003) 'Introduction', in M. Butcher and M. Thomas (eds) *Ingenious: emerging youth cultures in urban Australia*, Melbourne: Pluto Press.

Clarke, J. (1983) 'Style', in S. Hall and T. Jefferson (eds) *Resistance through Rituals*, London: Hutchinson.

Collins, J., Noble, G., Poynting, S. and Tabar, P. (2000) *Kebabs, Kids, Cops and Crime*, Melbourne: Pluto Press.

Cuneen, C. and White, R. (2002) *Juvenile Justice: youth and crime in Australia*, Melbourne: Oxford University Press.

Davis, M. (1999) *Gangland: cultural elites and the new generationalism*, 2nd edition, Sydney: Allen and Unwin.

Elley, J. and Inglis, C. (1995) 'Ethnicity and gender: the two worlds of Australian Turkish youth', in C. Guerra and R. White (eds) *Ethnic Minority Youth in Australia*, Hobart: Australian Clearing House for Youth Studies.

Friedman, J. (1994) *Cultural Identity and Global Process*, London: Sage.

Gibian, J. (2003) 'They're all wog rooms: the online chat of culturally diverse teenage girls in Western Sydney', in M. Butcher and M. Thomas (eds) *Ingenious: emerging youth cultures in urban Australia*, Melbourne: Pluto Press.

Guerra, C. and White, R. (1995) 'Introduction', in C. Guerra and R. White (eds) *Ethnic Minority Youth in Australia*, Hobart: Australian Clearing House for Youth Studies.

Hall, S. (1996) 'The question of cultural identity', in S. Hall, D. Held, D. Hubert and K. Thompson (eds) *Modernity: an introduction to modern societies*, Cambridge, MA: Blackwell.

Lally, E. (2003) 'Mods and overclockers: technology, young people and cultural innovation', in M. Butcher and M. Thomas (eds) *Ingenious: emerging youth cultures in urban Australia*, Melbourne: Pluto Press.

Livingstone, S. (2002) *Young People and the New Media*, London; Sage.

Noble, G., Poynting, S. and Tabar, P. (1999) 'Youth, ethnicity and the mapping of identities: strategic essentialism and strategic hybridity among male Arabic-speaking youth in south west Sydney', *Communal/ Plural*, 7(1): 29–44.

Pe-Pua, R. (1996) *'We're Just Like Other Kids!': street-frequenting youth of non-English-speaking background*, Melbourne: Bureau of Immigration, Multicultural and Population Research.

Poynting, S., Noble, G., Tabar, P. and Collins, J. (2004) *Bin Laden in the Suburbs: criminalising the Arab other*, Sydney: Institute of Criminology.

Pyong, G.M. and Kim, R. (2000) 'Formation of ethnic and racial identities: narratives by young Asian-American professionals', *Ethnic and Racial Studies*, 23(4): 735–60.

Tong, A. (2003) 'The art of wear: an east meets west perspective', in M. Butcher and M. Thomas (eds) *Ingenious: emerging youth cultures in urban Australia*, Melbourne: Pluto Press.

Vasta, E. (1994) 'Youth and ethnicity: the second generation', *Family Matters*, 38, August: 21–5.

White, R. and Wyn, J. (2004) *Youth and Society: exploring the social dynamics of youth experience*, Oxford: Oxford University Press.

Willis, P. (1990), *Common Culture*, Boulder, CO: Westview Press.

Wulff, H. (1995a) 'Inter-racial friendship: consuming youth styles, ethnicity and teenage femininity in South London', in V. Amit-Talai and H. Wulff (eds) *Youth Cultures: a cross-cultural perspective*, London and New York: Routledge.

—— (1995b) 'Introducing youth culture in its own right: the state of the art and new possibilities', in V. Amit-Talai and H. Wulff (eds) *Youth Cultures: a cross-cultural perspective*, London and New York: Routledge.

4 The social life of Japan's adolechnic

Todd Joseph Miles Holden

This chapter addresses key themes of the book by offering insights into the world of Japanese adolescents. As the hybrid term 'adolechnic' indicates, most Japanese youth make extensive use of communication technology. But do such technologies affect the rhythms and nature of their existence? For instance, does technological mediation enable youth to inhabit plural worlds? Does it bear on their socialization? And what insights might adolescent cell phone use shed on media theory? Here, answers emerge by examining matters of privatization, space, globalization, popular culture, subculture and social interaction.

This chapter primarily observes two Japanese adolescents during their earliest days using cell phones. Maya is a 14-year-old female; Alex, a 13-year-old male. Siblings, they live in the northern part of Honshu. Their city Sendai is rural, though fairly 'modern'. Maya and Alex are not 'typical' Japanese: their father is American, their mother Japanese; thus they are *hafu* (half), or *daburu* (double). Despite their difference in what is a rather exclusionary society, they have never experienced Japan's infamous *ijime* (bullying). This may be because they both attend private, Catholic schools – tightly controlled, with an emphasis on 'moral instruction' – although organized religion plays little part in their lives outside school. The kids lead busy lives. Typical of their peers, they fill their waking hours with scholastic and leisure activities: seven hours of schooling, five days a week, three hours of homework each day; weekly piano lessons for both, drums and soccer for Alex, and ballet (three hours a day, five times a week) for Maya. Unlike their friends though, who have carried cell phones for over two years, Maya and Alex only recently acquired them. And unlike their friends, the phones are shared with their parents.

Our discussion begins with a brief history of cell phones – *keitai* in Japanese. We subsequently witness two novices mastering the device's fundamentals then exploring its advanced capabilities. We see how peers assist knowledge-acquisition and the tool's rapid adoption as a central element in their daily routines. Above all, we trace how young Japanese forge connections with their educational, extra-curricular and leisure cohorts via a cell phone technology which has become 'indispensable' in the lives of Japanese youth (White Paper 2004: 43). Tracking *keitai* use enables the construction of a 'map' of the adolescent world in contemporary Japan. The map is social and cultural, derivatively economic and, invisibly, political. Contours are revealed via ethnographic methods, observation, group and individual interviews, text messages and content analysis of websites and materials downloaded. This data is neither systematic, nor 'representative' of all Japanese youth. Maya and Alex belong to variegated cohorts and are bounded by conditions pertaining to age, language, autonomy, social position, cultural and group identity, and financial, technological and intellectual resources. Yet, it is their comfort with, understanding of, and relationship to technology – cemented by the cell phone platform – that is most distinctly generational. Adolescents in contemporary Japan live lives inextricably linked to, and rooted in, technology; so much so they warrant the moniker 'adolechnic'.

The cell phone in Japan

The adolechnic belongs to the first generation of *keitai* user. Accounts of *keitai* development (Kohiyama 2003) point to a three-staged process (Holden and Tsuruki 2003): from *pokebell* (electronic pager) to PHS (personal handyphone system) to cell phone. Economic conditions were conducive to building a decentralized, non-fixed, subscriber network. With competition, prices dropped and *keitai* became available for younger users. Accordingly, between 1997 and 2003 subscribers doubled: from 46 per cent of all households (Joho Tsushin Tokei 2002) to 94 per cent (Joho Tsushin Tokei 2003). Some (see Lippit 1995; Suzuki and Best 2003) have argued that *kogaru* (stylish high school girls) were key in cell phone diffusion, as they perceived *keitai* as a fashion accessory, freedom statement and tool assisting their unfettered, peripatetic lifestyle. Others see innovation as a key: Japan has consistently led in *keitai* development – between 18 months to three years ahead of the global curve (Harrow 2000). By 2001, an astounding 81 per cent between age 10 and 19 carried *keitai*. A 2004 White Paper listed 86.65 million Japanese (68 per cent of the entire population) as carrying *keitai*.

Social consequences are significant. Context rationality has dictated that the younger generation is growing up with diminishing interest in the PC platform (Clark 2005). For young people with limited finances, apartment space, and time, it is more rational to plop down £50, sign a few papers, and receive a portable hand-held device which provides an email address and internet access – and the added luxury of mobility – rather than spend five times more to install a stationary, space-eating hard disk and monitor, with land-line dial-up, ADSL or cable. Through *keitai*, users transport voice, text messages, email, photos, films, sounds, software programs – anything digitally encoded. And it is email – rather than the phone function – that is most favoured by Japan's youth (Ito 2001). Indeed, as we soon consider, the technology has influenced how youth interact with peers and structure their worlds.

Characteristics of the adolechnic

As a youth culture phenomenon, the adolechnic has been little studied in Japan, and not very much in other countries. Significant work has transpired in Finland (Kasesniemi 2003) and Norway (Ling 2000; Pedersen 2002; Skog 2002), with Korea (Yoon 2003) and Japan (Ito 2001; Hashimoto 2002) considered only recently. Although mobile communication is the most prominent technology in the adolechnic's daily life, it is not the only one. These early teens engage in a lifestyle facilitated by machines – having been primed in childhood by role-playing games (RPG) on PlayStation, Nintendo, and Game Boy. Unlike earlier cohorts, who grew up on the comparatively passive technology of television, the adolechnic has learned to interact with technology proactively. Consequently, technology is less a mystery than a challenge – a tool for mastery and discovery. Technology has taught adolechnics that, by wielding machines, they can explore uncharted, rich, obscure spaces – worlds both imagined and 'real'. Adolechnic reality is nurtured through effort; made all the more actual and fathomable through enterprise. This fusion of technology and youth arises on the cusp of a child's social development, a time in which family ties become weaker as a correlate to their ever-widening external networks and ever-evolving social skills (Ling 2004: 86–97). Their group-shared technological expeditions remake their present world, if not create new ones.

Because adolechnics are inventors of worlds, they view technology positively, free of qualm or quandary. It is used to enhance, embellish and complete one's life. Understanding this, the adolechnic seeks information from instruction manuals, as well as fellow adolechnics, as a proximate means of improving the quality of their lifespace and activities. Unlike their elders, who often view technology as recondite, the adolechnic employs patience exceeding most other tasks in their lives, exhibiting curiosity, determination and goal-direction.

Entering the world of the adolechnic

About the observation

This research was initiated by observing my two children during their first days carrying *keitai*. Two phones were purchased on an *oya-ko denwa* (parent–child phone) plan, under which calls between the units, as well as home, are cheaper. With their approval, I was allowed to access a limited selection of their text messages, as well as photos they exchanged with friends. Observations were made in fixed locations – such as home, office, car and restaurants – and during transit between ballet, piano lessons, soccer and school. Common viewing times included during homework breaks, before and after dinner, prior to baths, before sleep, during visits to my workplace, and walking around town. These observations rather neatly divide into temporal sets. First, we can identify initial encounters – marked by a lack of facility with the technology. Second, a period marked by use of the device to establish adolescent identity and, accordingly, explore the world outside familiar family and age cohort groups. Let's consider each in turn.

First encounters: pre-organized activities

Obtaining a cell phone is an ordeal of sorts, bearing on social standing and demanding skills of persuasion. Social standing involves the age cohort – the majority already possess *keitai*; those who don't are viewed as 'uncool'. Obtaining *keitai* immediately readjusts status, as it calls attention to the owner and elicits sustained interaction with peers. Persuasion refers to parental authority – whose consent and continuing financial assistance must be secured. Often adolechnics have phones confiscated when monthly usage exceeds agreed-upon terms.

Immediately following purchase, the children opened the boxes and began working buttons. Gender differences seemed to emerge: Alex tried to do everything through intuition, while Maya went through the booklet step-by-step. After a short period of unco-ordinated activity, each working one phone, they agreed to proceed systematically together, only consulting the manual when they encountered a roadblock. In the ensuing week, they studied the instructions with greater frequency in order to fine-tune and personalize their machines. External guidance came from 'credible sources' – friends who were expert by virtue of prior experience. Temporarily, this knowledge gap engendered informal ranking in their cohorts. It only took these adolechnics a few days of intense use and select guidance to gain comfort with their machines. By the time they did, they were well into personalizing the machine – making it their very own (despite the fact that they were sharing it with their parents). Soon thereafter came a period of routinization, where operations were streamlined and rationalized.

Personalizing the machine

The earliest stage of *keitai* ownership is perhaps the most important – the phase in which the user renders the device to his or her specifications. Personalization is pervasive: the central assumption and selling point in contemporary *keitai* design (Natsuno 2002) – but adolechnics throw full weight into this activity. The tool becomes a 'possession' in a way that distinguishes the cell phone from ownership of other utilitarian technologies. The phones Maya and Alex wielded became 'sites of self': evidence of their existence, conveyers of their character, repositories of their individuality – worlds so personal that they ultimately sought to secure contents from parental view. Maya and Alex sank hours into refashioning the tool as avatar; in the process they transformed it into a customized library or portable bedroom with all the pictures, songs, sound bytes and mail that would normally be posted on walls or spread across desks. These customized clippings and sounds were carried into the world for the purpose of conjuring – as a means of announcing (and crafting), the bearer's 'authentic' identity.

The first stage of personalization resembles the pre-adventure stage of RPG, where teams are assembled, names created, colours, tools and provisions selected. Applied to the *keitai* this means making cosmetic alterations: buying accessories like straps, chains, coins, stickers, and miniaturized characters to attach to nodes on the phone. The 'characterization' stage mirrors findings on Japanese adolescent fashion (Holden 1994) and college cell phone users (McVeigh 2003), which has discerned: 'discreet statements of difference [by] those wishing to be considered as discrete statements' (Holden 1994: 206). The image crafting efforts of Maya and Alex were abetted by a trip to Tokyo Disneyland. There they purchased a silver Chip and Dale coin and a Tigger-figure strap for the red phone, and a gold Pooh coin and Mickey/Magician's Apprentice strap for the silver phone. The next day they bought Disney stickers – Tinkerbell, the Magic Kingdom and pixie dust – at a department store to adorn the exteriors. Maya accessorized even further, placing a ballerina on top, an apple with a bite removed on the main menu button, and peanuts and cashews on the submenu buttons.

Contemporaneous to external accessorization, these adolechnics worked through the various pre-set menus, assigning sounds and tones for every *keitai* function. This was an exacting process, tailoring announcements for incoming and outgoing mail and calls to correspond to particular folders, distinguished into groups of 'best friends', 'family', 'school', 'teachers', 'ballet', 'soccer', and so on. Sounds and tones were selected to signal successful downloads, keypunches, start-up and shut-down. As limited as the 17 pre-set noises and tunes seem, they enable hundreds of unique decisions. Thousands more possibilities exist on the web via download into the phone's memory.

The *keitai* assists customization. For instance, through a pre-set function called 'EZ-Web', Alex quickly located a category called 'Get Sounds, Pictures' offering a large number of downloads: songs, films, melodies, screen shots, photo albums, voices, karaoke, videos, promotional films, games and individual photos. Whether a fee is involved or not, ties to the economic world are undeniable – linking adolechnics to commerce in often invisible, unobtrusive ways. So, too, is the act of downloading associated with the configuration of the phenomenological world at levels of micro (or local) and macro (global) scale (see below). For now, consider that users can choose 'domestic classics' such as Spitz's *Robinson*, the Southern All Stars' *Ai no Kotoba*, and Oda Kazumasa's *Love Story wa Totsuzen Ni*, or 'global classics' like Queen's *We Are the Champions*, Bruce Springsteen's *Born in the USA*, and Gloria Gaynor's *I Will Survive*.

Keitai also facilitate identity discourse by demanding that users name, identify and declare themselves to the world. This is important to adolechnics, I discovered, when I made the mistake of creating the email handle: duck_princess@ezweb.ne.jp for the red phone. This caused indescribable consternation for Maya, who was appalled at the idea of being associated with fowl. Quickly expunging that handle, she redubbed her address sugerpop-scoobiedue@ezweb.ne.jp. Alex, being less particular, thought that my choice of buggsandelmer@ezweb.ne.jp was just fine. Given the malleability of adolescent identity, it is likely that six months later, alternative handles would be fashioned.

Another identity-related task is screen design. Although there are thousands available, Maya and Alex were intent on creating their own. They shot a number of photos with the built-in camera and selected one that they felt expressed their character. For Maya it was a stuffed Pooh doll; for Alex a succession of sports caps and ethnic *objets d'art* that I keep in my office. A simple image was clearly insufficient, but with the cell phone's 'art studio', they could dress up an image by inserting script, coloured font, stars and other icons. This was not altogether alien to them: such photographic embellishment is common practice for Japanese youth who frequent *purikura* photo booths. Within a fortnight, these adolechnics had reconfigured the device to reflect and assist them in constructing an individual identity. This process was abetted not only by pre-set options, but also by web-based material. Thus, Maya and Alex could be found daily surfing for pictures and text of their favourite singers and actors, as a means of refining their statements of self. Within two weeks the 'simple', generic cell phones their parents had purchased were transmuted into a device that exceeded tasks of sending and receiving text messages, phone calls and storing data. The *keitai* was now 'theirs'; it conveyed a portrait of the unique adolechnic user. So, too, by extension (and however unconsciously), it communicated a portrait of the social, economic, political and moral world surrounding the user.

Routinizing the machine

Parallel to the personalization process was the *keitai*'s integration into the normal rhythms of the adolechnic's life. As is common when fundamental changes in fashion and lifestyle transpire, one encounters a youth's casual denial that any substantive change has transpired. Observation suggests that the adolechnic seeks speedy normalization of the *keitai*; to make it a conspicuously inconspicuous part of everyday life. Stated alternatively: while *keitai* are astonishing machines that alter daily activities in significant ways, users adopt a blasé attitude towards the device's considerable influence over their everyday lives.

Normalization centres on constant use; not simply downloading and personalizing, but communication: human interaction and sharing information. For instance, when Alex and Maya first displayed their phones, their peers' response was '*me-ru chodai, ne*' (send me an email, OK?) or '*TEL kure*' (give me a call). Consequently, the early days of *keitai* possession were spent mailing and calling friends for the sole purpose of furnishing contact information. Beyond that, mail in the earliest days was of the following ilk:

4/11/04, 17:32 – Now I'm at Sendai Station. At position number 6
4/11/04, 17:44 – Now, I'm going home . . . I'm on the bus
(a friend of Alex's)

Such communications occurred about three times a day, but would increase fourfold in the coming months. They reflect a double form of routinization: *keitai* becomes a part of the everyday routine of life, while, paradoxically, serving to break the established pattern of an overly-routinized life. This echoes Ito's (2005) claim that 'heavy users of text messaging are beginning to inhabit an "always on" social environment where they can keep in ongoing, lightweight contact with their closest friends and families'. For the kids, prior to *keitai* acquisition, phone use had been occasional and utilitarian – merely to confirm a lesson time or check a school assignment – suddenly *keitai* formatics encouraged new ways of communicating with peers: instantly, at a distance. Consequently, the number of communication acts increased exponentially.

So, too, the manner of communication shifted. Alex found it most natural to text while walking from couch to table to a standing position in the living room, then into the kitchen and back to the couch. He also multi-tasked: talking and mailing while engaging in other activities, such as homework and television viewing. In fact, observing how much a part of their everyday actions *keitai* became, one might refer to these users as the *'nagara* (while doing something else) generation'.

For Maya, email was much more than words on a screen. Images, icons, attachments and photos were significant textual elements to be exchanged as part of the 'conversation' with friends. The *keitai*, of course, was designed to assist: its complement of 400 preset icons rendered web downloads unnecessary. Examples include a snowman, ghost, fire, SOS, cherries, knife and fork, baseball, camera, and television. Maya habitually uploads hearts into text, as well as her own 'original' combinations of 'thumbs up' alongside twinkling stars and a peace sign next to an upturned arrow. She also routinely inserts a blue star alongside the title 'It's Maya'. The problem with emoticons is that they are unreadable on regular PCs or phones from other (competing) phone companies. For this reason *kaomoji* (face-text) presets are available in seven categories, examples including: 'happiness' o(^-^)o, 'sadness' (;_;), 'anger' (-_-#), 'greetings' (★^o^★), 'stress' (f^_^;), 'surprise' (?_?) and 'others' (-.-)zzZ. Although Maya tends to eschew *kaomoji* as *'mendokusai'* (troublesome) the incompatibility issue does impinge on her mailing routine. Here, then, is evidence that the greater economic world 'out there' – beyond the adolescent universe – has a way of bounding and routinizing adolechnic behaviour.

Theorizing from observations

Keitai creates connections between adolechnics and the worlds of commerce and popular culture; moreover, a strong social dimension is discernible. As such, *keitai* phenomena can be evaluated sociologically. However, other social theories can also be employed to elucidate adolescent *keitai* use. The following section considers a few.

Communication theory

It is common in media studies to assess communication in terms of *form*, *content*, *types* and *uses*. If we consider *form*, *keitai* blends all forms – oral, written, printed, non-verbal, pictorial, and graphic/symbolic – into a comprehensive, multi-faceted communication. For instance, when Maya mails her friend after a long day of ballet, the following tapestry is woven:

> Song chimes indicating in-coming mail. Orlando Bloom appears on screen to introduce new mail. Maya unfolds the *keitai*, pushes her controller to surf to the correct folder, then clicks on the new mail. Sounds attend each action. After a short pause to read, Maya begins thumbing her finger pad. Her message reads:
>
> [*animated icon of a chicken hatching from an egg*] 'Thanks for the mail' [*another animated icon of the chicken hatching*] 'Ah, tomorrow (first period of school) is our level check test' [*cactus icons*] 'It's gonna be hell . . .' [*icon of a Japanese devil mask*] 'Well see ya then . . .' [*icons of hands waving goodbye*]

Turning to types of communication, five communication categories are often mentioned in media studies (Price 1996: 9–14). The mail above suggests that such categories are not analytically separable. What begins as an *intrapersonal* event becomes, through encoding–decoding–encoding–decoding, *interpersonal*. Moreover, given that machines serve as the ultimate encoders and proximate decoders in this exchange, *extrapersonal* communication also transpires. A pyramid-like structure has been held to capture communication events in contemporary society (McQuail 2000) – with intrapersonal at the base (the most extensive communication activity) and *mass* at the apex (reflecting the relative lack of societal-wide communication). The cell phone would seem to have altered the conical configuration of this model by increasing activity in every category. Intrapersonal communication is bolstered by greater stores of information received by and retrieved from *keitai*. Interpersonal communication is dramatically increased as users fill their moments riding buses, sitting in coffee shops, or pounding the pavement thumbing messages to friends (see message from Alex's bus-riding pal above). Furthermore, *group* communication has been influenced by a device that encourages the aggregation of individuals into named folders, thereby serving as the basis for common activity and interest. For example, after returning from dance, Maya's first hour is spent mailing her cohort – anywhere from three to ten dancers. To decompress the evening's events she contacts close friends; if the teacher or an adult leader wants to 'get the word out', Maya serves as conduit to the many names in her folder.

Another type of communication altered by *keitai* is *mass* communication, insofar as its connection to the internet has meant increased traffic between institutional sources and an audience seeking downloadable songs, screen images, icons and various economic services. Finally, the fact that these devices are available '24/7' as open-interface receptacles indicates that *extra-personal* communication also has increased. Certainly this is true of adolescent *keitai*-users.

If we turn to *uses* of communication, adolechnics employ *keitai* in ways that serve many of the acknowledged communication aims – socialization, social ritual, instrumental, expressivity (Price 1996). Socialization is perceptible in the following mail from Alex's friend, after their first day of Junior high school, 'Someone from my church is a second year student at [our new school]'.

The talk here is of *sempai* (senior in a vertical ordering), a Japanese word signifying bindingness, social organization and cultural meaning. Articulating *sempai* helps reproduce and fix status. Key institutional structures involved in socialization are mentioned – church and school – which transmit social values, roles, norms and practices.

Socialization into norms of sexuality, as well as outlets for budding sexual awareness, are also facilitated by the *keitai*. For instance, Maya routinely sends mails to her friends concerning Orlando Bloom. A sample mail, to which she attached a downloaded photo:

> 'Don't you think this guy is hot?!'
> 'This guy, Ohmygod--------------'
> 'I just love him sooooooo much!!!!'

Socialization is not the only dimension here. Ritual exchanges help establish psychological unity in a group. These may be *phatic* – ordinary exchanges that reinforce social contact and social status – or *emotive* – interactions that engender affective bonds among members. These can blend into each other, as when Alex sent his first mail after buying the *keitai*, 'Hey Genki listen up: give me your email address. And hey: until your knee is healed, don't be trying to do the impossible' [in soccer]'.

Maya also engages in such routinized reinforcement of ties, augmented by affect. Here, a friend sent a photo of her pet dog, along with the simple line, 'Really cute, isn't he (^_^)'.

Sharing intimate visual information as textual accompaniments is not uncommon. According to Okabe (2004: 17): 'the camera phone tends to be used more frequently as a kind of archive of a personal trajectory or viewpoint on the world, a collection of fragments of everyday life.' Moreover, communicators 'seem to take pleasure in . . . adding (intimate) visual information'.

While personal sharing is often unsolicited, the mail above was prompted by a conversation between the girls earlier at school: Maya indicated that she would enjoy seeing a picture of the pet, a request this mail addressed. In this case we see technology serving as an extension of social relations. Technology bridges and enfolds – connecting moments of physical proximity with those in which physical distance prevails.

Such interaction is endemic in adolechnic daily life, producing a regularized pattern of thought, interpretation, understanding and action. The emotional enfolding observed above, is often melded with the *phatic*, thereby consolidating peer/group ties through acts of utility and intimacy. This can be seen in an extended exchange between Maya and a fellow ballerina as they debrief after practice. What begins as a routine conversation, 'Yaho' [*star icon*] 'Good work in private practice' [*heart icon*] 'Let's work hard tomorrow!' moves to the ritualistic back-patting formatically embedded in Japanese language-culture, 'By the way, until the performance let's lose weight' [*three biceps flexing icon*] 'Well, you are so thin so . . . (you don't have to think about it)'.

Then to the mutual support so integral to this peer group. Maya's friend replies:

> 'I also worry about my leg thickness' [*sad face icon*] 'Truly, it doesn't get thinner . . .' [*crying face icon*] 'I also do massage . . . but even with my physical characteristics, the legs are the last to get thinner' [*tear drop icon*] 'But let's do our best' [*peace icon*] 'Both of us should make a goal to reach!!'

Although the superior dancer, she offers a window towards validating her mail partner by asking, 'Do you know the way to get taller? I can't grow taller'. To which Maya replies:

> 'Well, as for the body . . . teacher has also talked about how height has to be a goal . . . so, since the growth hormone comes out . . .' [*star icon*] 'at night . . .' [*moon icon*] 'I drink calcium at night (so that it will help me grow)? My aim is, first, 160 centimeters, but 165 is my ideal height, you know' [*heart mark icon*] 'Anyway, I think I have a copy of an exercise explanation regarding reducing leg thickness' [*tear drop icon*] 'If I find it, do you want a copy? Well, I should go . . . bye byyyyyye'.

The other dancer responds affirmatively and says good night. Thus, by the end of this exchange both girls have reinforced the emotional bond they share through collaborative information exchange.

Communication theory suggests that many exchanges are simply *instrumental*. Adolechnics certainly engage in such perfunctory exercises, as when Maya messaged me one day at work:

> 'Hi, dad. How's your/was your meeting' [*three smileys holding question marks*] 'We are at Royal Host and we are ordering' [*fried egg in pan icon*]

'Well, we are waiting for you' [*cat icon with swishing tail, meowing*] 'Love Maya' [*pink heart icon*]

Throughout these practical adolechnic communications the expressive dimension is clearly pronounced. Representation of personal feelings aesthetically – whether via icons or mismatched fonts – reflects creativity, and tends to emphasize the emotional over the cognitive. This element is facilitated – even encouraged – by the *keitai*, since the means for facilitating expressiveness are programmed into the machine. As such, *keitai* proves the perfect complement (and resource) for the adolescent personality seeking to give expression to personal 'voice'.

Interiority . . . or exteriorization?

In one of the few analytic works on youth *keitai* use, McVeigh (2003) theorizes the internet's connection to individualization, individuality and 'interiority'. He differentiates between 'external' and 'internal individualization', where the former refers to how individuals are constructed from exogenous sociopolitical and economic forces, and the latter refers to the 'internalness' (McVeigh, 2003: 24) that emerges when individuals respond to exterior forces. In speaking of 'personalized individualization' – built of fashion, sentiment, and privacy dimensions – he argues that consumerist and technological advances in society precipitate – if not necessitate – the emergent inwardness manifested by cell phone users. Profound though these postulates are, they do not appear to prevail for the adolechnics I observed. Reasons may stem from age, geographic or methodological differences. Still, my observations suggest that despite the personalization and subjectivity implicated in adolescent cell phone use, the greatest energy is expended in 'exteriorization' – linkage with worlds outside: school, friends, activity groups and the larger worlds of commerce and popular culture. In this way, rather than encouraging inwardness, *keitai* use appears highly integrative. It connects users to others – be they humans (peer group, cohort members) or societal structures (macro economic and consumer-cultural systems). Unquestionably, not all youth/technology interfaces do this. Adolechnic use of game consoles, *manga*, MD and CD players, and even the internet suggest there may be considerable interiority involved. Ultimately, this suggests that various media may differ in the amount of 'interiority' and 'exteriority' they encourage – even demand.

Net-working

A case for interiorization seems plausible, given the extraordinary attention paid to *keitai* personalization via accessories, sounds and songs, and the inordinate amount of picture-taking and downloading aimed at creating a unique inner space. At a macro level, the act of downloading signifies exchange rooted in a space and time beyond the immediate consumer. This enlarged scale is also apparent for peer-shared *keitai* photos. Even more telling, in the creation, organization and maintenance of externally-situated cohorts – the worlds of 'family', 'school', 'friends' and so on – one discerns a highly sophisticated web of social relationships, exogenous to the interior adolechnic space. Such extensive organization and sociability constitutes 'net-working': an active practice of web-spinning and maintenance. This activity is facilitated, and enhanced, by the technology, which not only makes the creation of groups easier, but increases opportunities to reinforce group ties. Still, more investigation would seem necessary, considering the paradoxical Japanese phenomenon of *minna-bochi/hitori-bochi* (persistence in being together while totally alone), hypothesized by Nagamine (2001). This condition, posited in a newspaper article, asserts that socially neglected Japanese youth seek connection with as many people as possible, while disdaining deeper ties. This ironic pairing of social linkage with isolation was not evident among the adolechnics studied here.

Space and non-space

Since McLuhan, media theory has emphasized technology's spatial dimension. His term 'global village' (1967) captured how communication devices transcend as well as compress space and time (see Harvey 1989). For urban Japanese youth *keitai* technology is not only capable of spanning space, but also of altering space-based relationships in other ways – for instance by providing a place of relative autonomy away from prying parental eyes in whose cramped quarters youth dwell. *Keitai* provide an insular world of undisturbed thought and invisible social interactivity, beyond the confines of an overly-constricted Japanese society. A relatively autonomous 'space of persistent connectivity' is created, operating within the 'power geometry of space-time compression' (Ito and Okabe 2005: 89–90) and altering the social dynamics inherent in obdurate institutions of family, school, public space, and peer group relationships. This goes beyond Morley and Robins' (1995) contention that media span boundaries. Practically, media work to *dis*place life by moving consumers into *non-space*. Youthful *keitai* users wield their communication tools intentionally, avidly constructing and colonizing non-existence place.

This emerged in the following conversation with Maya:

I: Can you talk a little about your mail conversations?
M: Like what?
I: Like, is it like regular conversations – you know on the phone or in person?
M: When I do mail, I'm just talking with that person . . .
I: Are you really 'talking' with them . . . I mean do you hear their voice?
M: No.

I: When they're talking to you are they in a specific place? In your mind – do you see them in the studio or school or . . .?
M: No. I don't see them in those places. They are just . . . out there.
I: You don't imagine them in a place?
M: Right.
I: Do you imagine their face or see the clothes they are wearing?
M: No, not really. Not at all.

Yet adolechnics' conversations are rife with concrete physical referents – the bus stand, ballet studio, pet photos, Orlando Bloom in *The Pirates of the Caribbean*. Essentially, while non-space is implicated in cell phone use, so too is 'real space'. So, too, is 'co-presence' (Okabe 2004; Ito and Okabe 2005). A marker of intimacy, this social practice is widely engaged in by close friends, family members and loved ones, helping to transcend space and time and forge affective links with one's social circle via the sharing of visual and real-time information. This is a practice widely pursued by adolechnics.

Mediated identity

Morley and Robins (1995: 172) observe that in the West, Japanese identity is associated with technologies of the future: screens, networks, robotics, artificial intelligence, simulation – thereby painting Japanese as cold, rational, calculating, unfeeling and barbaric. In fact, in post-industrial society the ubiquity of technology means that matters of identity intersect with, and are influenced by, increased bureaucratization, industrialization, liberalization and rationalization of everyday life. This is no more or less true for Japanese, though their 'hyper-consumerism' (Tobin 1992; Clammer 1997; McVeigh 2000) may constitute an additional influence on identity construction.

A key component of modern identity, of course, is individuation. Earlier we considered whether *keitai* liberates and/or exacerbates individuality – a matter with particular resonance for Japanese, who have historically been stereotyped as group-oriented. Though recently disputed, such an ontological claim would incline towards the notion of Japanese as 'naturally' amenable to technologies facilitating group interaction. To Castells (1996) though, this might be beside the point – as his elaborate theory of networks asserts bindingness *in* technology. While Japanese adolechnics may not employ *keitai* as a basis for group formation, as we have seen, it is integral to reproducing and strengthening group experience, and rehearsing and refining shared identity.

In other work (Holden 2003) I advanced the concept of 'mediated identity' to account for the negotiation and formation of identity in conjunction with contemporary media. My initial conception conceived media consumers as rather passive. Having observed the adolechnic, though, it seems wise to recast the concept to reflect user activity, as well as its locus: often within and with regard to the (sub)group. Thus, a more accurate definition of mediated identity would now be:

Interactions, in and through institutions, and involving significations, conveyed through representations of sameness and difference, by media, and brought into relief by: *users*' references to socially-constructed group traits, and *their* depiction of relationship(s) between *themselves, their group*, and/or *other* groups.

The logic for these amendments should be clear if one recalls Maya's conversation about weight and leg size with her fellow dancer. Beneath this dialogue were a number of 'givens' that did not require articulation – aspects that both dancers understood about the goals, beliefs, terminology, assumptions and practices of their particular group. So too, in the case of Alex, as we see in the following exchange:

> *I:* So, what do you talk about with your friends?
> *A:* Just stuff . . . lots of things.
> *I:* Like what kind of things?
> *A:* You know, things. About school. And teachers and other kids.
> *I:* Do you talk about girls?
> *A:* No, not really.
> *I:* Well, then, like what? Music?
> *A:* Yeah music. And, you know . . . stuff that kids my age talk about.
> *I:* So, could I see a mail or two about it?
> *A:* No, Dad. That's private!
> *I:* Private?
> *A:* It's just, you know, for us kids

Alex's identity is reflected in his group (kids, age peers, not teachers), in his spaces (school, private) and in his interests (music, not girls, stuff). These elements form an 'identity frame', an insular, bounded community to be patrolled and defended.

In observing adolechnic engagement with *keitai* technology, identity is clearly implicated. One sees a collective process of group identification during the course of cell phone use. Admittedly a fair amount of this activity would transpire without the *keitai*; nonetheless, the group employs the device positively, in the service of its collective process. Importantly, this mediated engagement transpires at two levels at once: cell phone use is individually executed, but collectively realized, experienced, shared, affirmed and reformed. Finally, though, the technology and the group mutually shape and reinforce identity; neither is necessarily determinative; so too, neither is neutral. Consider the following:

> *I:* How do you feel when you hold the *keitai*?
> *M:* Good.
> *I:* Good how?
> *M:* I don't know . . . different.

I: You mean like . . . cool?
M: Yeah. And . . . I don't know . . . I like how it feels to hold it.

What Maya may not know is that some of the differences she may be feeling concern class, materialism and consumption. For, the shiny, dazzling, relatively expensive communication tool she wields is a measure of status for an adolescent. The device also connotes a measure of individual skill, power and freedom out in the world. Possessing a *keitai* sends messages of adultness and efficacy. Thus, while the group plays an important role in mediated identity, it is difficult to look at Japan's adolechnic and endorse Willis' (1990) view that youth understand their creative possibilities and actualize them most often at the group level. After all, when it comes to *keitai* culture, groups are rather amorphous configurations – often simply a pair of interactants; sometimes, linked in chains of serial activity. Much of the adolechnics' creative actualization transpires in interactive aggregates of no more than two – abetted by technology.

In summary, the data above provides us with a view of adolescent socialization, ritual, creation and practice of social roles, and constitutive discourse. We can observe adolechnic integration into, and reproduction of, the economic system and culture (particularly popular culture), and strategies employed to exist in, but also to transcend physical place via technological mediation. I wish to emphasize the emerging reality of a life lived in 'nonspace'. In conclusion, I shall identify a few themes that have hovered behind stage throughout, as they bear on the future of the adolechnic in Japan.

Conclusion: the adolechnic in a globalizing world

We have considered the twin levels of individual and group activity in mediated identity. Two additional paired levels are implicated in adolechnic *keitai* use that merit mention: micro and macro, and local and global. Here I wish to sketch four spatially defined combinations arising out of the interplay between these latter dualisms. In each case, I perceive connection to an integral social entity or process.

Globalization: the macro-global

At the greatest remove, *keitai* facilitates globalization by channelling adolechnics into, and galvanizing them with, peer and subgroups. *Keitai simultaneously* connect adolechnics to larger social, political, economic and moral worlds: above all, the consumer-capitalist economy, and the popular cultural realm. Negatively, this carries the potential of 'ground(ing users) in the privatized discourse of commodified desire' (Goldman 1992: 14), by entrapping them in social, economic and political discursive spaces both hegemonic and repressive. It should be noted that my observations perceived little of this, yet without dispute, the complex economic processes that characterize globalization have influenced the life trajectory of young people. For Japan's adolechnics this has meant increased cultural options, recreational opportunities, access to knowledge, and ways of configuring life. As a conduit for macro-level, often exogenous, social content, *keitai* technology has altered the dynamics and patterns of youth organization, as well as group interaction and discourse. In short, contemporary Japanese youth experience is based largely on, and enhanced by, a technology that aids in constructing a popular culturally-based, consumption-conscious, network-configured, private-yet-public, energetic, cohesive subgroup.

Consumption: the global–local

Media consumers are 'cultural producers and cultural respondents to the social milieu' (Lewis 1992: 6). Applied to adolechnics, this insight moves us from a global-macro to a global-local orientation. Their milieu, Japan, has been characterized by 'hyper-consumption' (Clammer 1997); a 'consumutopia' (McVeigh 2000). This is unsurprising, as consumption has been said to be the defining experience of our age (Bauman 1988). Importantly, though, the adolechnic cohort consume without being overly consumed with the idea of consuming. Their acquisition and use is unreflective, unaware of what they are actively engaged in. Virtually no thought is invested in what lies behind the production that leads to their act of consumption. One might claim that they are consuming out of an impulse of unsatisfied yearning, but it seems more the case – to paraphrase Maya: 'I like how it feels'. In a word, adolechnics appear to consume out of the sheer joy of consuming the particular object of consumption.

Much, though not all of what adolechnics consume is western – the macro-global: pop songs, movie stills, mail icons and the English language. Adolechnics employ these materials for group cohesion. It is *not about tracing* or demarcating lines of taste or status difference, so much as sharing what is fashionable, cool and desired. It is not about speaking perfect English or actually possessing Orlando Bloom; rather, it inheres in the shared feeling engendered between mutually linked consumers, independently engaging in the identical act of consumption.

Subculture: the micro-global

This delivers us to the next level of globalization: the subculture within which localized adolechnic aggregates exist. Adolechnics devote considerable time to teaching one another how to belong to their groups, what it means to be a young adult-in-the-making, to be a consumer of popular culture, to become a member of an economic and cultural subgroup within society. So much of adolechnic behaviour can be understood as a process of mutual instruction and learning, reinforcing, integrating, connecting, group-forming. Those observed were protective of their subgroup, expressing reluctance to share information about the specific features of the worlds they had created with members in their network. Their adolescent cell phone 'non-space' was a private, secretive world.

However, while these groups were of adolechnic making, complete agency does not exist. The subcultural worlds adolechnics conjure are based on groupings to which they have access: school, extra-curricular activities and, less so, the communities in which they reside. Yet, regulation is everywhere. For instance, school in Japan is the domain of the state; extra-curricular activities are reflections of economic contracts between parents and cultural custodians; housing estates are domains of both private and public corporate interests. *Keitai* itself is the invention and province of macro-economic entities. While choice may be involved, it is only to the limited degree that a particular site/affiliation option exists within well codified, highly conscripted worlds.

Amae: *the micro-local*

Finally, we can speak of adolechnics in their atomized capacity – as individuals. Wielding *keitai* is both a means of effecting peer group connectivity, and also of defining self. Yet other Japanese social analysts express concern about the proliferation of communication technologies. Ito (1991), for one, sees not only a widening, but also a segmentation, of opportunities, ideologies, values, tastes and lifestyles. In such separation he perceives social fragmentation and, possibly, withdrawal. One of the forces that encourage withdrawal is what Doi (1971) identifies as *amae* – a parent–child relationship in which dependency induces desire for passive love and unfailing indulgence. As Doi persuasively demonstrates, in the past Japanese people were socialized into, and encouraged to engage in, *amaeru* behaviours and *amaeru* relationships. One manifestation of *amae* has been the creation of a dream world for youth – a protected space of enduring indulgence. It can be said that Japan's continued development towards a high-technology, consumption-oriented, middle-class society has done little over the past thirty years to alter this view of Japanese youth as pampered and insular.

Certainly in comparison with many other countries, adolechnics appear relatively privileged and secure. At worst, they can be said to exist in a typical contemporary 'post-modern' society – a complex milieu melding risk with unprecedented advantage. One indication of this is how older cell phone users often join on-line dating clubs to ensure security in the often dangerous, untrustworthy world of unaffiliated singles (Holden and Tsuruki 2003). In this way, cell phone technology, tied to legitimate economic/organizational contexts, can serve as a buffer against the trials and fears of everyday existence. Yet, for the younger user, the early adolescent not yet ready to engage in more complicated social acts in 'advanced' adult society, a more naïve sensibility appears to prevail. The technologically hybridized adolechnic of contemporary Japan is optimistic, inquisitive, playful, trusting, externally-oriented and pro-actively social.

Bibliography

Bauman, Z. (1988) *Freedom*, Philadelphia, PA: Open University Press.
Castells, M. (1996) *The Rise of the Network Society*, vol. 1, Oxford: Blackwell Publishers.
Clammer, J.R. (1997) *Contemporary Urban Japan: a sociology of consumption*, Oxford: Blackwell.
Clark, T. (2005) 'Japan's generation of computer refuseniks', *Japan Media Review: wireless report*. Online. Available: <www.japanmediareview.com/japan/wireless/1047257047.php> (accessed 23 January 2005).
Doi, T. (1971) *Amae no Kozo*; trans. J. Bester as *The Anatomy of Dependence*, New York: Kodansha International Inc.
Goldman, R. (1992) *Reading Ads Socially*, New York and London: Routledge.
Harrow, J.R. (2000) 'The tiny – changing the rules', *The Rapidly Changing Face of Computers*, Compaq Computer Corporation Online Journal. No longer available. <www.compaq.com/rcfoc/20001204.html> (accessed 4 December 2000).
Harvey, D. (1989) *The Condition of Postmodernity*, Oxford: Blackwell.
Hashimoto, Y. (2002) 'The spread of cellular phones and their influence on young people in Japan', paper presented at The Social and Cultural Impact/Meaning of Mobile Communication Conference, Chunchon, Korea: School of Communication, Hallym University, 13–15 July.
Holden, T.J.M. (1994) 'Surveillance: Japan's sustaining principle', *Journal of Popular Culture*, 28(1): 193–208.
—— (2003) 'Japan's mediated "global" identities', in. T.J. Scrase, T.J.M. Holden and S. Baum (eds) *Globalization, Culture and Inequality in Asia*, Melbourne: Trans-Pacific Press.
—— and Tsuruki, T. (2003) '*Deai-kei*: Japan's new culture of encounter', in N. Gottlieb and M. McLelland (eds) *Japanese Cybercultures*, London: Routledge.
Ito, M. (2001) 'Mobile phones, Japanese youth, and the replacement of social contact', paper presented at the Society for the Social Study of Science (4S), Boston, MA, November 4.
—— (2005) 'Always on, never alone: *Keitai* and youth peer relations', paper presented at Japan Youth Cultures in Transition, The Institute of Comparative Culture, Sophia University, Tokyo, Japan, March 5.
—— and Okabe, D. (2005) 'Technosocial situations: emergent structurings of mobile email use', in M. Ito, D. Okabe and M. Matsuda (eds) *Personal, Portable, Pedestrian: mobile phones in Japanese life*, Cambridge, MA: MIT Press.
Ito, Y. (1991) '*Johoka* as a driving force of social change', *Keio Communication Review*, 12: 33–58.
Joho Tsushin Tokei (2002) *Information and Communications Data Base*. Online. Available: <www.johotsusintokei.soumu.go.jp/tsusin_riyou/data/eng_tsusin_riyou02.pdf> (accessed 16 May 2005).
—— (2003) *Information and Communications Data Base*. Online. Available: <www.johotsusintokei.soumu.go.jp/tsusin_riyou/data/eng_tsusin_riyou02.2003.pdf> (accessed 16 May 2005).
Kasesniemi, E.L. (2003) *Mobile messages: young people and a new communication culture*, Finland: Tampere University Press.
Kohiyama, K. (2003) 'A decade of development of mobile communications in Japan', *Japan Media Review: wireless report*, 8 December. Online. Available: <www.ojr.org/japan/wireless/1059673699.php> (accessed 23 January 2005).

Lewis, A. (ed.) (1992) *The Adoring Audience: fan culture and popular media*, New York and London: Routledge.
Ling, R. (2000) 'The adoption of mobile telephony among Norwegian teens', Telenor notat 57/2000. *Kjeller, Telenor Research and Development*, May. Online. Available: <www.aber.ac.uk/media/sections/it05.php> (accessed 24 February 2005).
—— (2004) *The Mobile Connection: the cell phone's impact on society*, San Francisco: Morgan Kaufmann Publishers.
Lippit, T. (1995) 'Japan teens flip for private pager', *International Herald Tribune*, 10 April: 14.
McLuhan, M. (1967) *The Medium is the Massage*, New York: Bantam Books.
McQuail, D. (2000) *Mass Communication Theory*, London: Sage.
McVeigh, B. (2000) 'How Hello Kitty commodifies the cute, cool, and camp: "consumutopia" versus "control" in Japan', *Journal of Material Culture*, 5(2): 225–45.
—— (2003) 'Individualization, individuality, interiority, and the Internet: Japanese university students and e-mail', in N. Gottlieb and M. McLelland (eds) *Japanese Cybercultures*, London: Routledge.
Morley, D. and Robins, K. (1995) *Spaces of Identity: global media, electronic landscapes and cultural boundaries*, London and New York: Routledge.
Nagamine, Y. (2001) 'Isolation fears lead to phone addiction', *Daily Yomiuri*, 13 July: 6.
Natsuno, T. (2002) *à la i-mode*; trans. R. McCreery (2003) *The i-mode Wireless Ecosystem*, Chicester: John Wiley and Sons.
Okabe, D. (2004) 'Emergent social practices, situations and relations through everyday camera phone use', paper presented at Mobile Communication and Social Change, the 2004 International Conference on Mobile Communication, Seoul, Korea, 18–19 October.
Pedersen. P.E. (2002) 'The adoption of text messaging services among Norwegian teens: development and test of an extended adoption model', SNF-report no. 23/02. Foundation for Research in Economics and Business Administration, Bergen, Norway. Online. Available: <www.ikt.hia.no/perep/publications.htm> (accessed 3 January 2005).
Price, S. (1996) *Communication Studies*, Singapore: Longman.
Skog, B. (2002) 'Mobiles and the Norwegian teen: identity, gender and class', in J.E. Katz and M. Aakhus (eds) *Perpetual Contact*, Cambridge: Cambridge University Press.
Suzuki, T. and Best, J. (2003) 'The emergence of trendsetters for fashions and fads: Kogaru in 1990s Japan', *The Sociological Quarterly*, 44(1): 61–79.
Tobin, J. (1992) *Re-made in Japan: everyday life and consumer taste in a changing society*, New Haven, CT, and London: Yale University Press.
White Paper (2004) *Information and Communications in Japan: building a ubiquitous network society that spreads throughout the world*, Economic Research Office, General Policy Division, Information and Communications Policy Bureau Ministry of Public Management, Home Affairs, Posts and Telecommunications, Japan. Online. Available: <www.johotsusintokei.soumu.go.jp/whitepaper/eng/WP2004/2004-index.html> (accessed 29 April 2005).
Willis, P. (1990) *Common Culture*, Boulder, CO: Westview.
Yoon, K. (2003) 'Retraditionalizing the mobile: young people's sociality and mobile phone use in Seoul, South Korea', *European Journal of Cultural Studies*, 6(3): 327–43.

5 The reflexive youth culture of devout Muslim youth in Indonesia[1]

Pam Nilan

Clear evidence of the hybridity of social and cultural identity practices is the distinctiveness of local youth cultures in non-western countries and the selective choices evident in this cultural production. This chapter examines cultural hybridity in the lifestyles of devout young Muslims in Indonesia – how their distinctive youth culture includes both religious law and global popular culture trends. Data gathered from focus groups with Muslim youth in Sulawesi reveals the antithesis to western cultural hegemony, which they claim leads to moral decline of young people, and threatens Islamic cultural values. Survey data on popular culture preferences of Javanese high school students is used to consider these claims.

Some devout Muslim youth argued for a filtering and selection approach to popular culture, so that positive aspects of western modernity are retained and experienced, while culturally inappropriate aspects are marginalized. This implies a very conscious, focused selectivity in the construction of Muslim youth culture, a reflexive constitution of group identity. As an example of selective synthesis, the last part of the chapter examines the apparent construction of a 'parallel world' of mediated Islamic youth culture in a Muslim teen girls' magazine – *Muslimah*. It is concluded that distinctively Islamic youth culture icons, products and practices preserve traditional culture and religious faith. Yet they also articulate youth culture, related in genre and form to global youth trends and icons.

The complex hybridity of youth cultures

> Understanding these processes – how young people navigate their way between the various, often highly disjunctive influences operating in their lives – is crucial.
>
> (Dimitriadis 2001: 41)

There is a 'plurality of issues and circumstances' (Bennett 2000: 11) that inform the cultural practices of contemporary youth in a global sense. So the distinctive youth culture of devout Islamic young Indonesians is not explained by a series of statements about faith. Like young people everywhere, their constitution of local youth style cultures signifies the fractured process of identity-formation relevant to the active construction of a life trajectory in an uncertain world. While orthodox Islamic faith obviously provides a strong and reassuring sense of certainty to those youth committed to it, there are other aspects of their lives to be negotiated which are not easily ordered by tenets of religious faith. In creating their own 'reflexive biographies' to some extent (Beck 1992: 135), transitions to adulthood are increasingly 'fractured', even in countries like Indonesia which are not really 'post-traditional' (Giddens 1991: 20), because of the rapid socio-economic transformations of late (high) modernity.

Bolstered by global Islamist movements, and Muslim solidarity in the face of 9/11 and other jihadic terrorist events, Indonesian Islam not only retains its traditional authority but is undergoing an enthusiastic youth revival. So not only does tradition keep its '"binding" normative character', expressing a set of 'precepts about how things should or should not be done' (Giddens 1991: 145), it is being actively reinvented. Contemporary Indonesian Islam is being synthesized with some of the lifestyle characteristics of late modernity – urbanization, consumption for consumption's sake, dependency on technology, extended periods of education and training, later marriage, and the rapid expansion of the middle class – to formulate a youth market for distinctively Islamic cultural products and trends. Participation in this kind of morally-patrolled youth popular culture, like that of Christian surfers or bikers in the West, is subject to constant scrutiny and reflexive practice. Since contemporary roles in civic life are now not fixed, but constantly reinvented and constructed, these young people 'have no choice but to choose' (Giddens 1991: 81) in the seemingly inevitable process of consumption. But they exercise constant surveillance over their youth market choices to maintain faith.

They 'choose' youth culture in the form of appropriate *halal* cosmetics and hair products, *nasyid* music, Islamic clothing tweaked in the direction of modern trends, portable phones, IPods and other technology personalized with Islamist iconography, Koranic verses, and so on. The selective act of choosing expresses the 'reflexive habitus' (Sweetman 2003) of modern young Muslims, legitimizing and verifying identity claims in both the ontological direction of 'young', and 'Islamic'. Bourdieu (1984) points to relations of 'distinction' between 'consumption, social context and habitus, one that attempts to account for the relation between social conditions of existence, the formation of the person, and the practice of consumption as a construction of a life world' (Friedman 1994: 9).

In the current global context of the American-driven 'war on terror', young Muslim Indonesians, whether devout or not, often identify themselves as anti-American and anti-western. 'Choosing' distinctively non-western products in the moment of consumption simultaneously produces them as proudly Indonesian and Asian, confirming that the contemporary 'reflexive habitus' identified by Sweetman operates in the 'field' (Bourdieu 1984:

226) of national pride. This kind of national, regional or cultural 'closing ranks' as a recent generative disposition of reflexive habitus in many parts of the world seems logical. In the 'ontological' insecurity of late modernity (Giddens 1991: 84–201), people are driven by the need to find protective cover, a sense of group inclusivity which simultaneously connotes a category of people excluded from group membership. In this sense, devout Islamic youth culture constitutes a 'third space' (Bhabha 1994) not shared by non-Muslim Indonesian age peers, westerners or adults.

Devout Muslim youth in Indonesia actively constitute themselves as modern, but fundamentally different from other Indonesian youth, and western youth, because they observe Muslim religious laws in their daily life practices. In this chapter, the terms *devout* and *orthodox* are used, but not *radical* or *fundamentalist* because these terms do not describe the conservative ideological position. Devout Islamic families vary between ultra-conservative and progressive. The young people in the focus groups (FGs), consumers of *halal* cosmetics and *nasyid* music, represent the more progressive trend. The progressive devout youth in the focus groups openly discussed their religion in philosophical and practical terms, debating contentious issues such as dating, fashion, and women in paid work. As Muslims of strong faith, they believed every moment of their lives was accountable to God. However, the answer was not dogma, but careful consideration of their daily practices in terms of the moral and spiritual understandings of the religion – an example of quite intense reflexivity in the life trajectory.

The development of local discourses of culture/identity is a collaborative and collective practice that draws upon diverse sources and tools. Global marketing structures feed and shape the parameters of this meaning-making by offering readily available materials, both symbolic and actual, to be eagerly taken up by groups of young people and thereby turn a profit. Accordingly, products are modified to appeal to local norms and values (Klein 2000; Giroux 2000). Examples are 'Zam-Zam' and 'Mecca' Cola in the Middle East, guaranteed 'kosher' bottled water in Israel and 'Yasser Arafat' potato chips in Palestine. Similarly, enterprises in the region like the MQ group have been quick to seize the marketing moment and promote a range of *halal* and authentically 'Muslim' popular culture products – including non-alcoholic beer. Giroux (1997) argues that cultural industry marketing articulates a 'cultural pedagogy' that invites young people to think, desire and behave in ways which favour display, consumption and unsatisfied yearnings, no matter where they live, or one might add, which religion they follow. Nevertheless, we need to account for this in ways that do not connote youthful consumers as merely passive (Bennett 2000: 27).

The significant hurdle for transnational producers of youth culture products is sex. Western media and marketing have effectively relocated sex and sexual activities from the 'private' family realm to the more public realm of leisure, specifically the leisure domain of young people, emphasizing the body of the young person as a kind of marketable sexual commodity (Giroux

2000). It is exactly this aspect of western/global youth culture that offends Islamist youth most deeply, and drives the search for alternative popular cultural products and practices that do not locate sexual matters inside the discourse of youth culture, or promote the use of alcohol – hence the quest for an authentically 'Islamic' youth popular culture. However, discourses of fun, entertainment, flirting and courting in youth culture are much easier hurdles than sex and alcohol, so a ready market for 'Muslim' youth culture products is present in modernizing countries like Indonesia. For affluent Indonesians, as elsewhere, consumption is the crucial, defining experience of the age, whether they are devout Muslims or not.

A survey carried out by the newspaper group *Keker Fajar* in Makassar in 2002 found that the 'entertainment' and 'teenage issues' sections of the local newspapers constituted most favoured reading for youths of 16 to 24 years of both sexes. Both sections include fashion details either explicitly (teenage issues) or implicitly (celebrity profiles and photos). The local Makassar shopping mall Mall Ratu Indah is filled with clothing shops aimed primarily at young people. Youth flock to shopping malls in the early evening and on Sunday, and walk up and down, looking at shops and snacking, a significant leisure pastime. Like other countries in Asia, huge advertising billboards dominate the cityscape. In short, it is difficult for anyone, save the religiously secluded and the very poor, to avoid the discourse of avid consumption. Accordingly, membership of urban youth style culture for Islamist youth is typically signalled on the body, what you carry, where you go and what you do, how you speak and what you talk about, what music you prefer and who your heroes and heroines are. Devout Indonesian Muslim youth who even-handedly display and practice *both* selected symbols and rituals of Islamic culture, *and* selected symbols and rituals of western culture, in company with like-minded others, establish themselves as a morally superior category of modern young Indonesians, in solidarity with the globally-distributed discourse of progressive Islam. This hybridity challenges the assumption that cultural meeting points must *always* signify relations of domination.

The hybridity, yet singularity, of contemporary Islamist youth culture in Indonesia is not the outcome of an arbitrary, accidental process. Rather, as a process in itself, the curious mix of distance from much of the specific micro content of global popular cultural core products and practices, combined with an apparent copying of the macro forms and genres of those products and practices, suggest both an implicit resistance against globalizing western cultural hegemony, and a simultaneous desire not to 'miss out', but to create something of their own (Bennett 2000: 29). Nine years of research has convinced this researcher that religiously devout young Muslim Indonesians want to be acknowledged as modern. Middle-class youth have leisure, money, mobile phones, and are internet-savvy. They know a great deal about global youth culture and the glimpses of 'possible lives' (Appadurai 1990: 9) such things offer. They abhor western values but do not see themselves as backward or old-fashioned. They frame their identities not only in relation to western-derived global youth culture products and trends, but also in relation to the effect of global progressive Islam on all Muslim countries. Liechty (1995: 167) reminds us that the formation of identities is certainly local, but the shaping factors that influence this local process can come from sources on the other side of the world.

To a certain extent Indonesian youth cultures have always looked outside the country for trends and influences – for example the Jakarta jazz clubs of the 1950s. However, in the last ten to 20 years this popular culture 'borrowing' has taken place in the context of a highly political, polarizing discourse of Islamic versus western values, which imbue the hybridity and synthesis of local Islamist youth culture with far greater political significance. At the same time, life in the middle-class suburbs of Indonesia has not been easy since the economic crash of 1997 (Booth 2002: 7). Previously, the period of economic growth in Indonesia under the New Order government saw unprecedented urbanization and the rapid expansion of the middle class (Gerke 2000). In cities, most households became nuclear family units and it was common for both parents to work, and for children to remain in education until the end of secondary school at least. These patterns remain, but the cost of living and education is now much higher, corruption remains the same and the graduate job market holds no guarantees. Although politically now a democracy, Indonesia remains at 110th position on the Human Development Index (HDI), the same as in 1995 (UNDP 2002). We are reminded that when economic and political conditions are characterized by perceptions of substantial risk, young people are more open to the emotive urgings of ethno/local and religious separatist movements (Giddens 1991: 201). In a rapidly 're-Islamising' Indonesia (Robinson 2001), many young Muslims strongly identify culturally with the global 'tribe' (Maffesoli 1996) of orthodox Islam, and purposefully adjust their cultural practices to fit its real or perceived norms.

Methodology

One methodology used in research reported here is the focus group. Focus groups draw upon respondents' attitudes, feelings, beliefs, experiences and reactions in ways that would not be feasible using other qualitative methods. Focus groups elicit a multiplicity of views and emotional processes within a group context. Interaction between participants highlights their view of the world, the language they use about an issue, and their values and beliefs about a situation. The second kind of data used here is from a survey in a Javanese secondary school that included questions on popular culture, technology and lifestyle, designed to gauge patterns in life style and consumer preferences of middle-class Indonesian youth. The third form of data comes from ethnographic fieldwork: informant accounts, participant observation notes and local media texts – teen girls' magazines. Media sources engage people at particular points of cultural practice. Studying the context of local practices involving media is important for our understanding of the hybridity of youth cultures, since culture is communicated in the lived spaces of everyday life where local and global identities are mediated (Nilan 2001).

In 2002, five focus groups with Indonesian Muslim youth (aged 19 to 21) discussing modernity, identity and social change were conducted in Makassar, South Sulawesi. The mixed gender groups involved 4 to 5 participants. The criteria for recruiting participants were that they should be well educated, active on campus or in the community, and of strong religious faith. All focus groups were conducted by local co-researchers – native speakers. The author was present in all the interviews, and guided the translations that feature in this chapter. In 2004, a survey on life attitudes, ambitions and popular culture tastes was completed by 55 16- to 17-year-old students at SMA1 – a high-status public secondary school in Solo, Central Java. Supporting these two data sets, ethnographic fieldwork data was collected by the author between 1999 and 2004. All participants were middle-class city-dwellers.

Indonesian youth

Indonesia is the country with the most Muslims in the world – over 80 per cent (Hassan 2002: 23) of the population. Christianity, Hinduism and Buddhism are recognized in law and the secular constitution, but Islam dominates the nation. Once an economic Asian 'tiger', the 1997 economic meltdown continues to affect millions of people (Booth 2002: 7). In 2004, the country's major problems were described as lacklustre economic growth, poverty, massive unemployment, an education and health care record which was among the worst in Southeast Asia, and endemic corruption. Unemployment rose to 9.3 per cent of the population in 2003, and some two-thirds of the official jobless were young people between the ages of 15 to 24 (*The Jakarta Post* 2004). Indonesia has a relatively young population, and the number of young adults (20–4) is predicted to increase from 20.7 million in 2000 to 23.1 million in 2005 (Hull 2001: 109).

Two significant influences on Indonesian youth derive from global popular culture, on the one hand, and local/national discourses of ethnic and/or religious community on the other (Widja 1999; Robinson 2002). Since *reformasi* (the democratic period after the 1998 fall of Suharto) Islamist youth groups have assumed new prominence (van Bruinessen 2002; Nilan 2006). At the same time there has been a proliferation of youth lifestyle choices in the new atmosphere of cultural and political freedom. Cheaply available designer drugs are nothing new, but rave parties and television Pop Idol competitions are. In a city like Jakarta, trendy youth with dyed hair, wearing extreme flesh-revealing fashions, mingle at rush-hour with devout Islamic youth wearing the Muslim cap or veil, their bodies modestly covered. The focus group participants in this study were of devout Islamic faith. They clearly regarded their hedonistic, fashion-conscious Indonesian age peers with a mixture of concern and disdain.

Muslim youth and western culture

As elsewhere in the Islamic world, many Indonesian Muslims regard western culture as not only a threat to Islamic moral values, but as a debased and immoral form of culture (Atkins 2002).

> The hegemonic cultural patterns of the West appear to provoke strong resistance in Muslim populations which expresses itself in the reassertion of Islamic identity, which in turn reinforces cultural pride and self-esteem as well as consciousness of an Islamic history which once bore the signature of *superior* cultural traditions.
>
> (Hassan 2002: 224, emphasis mine)

There was much evidence of this discourse in the focus group discussions. Participants nominated western cultural values promoted through media and information technology as tainting the cultural traditions and morality of Indonesian youth, for example:

> I think young people make use of the mass media for entertainment, and other things which are not in accordance with the applicable norms of our society . . . Indonesian teenagers nowadays, they tend to follow the fashion trends in the mass media.
>
> (Yuliana, FG7, female)

Another participant was more specific:

> Communication technology has a strong influence on the behaviour of Indonesian people. There are too many examples of western lifestyles that are being imitated, or adopted into daily life – negative effects. The free life of a teenager, free sex and so on. Drugs and stuff. Those habits are from outside Indonesia and we imitate them. When youth imitate the behaviour of westerners, they become just like them.
>
> (Firman, FG1, male)

It is no exaggeration to say that United States-based transnational companies dominate the production and distribution of popular culture commodities on a global scale (Lent 1995: 3; Klein 2000). Certainly a great deal of Indonesian popular culture comes either from external sources, or if locally-produced, follows the conventions of global genres. Survey data collected from youth in Central Java tends to affirm Firman's implication of western cultural influence. When asked to nominate their favourite television shows, these high school 'teenagers' demonstrated affinity for popular culture products at odds with what the older devout Muslim youth were presumably defining as 'the applicable norms of our society'.

Table 5.1 shows that the five most popular kinds of television shows – cartoons, soap operas, sport, singing competitions and English language films dubbed into Indonesian, are all derived either directly or indirectly from sources outside Indonesia, to a greater or lesser extent. Very few cartoons are made in Indonesia. Japanese (*manga*-style) cartoons like *DragonballZ*, western cartoons like *Popeye* and *Rug Rats*, the German cartoon *Detektiv Conan* are watched keenly by Indonesian children and adolescents and all encode to some extent the cultural values of the countries where they were made. Soap operas (*sinetron*) are a thriving local production industry, but female viewers are equally enthusiastic about the genre (as long as it is dubbed) no matter where serials are sourced: South America, Europe, Taiwan, Japan, India, Malaysia and the Philippines. These shows share the plot and character conventions of western soaps such as *Dynasty*, *The Bold and the Beautiful* and *Passions* – romance, marital infidelity, intrigue, scandal, wealth, family conflict, ungrateful offspring, dubious paternity of children, and so on. They all star eternally beautiful women dressed in western-style fashionable clothing. A few Indonesian *sinetron* exclusively about orthodox Muslim families have been attempted, but they seem to have a very limited viewing audience, since most of the defining plot and narrative features of the genre listed above are necessarily absent, and the characters are all dressed in body-concealing Islamic clothing and headscarves. Recent Indonesian *sinetron* however, do seem to include a mixture of different kinds of characters and families, including orthodox Muslims and veiled female characters. This mixture of lifestyles seems to be better received by fans.

Although some Indonesian sport is televised, and some feature films are locally made, the majority of content comes from somewhere else. One of the most significant contemporary show formats to impact on Indonesian television is the singing competition modelled on the now global 'Pop Idol' format. The most popular is *Akademi Fantasi Indosiar* (AFI), one of the biggest rating successes of all time. For the purpose of argument here, suffice to say that the young male and female contestants are glamorous and dressed in fashionable western-style clothing. Off camera, contestants share a gender-segregated group house, and a daily broadcast AFI diary update profiles their personal lives, including any nascent or actual love interests. The elimination of contestants is achieved by SMS, and fan clubs form around regional loyalties. When it comes to other music shows, once again, whether Indonesian or from external sources, whether live concert or video clips, western-style clothing is worn. The performers are glamorous, sophisticated and often sexually suggestive (especially MTV and locally-produced *dangdut*).

As Table 5.2 indicates, the most popular films named by high school youth in Central Java, were those made by, and distributed by, Unites States-based production companies. Such films are significant sources of western cultural influence on fashion and cultural practices.

In contrast to films and TV, 'vernacular' music performers and bands were preferred by these Indonesian teenagers over the externally-produced

Table 5.1 Favourite television shows of 17- to 18-year-old Indonesian youth, 2004

Programme genre	Male	Female	All
Cartoons/kartun e.g. *Popeye, Sinchan, DragonballZ, Detektiv Conan, Si Yoyo, Duracell Explorer, pilem animasi*	12	15	27
Soap operas/sinetron e.g. *Chanda, Cinta SMU, Mi Gorda Bella* (Europe), *My Love Patty* (Taiwan), Indian films (Bollywood), *Serial Asia, Desah Malam, Ekspedisi Alam 6A1B, Tala*	3	17	20
Sport/ohlaraga e.g. soccer, Slam Dunk, Auto Club, Moto GP, motor sports, basketball, including direct telecast	18	1	19
Singing competitions e.g. *Akademi Fantasi Indosiar (AFI), Diary AFI* and *Indonesian Idol*	5	13	18
English language films (dubbed or subtitled) on TV mid-to late evening	7	8	15
Music shows/acara musik e.g. MTV, FTV – usually music variety shows, live concerts or music video clips	1	12	13
Science and nature shows e.g. Discovery Channel, Animal Planet, Technology World, Tomorrow Today, Killer Insting, acara tentang hewan, Gentayangan	10	3	13
Reality shows e.g. *Fear Faktor, Dibalik Lensa, Liputan 6, Survivor*	5	7	12
Comedy/komedia e.g. *Bajaj Bajuri, Bo Ho Ho*	2	6	8
Horror and supernatural shows/horor/misteri e.g. *Jejang Petulang, M-Zone, Dunia Lain, Percaya tidak Percaya, Disini ada Setan*	5	1	6
Infotainment e.g. *Berita Selebritas, Metro Hari Ini*	1	3	4
Hong Kong martial arts e.g. Jacky Chan	2	0	2
Fantasy/sorcery e.g. *Takeshi Castle, Ngelaba, Angling Dharma*	2	0	2
News e.g. *Berita Pagi*	1	0	1
Quiz shows e.g. *Kuiz, Family 100*	1	0	1

Notes:

Respondents were invited to name three items in each category.

n = 52.

Table 5.2 Favourite films of 17- to 18-year-old Indonesian youth, 2004

Film genre	Total
American or UK films rated R or above for sex and violence e.g. *The Fast and the Furious, Armageddon, Scary Movie 2, American Pie, Predator, The Matrix, American Beauty, The Godfather*	17
American or UK general viewing films e.g. the Harry Potter films, *Lord of the Rings, Home Alone, Jackass, Parent Trap, Indiana Jones, Titanic*	15
Indonesian films e.g. *Ada Apa Dengan Cinta? Dono – Kasino – Indro*	10
Animated films e.g. Disney films like *Shrek*	7
Asian films e.g. Jacky Chan and *DragonballZ* films	3

Notes:

Respondents were invited to name three items in each category.

n = 52.

product (Bennett 2000: 42). Nevertheless, it should not be assumed that these local Indonesian performers and bands are therefore in line with what Firman (from his devout Muslim position) implied were 'the applicable norms of our society' – modest and respectable behaviour. Some of the most popular male music groups (see Table 5.3) – Sheila on 7 and Slank for example – favour a wild, punk appearance; black clothing, long, dyed or dreadlocked hair, tattoos. Female singers such as scantily-clad Agnes Monica appear frequently in the gossip pages with a succession of boyfriends, and divorce or infidelity scandals follow them about. At least one member of Slank has taken a very public road to recovery after battling a drug habit, and is now selling more CDs because of it.

This brief snapshot of the tastes and preferences of some Central Javanese teenagers points to the strength of western cultural influence that devout Muslim youth complained about in the focus groups. They were particularly concerned about western-style appearance. As one participant explained about some of his male age peers:

> When they see some behaviours that they consider modern they imitate them. They tear their pants, or grow their hair long. And because westerners have blonde hair then they even dye their hair blonde, despite their dark complexion.
>
> (Akzar, FG2, male)

However, it was the western-style clothing and appearance of Indonesian young women that scandalized the focus group participants most, as comments from two different focus groups show:

Table 5.3 Favourite music groups or performers of 17- to 18-year-old Indonesian youth, 2004

Music genre	Male	Female	Total
Indonesian rock and pop e.g. Sheila on 7, Slank, Padi, Dewa, Audy, Glen Fedly, Rio Febrian, Agnes Monica, Inul Daratista, Siti Nurhaliza, Coklat, Iwan Fals, Ari Lasso	35	36	71
Western rock and pop – contemporary e.g. Lincoln Park, Blink 182, Red Hot Chilli Peppers, Westlife, Missy Eliot, Celine Dion, Britney Spears, Backstreet Boys, Limp Bizkit, Evanesence, Eminem	21	17	38
Western rock and pop – non-contemporary e.g. George Benson, Nirvana, the Beatles, Guns N' Roses, The Corrs, Queen, The Eagles	11	3	14

Notes:

Respondents were invited to name three items in each category.

n = 52.

> In the past, women dressed modestly, but then that was changed by external influences – through communication technology . . . but now, I'm sorry, the sexually provocative westerner way of dressing, it's really disgusting for us.
>
> (Muhammed Ibhraim Rifai, FG6, male)

> Some things are no longer considered as violations. For example, in Makassar, even if her clothes were tight a woman really covered up her body. But because of modernization, through television, magazines and the like, that custom has disappeared.
>
> (Saipul, FG3, male)

The modern process of filtering and selection

> We must be smart to choose the good from the bad.
> (Rina, FG6, female)

It seems indisputable that the character of postmodern global popular culture is complex, often contradictory, even 'collage-like' (Strinati 1995: 228). Non-western youth can, if they wish, engage only with those elements of this vast shifting landscape of products, preferences and practices which resonate with local contexts, and ignore or refuse other elements which do not. This implies a reflective and selective ordering of the landscape of consumption, in keeping with the point made above regarding the 'reflexive habitus' of young middle-class urbanites in late modernity. The devout Muslim youth in focus groups did not want to be seen as old-fashioned. Some argued quite passionately that their values were actually modern:

> We misunderstand the meaning of modernization. It is just a way of thinking, that our culture is not modern. Modern is always understood as referring to anything *not* practised in our society. So we look to customs from the outside world like America, or Europe. Modernity is always assumed to come from there, but this is *wrong*.
>
> (Anwar, FG7, male)

The kind of modernity they claimed for themselves was one in which a selective process of choosing and filtering was practised, as one young woman described it:

> It depends on how we deal with western cultural influences, 'this seems interesting, that is not right, this is not appropriate'. You see, we evaluate everything. In other words, we refuse what we think is not good, even though it's aimed at us.
>
> (A. Dartan, FG6, female)

The recommended practice for Islamic youth was to refer back to traditional norms and values when judging the suitability of modern trends and products, for example:

> It's OK to keep up with modernization, but we must take into account our customs and traditions. As people of the East, we have strong norms and moral values in comparison to westerners who have a very different way of life. We can keep up, but at the same time filter the influences; ignore what doesn't fit and take only the good parts.
>
> (Altrima, FG6, female)

To anyone who has listened to the regular Friday night sermons broadcast by loudspeaker from the local mosque, it is obvious that these young people are repeating some ubiquitous discourses of Muslim preachers addressing youth. This does not mean though, that they do not take these ideas as their own, or that they do not spend time thinking about these things and discussing them in Muslim youth groups in a highly reflexive and reflective fashion. While some of the focus group participants argued that cultural/religious observance should simply be enforced, 'those who have gone too far in following western culture must be made aware of the restrictions' (Altrima, FG6, female). Others admitted the inevitable attraction of popular culture for young people, for example, 'We live in the international world and the young follow modern trends. We can't stop that because they want to follow the latest styles, they want to call themselves modern' (Nailah, FG1, female) and:

In the region I come from around seventy percent of young people do not take an active role in religious and cultural traditions. They find these things boring. Norms and customs are viewed as just everyday mundane things because these youth have been touched by modernization. They want to do more challenging things, or try new things.

(Irwan, FG3, male)

In fact the focus group participants themselves embodied the kinds of ambivalence implied in these comments. Although, as religiously devout, they were disapproving of Indonesian youth who mimicked western behaviours and appearances, yet, at the same time as they were saying these things, they themselves were wearing jeans and footwear, and carrying items of technology which matched global popular cultural youth trends. We are reminded that young people's 'lifestyles' now draw upon highly diverse sources (Miles 2000: 32). These middle-class, well-educated young urban dwellers were dressed in fashionable (some brand name) jeans, shirts, watches and shoes, even the veiled young women. By their own account, they shopped in the mall, and in department stores, which now have Muslim fashion sections. They all carried cell phones and owned portable CD players, or more recently, iPods. Rather than inherently contradictory, this should be understood as a very modern cultural trope of middle-class, non-western youth in the contemporary world. In the non-western context, the cultural constitution of self – the defining of identity – largely occurs through the iteration of ethno/local/religious difference in relation to western culture, but this rarely means complete denial. In designing their appearance, symbols of non-western cultural practice were juxtaposed with western items. The young men had neat haircuts and wore crisp white cotton shirts, and did not have tattoos. During the focus group conducted in a room at the mosque, they wore skull caps. The young women wore veils and loose-fitting blouses. Their arms were covered, and their legs too – in jeans. Although several wore some make-up (see discussion below), in accordance with Islamic law they did not wear nail polish. By displaying some apparently acceptable 'global' youth culture commodities, while purposefully avoiding symbolically taboo others, they advertise themselves as simultaneously located in the dynamic modern 'now' of popular culture and the traditionally secure world of religious observance.

The parallel world of Islamic youth culture

For devoutly Muslim young people in Southeast Asia, there is an ever-expanding range of products, media, popular musical forms, fashion and cultural practices which approximate the usual activities of global youth while anchoring the youthful consumer firmly in pious religious observance. For example, Indonesian Muslim girls who cover most of their bodies and wear the *jilbab* (veil or headscarf) do not have to miss out on youth culture. There are magazines devoted to Muslim teen girls' culture such as *Muslimah* which cover more or less the same range of teen girl topics, themes and practices as the mainstream Indonesian girls' magazines *AnekaYESS*, *Gadis* and *Kawanku*, but the fashion models all wear the Muslim headscarf (*jilbab*) and cover up their bodies. As Driscoll (2002: 269) argues, marketing to teen girls has always built on complex relations between conformity and non-conformity. In the focus groups it was pointed out that 'On TV there are ads for cosmetic products. Girls want to try them out because they want to be beautiful' (Nailah, FG1, female).

Special make up and skin products for Muslim girls (including creams to whiten the skin) now address this need so devout girls need not miss out in the beauty stakes. Cosmetics advertised in *Muslimah*, for example the *Wardah* range, might be expensive but are guaranteed *halal* and hyper-allergenic. There are even beauty competitions which parallel the mainstream ones, like *Top Model Muslimah 2004*, which attracted 43 veiled young women to the Crowne Plaza in Jakarta for the final judging.

Music fans are not left out either. *Muslimah* includes photos of boy bands and profiles of their members, but these young men are religious *nasyid* singers who harmonize on traditional Islamic songs and arrangements. Recently, various kinds of pop and hip-hop beats have been added as backing for the traditional *nasyid* lyrics and arrangements (for example some tracks on Snada's recent album *Buka Mata Hati*). Fans are encouraged to put postings on the *nasyid* website, conveniently owned by the company that publishes *Muslimah*. The handy hints section in *Muslimah* includes new ways of wearing the trendy and colourful *gaul* style of headscarf – especially for Muslim festive occasions such as *lebaran*, or attending live *nasyid* concerts. For young men, the parallel world of Islamic youth culture includes *nasyid* music, concerts, fan clubs and websites. Special clothes include organically-grown pure white cotton robe and skullcap, or knee-length Nehru-collar coats in luxury fabrics and black velvet Indonesian hats for special occasions. They can buy trendy *halal* hair gel and shaving soap. Many of these *halal* products and Muslim clothes are sold in the 'Muslim' section of the menswear and womenswear sections of luxury goods department stores like Matahari. Of course, that means a trip to the mall, a western lifestyle practice deplored by at least one focus group member:

> Another thing which is against custom and tradition in Makassar is going to the shopping mall to socialize. Now that has became a habit.
>
> (Saipul, FG3, male)

Although Saipul refers to socializing, rather than shopping, for middle-class devout Islamic youth offended by the mall there are always tailors and dressmakers, and online shopping to acquire the desirable icons of Islamic youth culture. While online they can also order *nasyid* ring tones and sacred Koranic script decals for their cell phones. Furthermore, they can socialize in a non-western context on Islamic teen websites, such as KafeMuslimah, an offshoot of the magazine. KafeMuslimah certainly presumes devout Islamic faith, but the usual invitations to correspond found on mainstream teen websites like AnekaYESS (Nilan 2003) dominate, although postings are definitely more muted and moderate in tone and topic. In all Muslim youth chatrooms it is the absence of sexual innuendo that constitutes the contrast with mainstream youth websites.

Devout Indonesian parents appear to sanction these youth products and practices, probably employing the logic that if young people are forbidden any participation in teen culture at all, they may rebel against the faith at this critical stage in their adolescence and early twenties. Furthermore, it may seem a good way to meet a prospective (suitably devout) partner in an era when marriages are no longer arranged. Nevertheless, such apparently hedonistic products and practices do not find favour with some Muslim preachers, who make them a subject of warning sermons. Notwithstanding, Islamic youth culture gains in popularity all the time. Devout Islamic Indonesian youth use symbols of personal adornment and music preferences in group practice, both actual and virtual, 'to identify themselves and to claim power and space' (Moje 2002: 105). The cultural space provided by a distinctively Islamic youth culture allows for the symbolically powerful expression of a pan-global Muslim youth identity in the context of Indonesia as a secular state. Furthermore, we should not forget that the popular culture of youth always serves as a generational identity marker between the world of youth and the world of adults, which still prevails as a boundary it seems, even in orthodox Islam.

The Islamic teen girls magazine *Muslimah* has to avoid the danger of turning young readers off (see comments on the exclusively Muslim *sinetron* attempts above) if a hard line is taken. Editors obviously need to tiptoe carefully between adhering too firmly to the orthodox position, and endorsing inappropriate frivolity and consumerism. The debate over birthday parties is a good example of this delicate negotiation between discourses. Mainstream Indonesian teen girls' magazines such as *Kawanku* make much of teenage birthday parties, advising on themes, guest lists, menus, party clothes and so on. However, it seems that birthday parties are the subject of critical scrutiny under Islamic religious law, so *Muslimah* takes a different line. In the birthday edition of the magazine, birthday parties are debated, readers' views are aired, and the opinions of three youthful Muslim celebrities (Indonesian *sinetron* actors) are sought. The verdict is that big birthday parties are out, but a small, self-catered celebration for family and close friends is permissible. Recipes for a *halal* Strawberry Chocolate Forest birthday cake and hot chocolate are featured (with colour photos). The brief editorial paragraph in the birthday edition of *Muslimah* demonstrates the distinctive hybridity of the discourse of Islamic youth culture:

It doesn't feel as though *Muslimah* has been going for three years, right? The magazine is still way young, but God willing [*Insya Allah*], we will continue to have your support, dear readers. Many wonderful things have happened during this time. From the beginning we grew and grew until we had to move premises. Our loyal readers know that there have been significant changes to our layout. At last our magazine has settled into its final form. Right from the start we brought you stories, information, fashion, even recipes. Changes have been made in printing and editing, so the magazine is now much more dynamic and lively, in its initiative, ideas, inspiration, in its jokes and serious matters (usually involving deadlines ha ha). In this special birthday edition, as your guiding friend, we brighten your day with an inspiring spread from the world of Muslim women's fashion. We also debate birthdays. Three celebrities talk about birthday parties. In fact, dear readers, they all agree that money should not be squandered, only just enough spent to celebrate the day. In the future, *Muslimah* wants to continue to be a supportive friend to all our readers, so look out for us all through the year, identify with us, keep supporting us. Hey, you are the voice of our crusade, right? Whatever happens, our goal is the same, to promote the rapid expansion of Islam. Happy reading!

(Editorial in *Muslimah* 2004: 4)

The translation here tries to capture the light-hearted, chatty tone of the original editorial. Slang terms commonly used by youth like *banget, lho, tapi, kok, nggak, nih* are employed rather than the formal Indonesian words. There is a serious message in there about being part of the global Muslim 'crusade', but it is somewhat undermined by being partly expressed in *bahasa prokem* (youth slang).

Clashing juxtapositions of this kind are also to be found on the *Muslimah* reviews page. The blockbuster Hollywood film *The Day after Tomorrow* is reviewed, and praised for its spectacular special effects which readers will find thrilling. Just above, the book *Ketika Mas Gagah Pergi* (*When Mr Gagah Went Away*) also receives a glowing review. It is claimed that many young readers took to wearing the Muslim headscarf after reading this love story. A young female civil engineering student meets an older male student who teaches her more and more about Islam until she finally reaches the decision to wear the veil. When she does, he falls in love with her.

Muslimah is published in both Indonesia and Malaysia by the Malaysia-based Variapop group which is not an exclusively Islamic business enterprise as such. Variapop owns a number of different media enterprises, publishes a secular men's magazine of the same name, and manages a number of musicians and bands, including *nasyid* performers. Variapop's mainstream publications and fanzine websites use the same kind of light-hearted, chatty tone and proliferation of slang terms as those translated from the *Muslimah* editorial above. So, while *Muslimah* discursively positions itself as a text that forms part of the Muslim struggle in Indonesia, seen differently it is really just a niche product in a stable of profitable popular culture publications and management enterprises in Southeast Asia as a whole. Like teen girl magazines anywhere, *Muslimah* is an index of specific technologies of the self (Foucault 1988; Driscoll 2002: 283).

Heavily hybridized Islamic popular culture products like *Muslimah*, no matter what the material actuality of their commercial production, occupy important semantic space in the development of legitimate Muslim youth identities in Indonesia. As a page 17 fashion advertising spread of colourful tunics and headscarves claimed (in English) 'The clothes that secure you!!' Certainly, Islamic youth culture icons, products and practices do 'secure' Muslim youth in the strong laws and norms of their religion and, simultaneously, in the powerfully legitimizing arena of mainstream popular culture. This hybridity is further symbolized by the frequent use of both English language phrases and Arabic script phrases in the text. *Muslimah* invites teen girl readers to exercise a form of dual surveillance over the textually-mediated creation of a viable self anchored in both 'worlds'.

Conclusion

In this chapter, it has been argued that the distinctive youth culture of devout Islamic young people in Indonesia draws upon both religious law and global popular culture trends, to create hybrid youth products and practices that serve to anchor the young person securely in the apparently antithetical worlds of orthodox Islam and global teen popular culture. Devout Muslim youth in South Sulawesi expressed their disapproval of western cultural influences on Indonesian youth, arguing for a filtering and selection approach to global popular culture products and trends. Survey data from Central Java appeared to affirm the claim that (with the possible exception of music) for mainstream Indonesian youth, popular culture texts and products from the West, or derived from western genres, were more popular than local cultural materials which bowed to tradition and religion.

Since devout Islamic youth eschew western cultural hegemony, especially rampant hedonism and the location of sexuality and sexual activities in the realm of youth leisure rather than marriage, they constitute a ready market for a 'parallel world' of Muslim youth culture – a hybridized range of products and implied practices that follow the broad parameters of Islamic law. Islamic youth culture products and trends (embodied in publications like *Muslimah* and musical forms like *nasyid*) are particularly popular with devout but progressive, middle-class Muslim youth who proclaim their modernity, while negotiating a reflexive biography anchored to both moral ascendancy and material success. The business enterprises behind Islamic youth culture products and trends strive to ensure that young Indonesian Muslims never need to feel they are missing out in comparison to their age peers. According to *Muslimah* they can have their birthday cake and eat it too, on the right side of Islamic orthodoxy. Distinctively Islamic products and practices appear to preserve traditional culture and religious faith. Yet this is still most emphatically youth culture, closely related in genre and form to global youth trends and icons.

In non-western countries, young people in their local contexts do not come empty to moments and sites of engagement with global popular culture. They bring with them a strong sense of who they are – primary identity markers – which derive from family and local reference frames, from history, race, class, gender, nation, tradition and religion. Primary identity orientation at the local level shapes how that young person engages with the field of global popular culture, and how this in turn affects their own process of self-legitimation and identification within youth culture. However, while devout Muslim youth in Indonesia do understand themselves as 'local' in the sense of Indonesian, and most certainly as ethnically Makassarese or Javanese, they also identify very strongly with the global 'tribe' of Islam, and this is a significant component of their reflexive habitus. Accordingly, they tend to filter the products and trends of global youth culture not only through the cultural lens of the local (Indonesian–Javanese for example), but also through the global cultural lens of Islamic law, and contemporary worldwide Islamist discourses, which seem to constitute culturally distinct generative dispositions in their habitus.

As an instance of hybridity, the example in this chapter of the constitution of a distinctive youth culture for devout, yet progressive, young Muslim Indonesians illustrates Bhabha's (1994) point that such emerging cultural patterns do not represent the coming together of two authentic and original sets of practices to form a variation on biculturalism. Rather, the process of hybridization looks towards an ambivalent and complex third space of cultural practice, in which new authority structures pull young people towards different narratives of identity. Furthermore, practising devout yet progressive Islam means these young Indonesians do not rest within the confining strictures of orthodoxy, but subject themselves and their social practices to constant surveillance, monitoring and debate. As shown above, it is these very qualities of hybridity, and self-conscious construction of a reflexive biography, that characterize contemporary and future Islamic Indonesian youth culture as a compelling topic of research.

Note

1   Dedicated to the memory of Asmaun Aziz – Indonesian youth researcher.

Bibliography

Appadurai, A. (1990) 'Disjuncture and difference in the global political economy', *Public Culture*, 2: 1–24.

Atkins, W. (2002) *The Politics of Southeast Asia's New Media*, London: Curzon.

Beck, U. (1992) *Risk Society: towards a new modernity*, trans. M. Ritter, London: Sage.
Bennett, A. (2000) *Popular Music and Youth Culture*, Basingstoke: Macmillan Press.
Bhabha, H. (1994) *The Location of Culture*, New York: Routledge.
Booth, A. (2002) 'Crisis and poverty', *Inside Indonesia*, 69: 7.
Bourdieu, P. (1984) *Distinction*, trans. R. Nice, London: Routledge and Kegan Paul.
Dimitriadis, G. (2001) '"In the clique": popular culture, constructions of place, and the everyday lives of urban youth', *Anthropology and Education Quarterly*, 32: 29–42.
Driscoll, C. (2002) *Girls: feminine adolescence, popular culture and cultural theory*, New York: Columbia University Press.
Foucault, M. (1988) 'Technologies of the self', in L. Martin, H. Gutman and P. Hutton (eds) *Technologies of the Self*, London: Tavistock.
Friedman, J. (1994) 'Introduction', in J. Friedman (ed.) *Consumption and Identity*, London: Harwood Publishers.
Gerke, S. (2000) 'Global lifestyles under local conditions: the new Indonesian middle class', in Beng-Huat Chua (ed.) *Consumption in Asia*, London and New York: Routledge.
Giddens, A. (1991) *Modernity and Self-identity: self and society in the late modern age*, Cambridge: Polity Press.
Giroux, H. (1997) *Channel Surfing*, Basingstoke and London: Macmillan.
—— (2000) *Stealing Innocence: corporate culture's war on children*, New York: Palgrave.
Hassan, R. (2002) *Faithlines: Muslim conceptions of Islam and society*, Oxford: Oxford University Press.
Hull, T. (2001) 'First results from the 2000 population census', *Bulletin of Indonesian Economic Studies*, 37: 103–11.
The Jakarta Post (2004) 'Next Indonesian leader faces a nightmarish list of problems'. Online. Available: <www.thejakartapost.com/detaillatestnews.asp?fileid> (accessed 28 June 2004).
Klein, N. (2000) *No Logo*, London: Flamingo/HarperCollins.
Lent, J. (1995) 'Introduction', in J. Lent (ed.) *Asian Popular Culture*, Boulder, CA, and Oxford: Westview Press.
Liechty, M. (1995) 'Media, markets and modernization: youth identities and the experience of modernity in Kathmandu, Nepal', in V. Amit-Talai and H. Wulff (eds) *Youth Cultures: a cross-cultural perspective*, London: Routledge.
Maffesoli, M. (1996) *The Time of the Tribes: the decline of individualism in mass society*, London: Sage.
Miles, S. (2000) *Youth Lifestyles in a Changing World*, Buckingham and Philadelphia, PA: Open University Press.
Moje, E. (2002) 'But where are the youth? On the value of integrating youth culture into literacy theory', *Educational Theory*, 52: 97–121.
Muslimah (2004) No. 25, Year 3, August. Jakarta and Kuala Lumpur: PT Variapop Grup.
Nilan, P. (2001) 'Gendered dreams: women watching *sinetron* (soap operas) on Indonesian TV', *Indonesia and the Malay World*, 29: 85–98.
—— (2003) 'Romance magazines, television soap operas and young Indonesian women', *Review of Indonesian and Malaysian Affairs*, 37: 45–70.
—— (2006 forthcoming) 'Indonesian Youth Activism', in L.R. Sherrod, C. Flanagan and R. Kassimir (eds) *Youth Activism: an international encyclopedia*, Westport, CT: Greenwood Publishing.

Robinson, K. (2001) 'Gender, Islam and culture in Indonesia', in S. Blackburn (ed.) *Love, Sex and Power: women in Southeast Asia*, Clayton, Victoria: Monash University Press.

—— (2002) 'Inter-ethnic violence: the Bugis and the problem of explanation', in M. Sakai (ed.) *Beyond Jakarta: regional autonomy and local society in Indonesia*, Belair, Adelaide: Crawford House Publishing.

Strinati, D. (1995) *An Introduction to Theories of Popular Culture*, London: Routledge.

Sweetman, P. (2003) 'Twenty-first century dis-ease? Habitual reflexivity or the reflexive habitus', *The Sociological Review*, 51(4): 528–49.

UNDP (2002) *The Indonesian Human Development Report 2001*, Jakarta: United Nations Development Program.

van Bruinessen, M. (2002) 'Genealogies of Islamic radicalism in post-Suharto Indonesia', *South East Asia Research*, 10: 117–54.

Widja, I.G. (1999) 'Kebhinekaan masyarakat Indonesia dan peranan pendidikan nilai di masa depan', *Aneka Widya*, 1(XXXII): 1–7.

6 Youth subcultures in post-Revolution Iran
An alternative reading

Mahmood Shahabi

This chapter explores the emergence of a postmodern cultural bricolage among urban youth in the Islamic Republic of Iran. It takes as understood that the process of cultural mixing has been 'very much on the increase' during the past decade, producing 'concepts such as bricolage, syncretism, and hybridity' (Wulff 1995: 63), as opposed to 'cultural imperialism', 'Americanization' and 'McDonaldization' (Foster 1991; Barber 1996). To comprehend the everyday life of Iranian young people, it is essential to examine the confrontation between official and unofficial youth discourses in both pre- and post-Revolutionary Iran. Youth have been viewed and defined by dominant official culture, yet Iranian youth themselves have constructed their own cultural world. The discussion below offers fresh evidence for Sreberny-Mohammadi and Mohammadi's (1991) claim that Iran constitutes one of the most extreme examples of Third World post-modern cultural bricolage.

Three categories of urban Iranian youth (locals, cosmopolitans and activists) are typified below according to their lifestyles, their relationships to each other and to the dominant social order. In the second section, three different 'readings' or explanations for the existence of cosmopolitan youth subcultures in post-Revolutionary Iran are offered, and their relation with popular culture is explained. The first is a 'mass culture' reading, the second a resistant or politicized reading in the tradition of 1960s and 1970s British youth cultural studies, and the third – my alternative reading – is a postmodern reading of cultural bricolage. The interpretive question relevant to the point made by Mohammadi and Sreberny-Mohammadi above, is whether processes of cultural mixture and hybridization are politically intended and conscious enough to talk of an *active* bricolage in Iranian youth subculture. Data collected relative to this question certainly reveals that some processes of postmodern accommodation of the different contradictory worlds of localism and cosmopolitanism are happening in post-Revolutionary Iran, in young people's everyday lives. These arguments are supported by qualitative data (observation, interviews and focus groups) gathered in July 2004 in Tehran.

Background

The definition of a 'youth problem' in Iran can be traced back to rapid urbanization in the 1960s when land reform under the Shah sparked an influx of migrants from the countryside to urban areas. Rural migrants experienced a tremendous change from traditional ways of life in clothing style, education, social relationships, food habits and leisure patterns. The influx of unemployed rural youth created problems for Tehran, particularly social disorganization. Rapid urbanization was coupled with forced westernization. Agents included radio and television, cinema, advertising, architecture, clothing style, food habits, education, youth clubs and organizations. Iranian popular magazines promoted 'beauty pageants, American-style contests, new sexual liberation *à la California*, and the latest cosmetics, dresses, and Hollywood gossip' (Mowlana 1979: 108). Youth were enticed by glamorous images of local and global film stars and popular singers. 'Modern society was hastening the sexual maturity of children. Radio, films, and books were inducing greater sexual awareness among young children' (Rejali 1994: 87). The dual processes of rapid urbanization and forced westernization provoked a harsh clash between the forces of continuity and change.

The youthful winners of this battle were unanimous about what they were rejecting: the Shah and his style of modernization. The Islamic Revolution of 1979 resulted in a mass of radicalized youth who had 'acquired arms, established grassroots organizations and were poised to take radical initiatives' under the clergy's control (Paidar 1995: 225). In May 1979, Khomeini established the Revolutionary Guards Corps 'to mobilise revolutionary youth in a pro-clergy army' (p. 225). It became the largest and best organized mass organization in Iran, playing a crucial role against militant opposition groups and ethnic separatist minorities, and later in the 1980s Iran-Iraq war. Youth were also active in Islamic Societies – *Anjoman Eslami* – which flourished in offices, factories and educational institutions to encourage Islamization and 'purification of the work place' (Paidar 1995: 225). In short, young people played a significant role in the revolution and subsequent rebuilding of the nation. Unlike the Shah's regime, the Islamic Republic emphasized the necessity of participation and politicization by the young. Youth were active in many social and political organizations created for them after the Revolution, for example Basij-e-Mostaz'afin (Mobilized Force for the Disinherited) and Jihad-e-Sazandegi (Reconstruction Struggle). Moreover, through participation in elections and pro-government demonstrations, young people contributed significantly to the popularity and stability of the Islamic government.

Undoing Pahlavi-style modernization: re-Islamization of youth

Socio-cultural changes resulting from the Islamic Revolution of 1979 affected youth in general, and women in particular. Through the Islamization programme, the new Revolutionary government attempted to 'cleanse' and 'purify' the society from the alleged vices and evils of modernity and to bring up youth according to Islamic ideological and social values (Beyer 1994). Changes included Islamization of educational textbooks; Islamization of family and gender relations; instituting a dress code for women; sexual segregation policy in education (except in the universities); sexual segregation and restrictions in sport and leisure; banning non-Islamic entertainment and recreations such as discothèques, bars, night clubs and casinos; and supervising approved entertainment centres such as parks (Paidar 1995: 336–55). Instituting and enforcing traditional gendered dress code was the most visible sign of Islamization of appearance. For men, ties and short-sleeved shirts in public were initially banned although they are tolerated now. Several days' growth of beard and a tie-less shirt buttoned at the neck symbolized an ideal or officially-favoured youth. In the name of 'public chastity' people were subject to surveillance either by police patrolling the streets or by 'promoters of good and forbidders of evil': groups composed of politically active and militant youths. However, these efforts proved less than effective among yet another cohort of Iranian young people.

Typology of Iranian youth lifestyles

Iran has one of the youngest populations in the world. Roughly half of the 70 million Iranian population is under 29. Looking at structural, sectional, religious, gender and ethnic variations, different youth lifestyle patterns can be identified: rural/urban, upper/lower-class, Muslim/non-Muslim (Jews, Christians, Zoroastrians), boys/girls, religious/non-religious or 'westernist', and different ethnicities (Persians, Kurds, Lors, Turks, Torkmans, Baluchs and Arabs). While some experiences and problems are common, the specific lifestyles of Iranian youth cohorts differ depending on their membership of the above-mentioned categories.

Yet this is not the full story. For analytical purposes, I developed the following typology of youth cultural lifestyles using the concept of 'Ideal Types' from Max Weber. The typology is also informed by the notion of 'cultural deviance' offered in Iranian official culture. By cultural deviance, I do not mean delinquency but elements of youth lifestyle not sanctioned by the official culture: dating, attending private mixed parties, engaging with certain types of western music – such as rap, heavy metal and rock 'n' roll, favouring western styles of clothing or grooming or, in the case of women, improper dressing (*bad-hejabi*). While there are many young people not involved at all in these youth cultural activities, for others, involvement is a matter of degree rather than either/or. Three major youth lifestyles are identified. First, locally-oriented conventional youth. Second, cosmopolitan or subcultural youth. Third, politically radical or activist youth (*basijis*). I examine each in turn below.

Locally-oriented conventional youth

The great majority of Iranian youth is conformist, convinced by Islamization programmes. They have internalized the key concepts, passing through adolescence and their twenties without being involved in any non-conformist youth cultural activities. They are 'conventional youth' to use Rosengren and Windahl's (1989: 167) terminology, or 'conformists' to use Robert Merton's goals/means typology of deviance and innovation, in respect to most aspects of official or mainstream culture. Their opinions, values, attitudes and lifestyles are consistent with traditional reference groups and with adult standards for teenage behaviour. Their identity is shaped by the cultural elements offered by parents, schoolteachers, national media and other representatives of Islamic authority. Intergenerational continuity exists between this group of young people and the older generation.

Cosmopolitan or subcultural youth

Nevertheless a portion of the post-Revolution generation, mainly from upper and middle-class origins, indicate that state youth policy is not deeply embedded in their minds. Despite the government's pedagogic efforts, a significant number of Tehran youth have their own definitions of normality and the good life. Uninterested in ideology and politics, they tend to be materialistic, hedonistic consumers of mass popular culture. While radical, militant and revolutionary youth were constructed as 'other' during the Shah's rule, in the aftermath of the Revolution it has been cosmopolitan or subcultural youth who have been defined as 'other' from mainstream Iranian culture. This latter group is influenced by more extensive contacts with the outside world through foreign travel, books, magazines, video, satellite television channels and the internet.

Rapid expansion of communication technology and a breakdown in traditional authority have resulted in a greater role for mass media culture in the process of Iranian youth socialization. Global media sources are used by cosmopolitan or subcultural youth as guidelines for standards of behaviour – hairstyles and clothing trends are diffused via popular music stars and other entertainment heroes. These young people identify with distant icons, rather than the proximate role models favoured by official Iranian culture. Being popular among their peers requires becoming familiar with, and involved with, global media culture. International media sources provide cultural food for subcultural youth identities, which are not usually served or represented via national media, although we may note that in 1995, two popular youth-oriented programmes were broadcast on Iranian television: *Sale-khosh* (Happy Year) and *Sa'at-e-khosh* (Happy Time). Both were criticized by the official press (for example *Jomhuri Eslami*) and some authorities on the grounds that these programmes introduced and represented punk and rap fans. We may also note that in April 2004 a youth festival was organized by the National

Youth Organization (NYO) for the first time after the Revolution. It was highly criticized by 29 members of Parliament (in a letter to President Khatami) on the grounds that at this festival young men and women mingled and their appearance violated the Islamic *hejab*. Processes of marginalization can also be seen in the way some public places (shopping malls, for example) are policed. Cosmopolitan boys (not girls) are subject to various regulatory practices, including various forms of temporal and spatial curfews exerted by the private security forces.

The lack of any institutionalized youth subculture in Iran means that counter-cultural youth live an underground existence, constantly negotiating with the official version of culture. No part of this minority underground youth culture falls within tolerable limits of current state ideology. For example, despite official disapproval, dating is considered normal by these young people. One can estimate the prevalence of dating behaviour by the number of Valentine cards or gifts bought on 14 February each year. Surreptitious satellite television viewing also takes place, despite its official ban. Western music genres such as heavy metal, rap and punk are popular. CDs and cassettes of many western singers and groups circulate among counter-cultural Tehran youth. Increasingly, the names and symbols of these musicians and bands are appearing as graffiti in public places. While these young people are, during the daytime, exposed to Islamic teachings through textbooks and extra-curricula programmes at single-sex schools, in the evening some teenage boys and girls gather together, often for birthday parties, to enjoy western music, dance, drinks and, for some, ecstasy pills.

In recent years they have even claimed some visibility in public space, both in individualized and collective (crowd) forms, and also in real and virtual public spaces. Apart from displaying an apparently subversive appearance in the streets, some subcultural young women don't bother to cover their hair with headscarves while driving or when seated in their cars. The once sinful and daring scene of handshaking between unrelated young men and women in public has now become relatively common. They use the internet for subcultural purposes (net dating and intra-group communication). Moreover, their claim for socializing space has propelled partying from the private to the public sphere. Formal occasions for public revelry are only three: Chaharshanbeh Souri (Tuesday night celebration), Shabe Ashura (the night of Ashura) and Valentine's night, unless Iran wins an important football game, and then there are four. Chaharshanbeh Souri is a pre-Islamic fire festival with a night of dancing, flirting and fireworks throughout the country. Shabe Ashura is the day Shi'ites solemnly commemorate the martyrdom of Imam Hossein, the Prophet's grandson in AD 680. Significantly in 2004 and 2005, some of Tehran's subcultural youth gathered in trendy Mohseni Square to disobey the rules and turn the religious ceremony into carnival and celebration, a bold practice indicating they have become more secular than ever before. Valentine's night is another occasion for public revelry which has recently provoked harsh reaction on the part of disciplinary forces. And finally football mania. In November 1997, football-crazy Iranian young people poured into the streets to celebrate the 2:2 tie with Australia, which qualified Iran for the 1998 World Cup. The subsequent thrilling 2:1 victory over America created another chance for public revelry by youth in Tehran. In June 2005 there was more public celebration after the 1:0 victory over Bahrain again qualified the national team for the 2006 World Cup.

While various western music genres like rock and roll, pop, jazz, soul, folk and reggae have their share of fans, four more extreme genres of western music – pop, *techno*, heavy metal and rap – and their associated styles of dress and hairstyle, are the core of current subversive Iranian youth subcultural identities, and are the least tolerated. Commitment to a particular genre of music defines membership of individuals within the range of youth groups. It is the focal point by which the group both defines itself – by creating a self-image – and is defined as such by outsiders. Members are labelled by conformist youths as *rap-iha* (rap people) and *hevi-ha* (heavy metal people), for example. Grossberg (1986: 115) refers to these as 'nomination groups'. The particular dress and hairstyle associated with nomination groups function as identity markers. Subcultural music sources are not only western. The home-grown underground pop music sung by a Tehrani female teenager known as 'DJ Maryam' has been popular with Tehran youth since 2004. There are also officially sanctioned home-grown mixed gender pop groups like Arian – a nine-piece band that has been permitted to play, tour and publish music in Iran, even though their music is not broadcast on national radio and television. They are now touring Europe and have opened the door for other local bands. Finally, there are Persian pop music audio and videocassettes and CDs produced by Iranian expatriate musicians abroad and sold by street vendors in Tehran illegally, or broadcast globally via ever-expanding Persian-speaking satellite television stations based in America. Engaging with this wide range of music options constitutes the most important form of cultural expression for Iranian subcultural youth. For those young people who can afford foreign travel, attending the annually held huge pop music concert in Dubai during the Iranian New Year festival in March is considered a ritual not to be missed.

Data obtained from participant observation, interviews and local press indicates that male Iranian rap and punk fans grow a goatee or stubbly beard and long sideburns, part and grease their hair, wear sunglasses, tight jeans and shirts or t-shirts bearing English words and terms. They have their own *argot*, slang, gestures and body language which differs from that of *basiji* youth (see below). Since they usually come from rich families, they drive their fathers' cars and use it for subcultural activities, they go abroad on holidays to western countries with their parents and generally imitate western life-styles. Their leisure time pattern differs from that of *basiji*. Subcultural male youth usually hang around shopping malls in affluent areas of Tehran, trying to attract the opposite sex, making dates in the streets, dining out at restaurants and coffee shops and playing western *techno* music on their parents' car stereos loudly enough for everyone to hear.

For young subcultural women, the public expression of global fashion is, of course, a subject of greater negotiation with local conventional rules. Women's *hejab* – dress code – became legally compulsory in 1983, with 10 days to two months imprisonment as punishment for lack of strict observance. The list of infringements included uncovered head, showing of hair, make-up, uncovered arms and legs, thin and see-through clothes and tights, tight trousers without an overall over them, and clothes bearing foreign words, signs or pictures (Paidar 1995: 344). This law, like the law banning satellite television equipment, has been frequently subject to negotiation depending on the nation's socio-political atmosphere and interfactional disputes. *Bad-hejabi* – inappropriate female dressing – is a major site of female youth subcultural practice and involves wearing bright colours; lighter and finer stockings; fashionable trousers, shoes, or bags; and revealing some hair beneath the headscarf. Even wearing jeans – a key youth symbol – is negotiated within Islamic dress code. While the *chador* – an overall black garment covering the body – is officially preferred, women can also wear a *manteau* – a large garment like a rain-coat. Subcultural girls choose the latter. A *roosari* – large headscarf – is also mandated, but subcultural girls choose a colourful one and tie it loosely. Young women's clothing style therefore indicates their position in the urban cultural divide. Devout young women wear the all-concealing black *chador*, or dark-coloured *manteau* and matching neat headscarf over a tight bun, while cosmopolitan young women wear tight, tunic-style vibrant pink or turquoise *manteaus* worn knee-length, and high heels. They wear their hair curly and dishevelled under the sheer headscarf, sometimes allowing dyed-blonde hair to frame heavily made-up faces.

Radical or activist youth

Unlike the two categories of youth above, the third – *basiji* – is politically involved. As mentioned earlier, activist youth played a crucial role in the Revolution. Since then, they have focused on 'promoting the good and forbidding the evil' in the country's urban environments – waging a campaign against cosmopolitan or subcultural youth. Currently *basiji*-volunteer militias serve under the Revolutionary Guards, now an organized regular army. *Basiji* lifestyle is organized around meeting places like mosques and military units. They attend mosques not only for prayer but also for ideological, technical and art courses. They tend to be found mainly, but not exclusively, among Tehran's lower class and traditional middle class. *Basijis* believe they possess the right to supervise and guide 'misled' youth (as well as adults and even certain governmental authorities and institutions) onto the right path and make them act along certain lines.

They claim that the revolutionary ideals for which so many Iranians suffered are threatened by western cultural invasion, represented partly by cosmopolitan youth subcultures. Their aims are to re-Islamize Iranian society, to restore the revolutionary zeal of the early days of the Islamic Revolution and expand the 'culture of *Jebhe*' – war zones during eight years warfare with Iraq from 1980 to 1988 – into the inner city. *Basijis* want to reconstruct wartime values disrupted by Iran's acceptance of United Nations Resolution 598 in 1988 and shape social values in full accordance with their perceptions of Islamic teaching. They assign themselves the role of guardians of Muslim morality. Urban spaces in large cities – notably in affluent north Tehran – are the scene of periodic confrontations between cosmopolitan and subcultural youth, and are main sites identified for 'purification'.

Reading Iranian youth cultures

Two contrasting interpretive positions can be taken to explain the relationship of cosmopolitan or subcultural Iranian youth culture to popular culture. It is either unthinking, passive, uncritical, manipulated, hedonistic and consumerist (Adorno and Horkheimer 1977), or conscious, creative, autonomous, selective, significant, symbolic and meaningful (Johansson and Miegel 1992: 113). The first reading is associated with Frankfurt School theorists and American media critics like Postman. The second reading is associated with British youth cultural studies (Hebdige 1979; Willis 1990), American cultural studies (Fiske 1994), as well as some French cultural theorists (de Certeau 1984) and Scott (1990) in political science. Both are relevant to readings of Iranian youth subcultures and popular culture. For instance, the idea of subcultural youths as cultural dupes or passive consumers has been promoted by Iranian authorities and official media. Conversely, the image of subcultural youth as conscious and resistive *bricoleurs* has been promoted by critical Iranian academics, particularly feminists, outside the country. These positions are discussed below and a third, alternative approach is offered.

Mainstream Iranian cultural authorities consider cosmopolitan or subcultural youth as 'cultural dupes' or victims of 'western cultural invasion' who blindly and imitatively consume imported foreign cultural products. They are depicted by the official media as *sousoul* (sissy or effeminate boys), 'deviants' – 'corrupt'. *Bad-hejab* young women are demonized as *gharbzadeh* – 'westoxificated', 'cultural traitors', typifying 'all social ills', 'dependency on the West', 'cultural imperialism', 'consumerism', even 'imperialist fifth column' (Moghadam 1993: 245). In short, the official image of Iranian youth subcultures matches the notion of 'folk devils' (Cohen 1972).

At the same time, academic literature on youth subcultural life in Iran is dominated by politicized readings of the popularity of punk style in Iran, *bad-hejabi*, and underground cultural consumption patterns of videos, internet and satellite television. These readings have one point of analysis in common: owing to the lack of formal and institutionalized channels for overt political expression, culture, particularly, popular culture, has become politicized. Certainly oblique or symbolic resistance has been at work in Iran for a long time. Behnia (1993) argues that in pre-Revolutionary Iran, the use of both 'horizontal voice' (addressed to all of civil society) and 'vertical voice' (addressed to the top by citizens) was inhibited and instead the use of 'oblique voice' or 'symbolic language' (O'Donnell 1986) was prevalent under the Shah. Between 1977 and 1979, Iranian revolutionaries used 'religious language, traditional symbolism' (Sreberny-Mohammadi and Mohammadi 1991: 133) and religious popular culture – for example parables and stories – to mobilize the masses in mosques and other traditional meeting places. This was really disguised opposition to authority and a form of covert communication between revolutionaries.

Similarly, the subversive politics of the veil have been repeatedly at work in Iran. Under Reza Shah in 1935 all women were forced to remove their veils, a brutal policy which engendered resentment. Before and during the Revolution of 1979, some activist women with secular liberal, or radical inclinations adopted veiling who had never done it before, unlike the Islamist women activists. For both, the veil constituted a symbol of solidarity, a sign of resistance (Fantasia and Hirsch 1995) – opposition to imposed westernization (Tohidi 1991). However, after the Revolution, non-Islamist women came to consider the veil as a symbol of women's subjection and questioned the legitimacy of gender policies of the new government. Certainly veiling was read by the new state apparatus as a sign and symbol of commitment to the Islamic Republic. That is why Iranian women's violation of dress code has been interpreted by some (including Friedl 1994) as subversive to the rule of *hejab*. Mir-Hosseini (1995: 156) argues the *hejab* has empowered those whom it was meant to restrain, and that its enforcement 'can be as empowering as its ban'. Both writers find similarity between Iranian women's resistance to female dress code and what Scott (1985) describes as 'weapons of the weak'. This resistance 'lacks any kind of organisation and indeed needs no co-ordination or planning' (Mir-Hosseini 1995: 157)

These interpretations echo de Certeau's (1984) analysis of popular culture. Although hegemonic cultural structures are produced for controlling meaning, there is a possibility that they may be used against themselves. For example, 'the headdress which is meant to conceal has become an ornament; the intent is subverted and the woman who wears it makes a political statement by turning an object of control into one of protest' (Friedl 1994: 156). According to de Certeau, subversive popular culture does not express itself through overt political opposition but by a disguised act which does not necessarily lead to wholesale social transformation. In summary, some Iranian youth subcultural activities function this way – they are not motivated by political intention but may have a slow-acting effect of political change.

Criticisms of political readings of Iranian youth cultures

The popularity of punk subculture in Iran has been considered by some Iranian sceptics as direct resistance against the Islamic government, but reading the phenomenon politically at all is open to question. The most explicit politicized reading of popular culture in Iran has been offered by Sreberny-Mohammadi and Mohammadi. Discussing media politics, they claim that owing to the absence of institutionalized and 'overt channels of collective political expression' in post-Revolution Iran, political dissent has manifested itself through 'individualized', 'passive' and 'fragmented forms of cultural resistance' to the 'fanaticism and puritanism of the official Islamic culture' (1991: 47; see also Boyd and Straubhaar 1985). The latest reading of this kind has been offered by Moaveni (2005) a young American-born Iranian freelance journalist. In *Lipstick Jihad*, she describes an underground, gradual movement among young Iranians, especially women, which she believes will be the country's saving grace.

Many politicized readings of popular culture are based on the notion of bricolage as a process of cultural selection. This is quite useful for considering the phenomenon of Iranian youth subcultures. Bricolage (Clarke 1976; Hebdige 1979) refers to the creative construction of meaning through an appropriation of prior discursive elements:

> Together, object and meaning constitute a sign . . . within any one culture, such signs are assembled, repeatedly, into characteristic forms of discourse. However, when the bricoleur relocates the significant object in a different position . . . a new discourse is constituted, a different message conveyed.
>
> (Clarke 1976: 177)

However, while punk culture in Iran seems a good example of bricolage, the problem with politicized readings of youth subcultures and their relations with popular culture is that they indiscriminately consider all youth popular cultural activities as conscious or disguised politically-motivated acts. Although it is true that individual taste and pursuit of urban fashion have resulted in alteration and modification of *hejab* details (length, colour, model and so on) by a section of Iranian upper middle-class young women, one cannot infer or speculate from this any politically-motivated challenge to mainstream notions of Iranian clothing style. Thus, while the adoption of western cultural forms by Iranian youth is really driven by a plurality of motives and factors, it has been read in a reductionist way both by admirers and detractors as an expression of either oblique or direct resistance against the extremism of hegemonic, official culture.

Furthermore, we should note that globally-derived subcultures carry little of their original political or social content in Iran. In the United States, youth cultures have often been defined by ethnicity, and in Britain by class, but in Iran non-conformist or cosmopolitan youth subcultural activities are not synonymous with western counterparts. Iranian youth subcultures are copied from the West at first remove. When the style of punk was imported – although in a hybridized form – to the country in the early years after the Revolution, it was evident from the outset that it did not carry the same political meaning. There was no socio-cultural base for a movement dedicated to subverting the consumerist lifestyle in a developing country with a different level of development and affluence. Similarly, there is great love of rap music among a segment of Iranian youth but there is no social base for a movement challenging racism in a society where different ethnicities and faiths have a long history of peaceful co-existence. Although they were resistant subcultural styles in their original contexts – punk in Britain and hip-hop in America – they have been brought into the mainstream and, stripped of their initial political connotations, made into an accessible consumer item by mass culture industries.

So we have to recognize that even though youth subcultures in Iran exist outside the mainstream, this does not imply direct political resistance or subversion. Owing to their non-organized nature, youth subcultures in Iran lack any focus to formally challenge existing political structures. Since these hedonistically-oriented subcultures are culturally marginalized at present, members are not quick to attach any overt political meaning to their activities – as a group of my teenage interviewees put it. One said his youth style signified:

> Thoughtlessness, convenience, carelessness toward everyday difficulties, and being happy and having fun.
> (Iranian punk fan, Tehran, 2004)

When I asked a female interviewee in downtown Tehran the reasons behind her excessive make-up, she said:

> Nowadays wearing make-up is fashionable, those who don't wear it will be looked down on as old-fashioned. I feel good about myself whenever I make up. My mum says it is sinful for a modest girl to make up, but I think she is not aware of the present society, nowadays wearing make-up is not as bad as it used to be.
> (non-conformist young woman, Tehran, 2004)

Another (who seemed very make-up literate) replied:

> I like western pop music singers like Madonna particularly because of their dress style and make up. I have modelled many night gowns upon Madonna's video clips.
> (non-conformist young woman, 20, Tehran 2004)

Yet another favoured Turkish style:

> I like Turkish female music singers and the way they dress, so I usually adopt their clothing style.
> (married non-conformist young woman, 24, Tehran 2004)

As these quotes indicate, cosmopolitan Tehran youth make no political claims and their subcultural activities are not self-consciously organized to achieve political change. While they demand more tolerance in social life, they do not intend to reach this goal through violent channels. Indeed the huge turn out of the young, including subcultural and marginalized youth, in the presidential elections of May 1997, June 2001 and June 2005 indicates their quest for both change and continuity through democratic channels.

To them, the occasional experience of being chased by the anti-vice squad is rather an exciting game – a sort of 'rite of passage'. They quite like the daring image that goes with being stopped, lectured and even detained temporarily for their subcultural activities. The punitive reaction of the dominant culture contributes to the self-definition of Tehran youth subcultures. Cosmopolitan Tehran youth normally don't fight back, they just run away from any confrontation with the anti-vice squad or with conservative *basiji* youth. It is the event of the confrontation itself that proves youth rebelliousness to individual youth and to their peers. The status of having an image daring enough to provoke a confrontation enhances their position in the group. Confrontations also contribute to an 'us and them' attitude on the part of cosmopolitan youth, especially towards *basiji* youth – who are the same generation. Nevertheless, while hardly any youth subcultural activities in Iran are politically motivated or consciously directed at bringing down the state, this does not imply that everyday youth subcultural activities lack any sort of political *consequences*.

Iranian subcultures and multiple uses of popular culture

The central argument here is that neither the 'passive dupes' position, nor the various politicized positions on youth subcultures, offers a productive reading of the phenomenon. I favour the balanced position taken by Swedish sociologists Johansson and Miegel (1992) between an overstated image of youth cultures comprised of passive consumers of mass culture or 'passive slaves of fashion' (Johansson and Miegel 1992: 104), and the equally overstated image of youth cultures as comprised of potentially politically subversive, creative users of popular culture. Johansson and Miegel claim popular culture is a multidimensional phenomenon, including both these possibilities (1992: 106–13). We should never lose sight of the fact that the world market is dominated by the new youth-oriented leisure industries whose success is dependent on monopolized control over advertising and global marketing, rather than on their quality (Johansson and Miegel 1992: 113). But equally we should never forget that different people may use popular cultural elements creatively for different reasons.

Ordinary people pick from other cultures – even hegemonic cultures – only those pieces that suit themselves and adapt to local conditions. Moreover, the metropolitan culture is selected and reshaped by the periphery, 'enrich-

ing it with some local values, giving local interpretation to received ideas
. . . a unique fusion or amalgamation of indigenous and imported elements'
(Sztompka 1993: 94). For example, a Tehrani middle-class teenage boy distinguished himself from his western counterparts by saying:

> We are not exactly like rap fans or heavy metal fans in the West, they do lots of strange things, but we don't. We only like their clothes and styles.
> (middle-class youth, Tehran, 2004)

A Tehrani girl told me during her interview:

> I like to wear boots and jeans. I like to follow world's fashions providing they conform with my beliefs and standards. I don't follow, for example, fashions like wearing torn jeans, because it contradicts my beliefs.
> (upper-class teenage girl, Tehran, 2004)

A similar point is raised below:

> I know most of the western rap and punk groups and bands and I like some of them, but I cannot, for example, dye my hair green, because I don't want to make fun of myself or attract male harassment in the street.
> (female university student, 21, Tehran, 2004)

Similarly:

> We take a western fashion and add something Iranian to it to make it conform with the revolution.
> (Iranian teenager quoted in Faramarzi 1997)

As these quotes indicate, cultural flows meet one another and form new combinations or hybrids. Mediating this process, Sztompka tells us, 'are local cultural entrepreneurs, who select and reshape imported products in line with their own local cultural competence and sensibility and the needs of the local market' (1993: 94). He credits an equally important role to the ordinary people in this process – they fill the global form with local content. In short, there are always possibilities of cultural bricolage by active users or consumers. This implies that the presence of western popular culture in Iran will not lead to full cultural homogenization.

Postmodern bricoleurs

I turn now to the analysis of the relationship between Iranian and western cultures, and the part recipient youth cultures play in the process of cultural globalization. The term 'globalization' implies the implosion of time and space, as well as cultural homogenization (McLuhan 1964; Crane 2002). This assumption has cultivated fear in subordinated and marginalized cultures and hope in western-based global cultural industries. Such fear is visible in Iran, particularly since 1993 when a campaign against 'western cultural invasion' was announced. We certainly are witnessing a progressive internationalization of cultural consumption patterns and standardization of cultural tastes and preferences. Moreover, new communication media technologies, the internet and audio-visual media – satellite television channels, videocassette recorders, DVD burners – have widened the extent of cultural contacts and experiences. However, there are various interpretations of this process. For some, cultural globalization is simply the corollary of modernity. Most imply the 'history of globalization begins with the history of the West' (Pieterse 1994: 163) – the colonizing, hegemonic process of global diffusion of cultural forms which have uniform effects on all recipient cultures.

However, historically cultural forms are always modified by local context. Hannerz (1987), Pieterse (1994) and Lull (1995) interpret globalization processes as hybridization. Local and indigenous cultures do not disappear or become extinct in the face of foreign cultures, but adapt, absorb and synthesize. For example, musical hybridity, as García Canclini (1989: 283, cited in Lull 1995: 155) argues, can be present in already synthesized cultural products or it can be produced by the consumers making a mixed repertoire of discs and cassettes. So from this perspective, globalization means increase in 'the range of organizational options' without any 'necessary overall priority or monopoly' among them (Pieterse 1994: 167–8). The account in this chapter of youth subcultures in Iran and their relation with global popular culture is influenced by this concept of globalization process, as well as by the notion of bricolage.

Transcultural mix in the 'production moment' can be seen in the appropriation of rap music format and attitude within underground Persian music produced by Iranian expatriate musicians abroad, mainly in America. Recent hits indicate that while songs are sung in Persian and lyrics refer to locally-familiar icons, personalities and situations, the attitude and format of Black American rap dominates. A new hybrid form of music has been created. Another type of hybridity is present in the 'consumption moment'. A subset of Iranian young people equip their home with a repertoire of discs and cassettes spanning a range of western music genres (including rap, punk rock and heavy metal), and even Turkish, Indian and Persian music, both official and underground.

Transcultural mix in the 'consumption moment' of cultural elements from different worlds and times was very apparent in the data. A 24-year-old tailor in a poor area in south Tehran was fasting in the daytime during the Muslim month of Ramadan in January 1996, and watching Turkish television programmes via satellite, in the night-time. Yet 'it is not the contrast between the elements that is striking; it is the lack of contrast, the clever, and taken-for-granted integration' (Davis 1990: 12, quoted in Srebreny-Mohammadi and Mohammadi 1991: 133). Practising religious rituals connects the devout young tailor to his familiar traditional past, while watching commercial satellite television links him to his global postmodern generational peers. 'Mixing the traditional with the modern is fully reasonable and practical in the range of contemporary cultural possibilities' (Lull 1985: 155).

Perhaps the youthful satellite television enthusiast was able to compartmentalize his various identities and thereby respond flexibly to the changing socio-cultural circumstances of contemporary Tehran. In so doing he has perhaps the best of two worlds – keeping his ties of belonging to the surrounding Islamic community, yet asserting his individuality through adventurous and imaginary tourism beyond community territory and approval – a splendid amalgam of particularism and cosmopolitanism, localism and globalism, inside and outside. Perhaps his subjectivity was constituted between the official and the unofficial, between the purified and the defiled, between proximity and remoteness, between continuity and discontinuity. This constitutes a postmodern lifestyle, based on bricolage of elements from different cultural worlds – combining 'parts of several world views into a meaningful entity' (Riis 1993: 376).

Conclusion

The very existence of youth subcultures in Iran suggests that post-Revolutionary Iranian society is not as monotonously dreary as imagined by some global observers. Using political jargon like 'closed society' (Bogert 1995) or 'fundamentalist society' (Boethius 1995) are misleading. Such judgements of Iran ignore minority groups and subcultural identities on the one hand, and dynamic social and cultural developments and contradictions in the dominant Islamist discourse, on the other. The acknowledged presence of youth subcultural identities in Iranian society signifies that while the official culture has been successful in fostering its values, and implementing its hegemony among the majority of youth, at least a portion of the young do not conform fully to the Islamic way of life promoted and pursued in official cultural policies.

Over the past two decades, Iranian youth have grown up under conflicting conditions of domestic and international pressures for conformity. The youth generation in Iran has constituted the main target for *endogenous* (internal) forces of socialization – Islamization – on the one hand, and for *exogenous* (external) forces of socialization in the form of globalization - through the activities and products of transnational popular culture industries. Between these two opposing forces are Iranian youth identities. Escaping from certain parts of the local socialization thrust, a significant minority of Tehran youth have attempted to fulfil their personal identity in subcultural bricolage. Struggles are fought out around differential sources for the construction of cultural identity and its political consequences: the official definition of national or religious identity, as opposed to the unofficial definition of personal, and small group identity.

In this partial escape, the ubiquitous character of popular culture and media provides individuals with greater opportunities for expression without involving geographical mobility, a phenomenon which Hannerz (1990: 249) describes as becoming 'a cosmopolitan without going away at all'. By providing Iranian underground youth culture members with an unprecedented opportunity to choose from among global popular cultural elements – Arabic, Turkish, Indian, western, Iranian – and shape their own hybridized cultural environment, new media (VCRs, satellite televisions and the internet) contribute to the development of a variety of youth subcultures in Iranian society. Global cultural elements are appropriated according to local needs, constraints and circumstances – cultural indigenization (Lull 1995: 153–9).

However, from the dominant ideological point of view, even an indigenized version of global youth culture is only tolerable and recognizable within certain limits. So making ideological compromises or liberal re-readings of religious text to accommodate all or some of the new generation's demands for more cultural freedom cannot go beyond the so-called 'red zones'. This implies that some subcultural identities or cultural practices will remain hidden in the underground. However, the official culture has not so far resorted to a new quest for purity or absolute authenticity, despite *basiji* urgings, but has continued to try to regulate the pace and the direction of socio-cultural change. The 1979 Revolution was not simply a nostalgic regression to the pure authenticity of the Islamic past. Rather it was engaged in what Karl Rahner (in Marty 1988: 21) calls the 'selective retrieval' of this past through redefinition, 'reinterpretation' and 'adjustment' (Afshar 1996: 122). In fact the Revolution's ambivalence towards the West, and its selective approach towards modernity in general, had bearings on many social formations, and created many mixed and contradictory entities. For example, the Islamic Republic's constitution is an eclectic combination of democracy and fundamentalism.

In recent years Iran has modified many policies through official reinterpretation of religious texts, following a pragmatic approach in the face of internal or external pressures. It has been a matter of 'becoming' rather than 'being'. The initial ban and later approval of chess, musical instruments, and private use of video, indicate flexibility in the face of the demands of the modern age. Moreover, the Islamic Republic has never disconnected itself from the world's perceived 'good', especially western high culture and even some elements of popular culture. Tehran bookstores stock translations of Heidegger, Marx, Althusser, Gramsci, Marcuse, Toffler, Fromm, Freud, Karl Popper, Kant, Foucault, Simone de Beauvoir and many others. Western classical music is performed by Iranian symphony orchestras and broadcast on national radio and television. Edited versions of western films such as *Dances with Wolves* and *Jurassic Park* are screened in cinemas and on television. However, while the softening of cultural policy has narrowed the gap between the official ideology and actual popular cultural practices and demands, it still falls short of many Iranians' expectations, especially the young. While the presidential election of May 1997 resulted in the victory of the modernist camp, igniting hopes among the young – whose votes were instrumental in the outcome of the election – for progressive change, the presidential election of June 2005 resulted in the victory of the traditionalist camp in which *basiji* young people's campaigning and votes were crucial.

While some Iranian authorities responsible for youth socialization have made positive responses to demands for change, and while some Ayatollahs have explicitly expressed the necessity for lifting restrictions and rigid limitations on young people's appearance, hair and clothing styles, and gender relations – restrictions which according to them have nothing to do with Islam, others have expressed concern about the extent and consequences of such laxness. It remains to be seen how future governments will handle the commonplace, yet highly-differentiated demands of youth. For the present, uneasy coexistence of official and unofficial youth culture seems likely to continue. It is highly probable that over time Iranian youth subcultures will provide mainstream society with a number of possibilities for gradual, irreversible and sustainable cultural change. This chapter ends with the prediction that the ultimate result will be cultural hybridization at two levels. The first will be brought about by the agents of official culture through reinterpretation of religious texts or appealing to hermeneutical solutions. The second will be brought about by the youthful agents or users of popular culture themselves through practising the sort of postmodern bricolage described above.

Bibliography

Adorno, T. and Horkheimer, M. (1977) 'The culture industry: enlightenment as mass deception', in J. Curran, M. Gurevitch and J. Woollacott (eds) *Mass Communication and Society*, London: Edward Arnold.

Afshar, H. (1996) 'Introduction', in H. Afshar (ed.) *Women and Politics in the Third World*, London: Routledge.

Barber, B. (1996) *Jihad versus McWorld: how globalism and tribalism are reshaping the world*, New York: Ballantine Books.

Behnia, B. (1993) 'Reflections on the reproduction of dictatorship in Iran: communication and dictatorship', *Alternate Routes*, 10: 85–111.

Beyer, P. (1994) *Religion and Globalisation*, London: Sage Publications.

Boethius, U. (1995) 'Youth, the media and moral panics', in J. Fornas and G. Bolin (eds) *Youth Culture in Late Modernity*, London: Sage Publications.

Bogert, C. (1995) 'Chat rooms and chadors: Iran – will the internet open a closed society?', *Newsweek*, 21 August 1995.

Boyd, D. and Straubhaar, D. (1985) 'Developmental impact of the home video cassette recorder on third world countries', *Journal of Broadcasting and Electronic Media*, 29(1): 5–21.

Clarke, J. (1976) 'Style', in S. Hall and T. Jefferson (eds) *Resistance Through Rituals: youth subcultures in Post-War Britain*, London: Hutchinson.

Cohen, S. (1972) *Folk Devils and Moral Panics: the creation of mods and rockers*, Oxford: Blackwell.

Crane, D. (2002) 'Culture and globalization: theoretical models and emerging trends', in D. Crane, N. Kawashima and K. Kawasaki (eds) *Media, Arts and Globalization*, New York and London: Routledge.

Davis, H. (1990) 'American magic in a Moroccan town', *Middle East Report*, 19(4): 12–18.

de Certeau, M. (1984) *The Practice of Everyday Life*, Berkeley, CA: University of California Press.

Fantasia, R. and Hirsch, E. (1995) 'Culture in rebellion: the appropriation and transformation of the veil in the Algerian Revolution', in H. Johnston and B. Klandermans (eds) *Social Movements and Culture*, London: UCL Press.

Faramarzi, S. (1997) 'Young Iranians help elect moderate', *Associated Press*, 23 October 1997.

Fiske, J. (1994) *Media Matters: everyday culture and political change*, Minneapolis, MN: University of Minnesota Press.

Foster, J. (1991) 'Making national cultures in the global ecumene', *Annual Review of Anthropology*, 20: 235–60.

Friedl, E. (1994) 'Sources of female power in Iran', in M. Afkhami and E. Friedl (eds) *In the Eye of the Storm: women in Post-Revolutionary Iran*, London and New York: Tauris Publishers.

García Canclini, N. (1989) *Culturas Híbridas*, Mexico: Grijalbo.

Grossberg, L. (1986) 'Is there rock after punk?' *Critical Studies in Mass Communication*, 3(1): 111–23.

Hannerz, U. (1987) 'The world in creolisation, Africa', *Journal of the International African Institute*, 57(4): 546–59.

—— (1990) 'Cosmopolitans and locals in world culture', in M. Featherstone (ed.) *Global Culture: nationalism, globalisation and modernity*, London: Sage.

Hebdige, D. (1979) *Subculture: the meaning of style*, London: Methuen.

Johansson, T. and Miegel, F. (1992) *Do the Right Thing: lifestyle and identity in contemporary youth culture*, Södertälje: Almqvist and Wiksell.

Lull, J. (1985) 'The naturalistic study of media use and youth culture', in K. Rosengren, L. Wenner and P. Palmgreen (eds) *Media Gratifications Research: current perspectives*, London: Sage.

McLuhan, M. (1964) *Understanding Media*, New York: McGraw-Hill.

Marty, M. (1988) 'Fundamentalism as a social phenomenon', *Bulletin of the American Academy of Arts*, 42: 15–29.

Mir-Hosseini, Z. (1996) 'Women and politics in post-Khomeini Iran: divorce, veiling and emerging feminist voices', in H. Afshar (ed.) *Women and Politics in the Third World*, London: Routledge.

Moaveni, A. (2005) *Lipstick Jihad: a memoir of growing up Iranian in America and American in Iran*, New York: Public Affairs Books.

Moghadam, V. (1993) 'Rhetorics and rights of identity in Islamist movements', *Journal of World History*, 4(2): 243–64.

Mowlana, H. (1979) 'Technology and tradition: communication in the Iranian Revolution', *Journal of Communication*, 29(3): 107–12.

O'Donnell, G. (1986) 'On the fruitful convergence of Hirschman's exit, voice, and loyalty and shifting involvements: reflections from the recent Argentina experience', in A. Foxley, M. McPherson and G. O'Donnell (eds) *Development, Democracy, and the Art of Trespassing: essays in honour of Albert O. Hirschman*, Indiana, IN: University of Notre Dame Press.

Paidar, P. (1995) *Women and the Political Process in Twentieth-century Iran*, Cambridge: Cambridge University Press.
Pieterse, N. (1994) 'Globalisation as hybridisation', *International Sociology*, 9(2): 161–84.
Rejali, D.M. (1994) *Torture and Modernity: self, society and state in modern Iran*, Boulder, CO: Westview Press.
Riis, O. (1993) 'The study of religion in modern society', *Acta Sociologica*, 36: 371–83.
Rosengren, K. and Windahl, S. (1989) *Media Matter: TV use in childhood and adolescence*, Norwood: Ablex Publishing Corporation.
Scott, J. (1985) *Weapons of the Weak: everyday forms of peasant resistance*, New Haven, CT: Yale University Press.
—— (1990) *Domination and the Arts of Resistance*, New Haven, CT: Yale University Press.
Sreberny-Mohammadi, A. and Mohammadi, A. (1991) 'Hegemony and resistance: media politics in the Islamic Republic of Iran', *Quarterly Review of Film and Video*, 12(4): 33–59.
Sztompka, P. (1993) *The Sociology of Social Change*, Oxford: Blackwell.
Tohidi, N. (1991) 'Gender and Islamic fundamentalism: feminist politics in Iran', in C. Mohanty, A. Russo and L. Torres (eds) *Third World Women and the Politics of Feminism*, IN: Indiana University Press.
Willis, P. (1990) *Common culture*, Milton Keynes: Open University Press.
Wulff, H. (1995) 'Inter-racial friendship: consuming youth styles, ethnicity and teenage femininity in South London', in V. Amit-Talai and H. Wulff (eds) *Youth Cultures: a cross-cultural perspective*, London: Routledge.

7 Music is the connection
Youth cultures in Colombia

Germán Muñoz and Martha Marín

> Music is fundamental for skinheads because it is like the sound track of the movement. When one is walking along the street . . . or when the first '69 skinheads were on the street doing their thing, they had a song in their heads and that song was like everything they were living. If that song had not existed, that medium of expression from which the movement emerged, we might not have existed.
> (Freddy, Bogotá RASH skinhead, and Skandalo Oi, singer, 2004)

This chapter addresses the relevance of music in Colombian youth cultures from an unusual perspective, taking the view that music is the key to the construction, weaving and constant transformation of global youth cultures such as skinhead, hip-hop, punk and hardcore. In particular, we will examine the musical dynamics that connect these global youth cultures to their local versions found in the Colombian setting.

The active and creative engagement of young people in the production of meanings, and of other ways of existing within their own cultures, has been a long-neglected topic within the social sciences. The concepts, theoretical models, research practices and disciplinary emphasis through which the current thinking about youth is built does not let us see much of young people as creative social actors and producers of culture. There are some highly influential, uneven and arbitrary views of youth as people 'in the process of becoming someone'. They are seen as people who are to be objectified and transformed over time into mature adults: as primarily passive receptors of adult culture and the mass media; as trivial members of a unified system of meaning dominated by consumerism; and as predelinquents or youngsters at risk, in need of adult direction, punishment or protection.

We move away from these notions and broaden the scope in order to analyse youth cultures from the aesthetic dimension, understanding it as a creative dimension which has transcended the boundaries of Art (written with a capital) in the twentieth century, to install itself in the fields of existence and experience. This dimension focuses interest on life considered as a work of art, on the ways in which young individuals actively constitute themselves. It is the act of creating one's self or self-styling, defined by

Foucault (1987: 106) as 'the exercise a subject does over him/herself and by which he/she attempts to elaborate, transform and accede to a certain way of being'. The dimension of creation comprehends the practices of self-styling or self-creation, and the search for, and construction of, new ways of being – means of artistic expression and alternatives – in social, political, economic and cultural arenas.

From this perspective it is possible to perceive that the creative potential of youth cultures transcends the simple composition of styles and gives them primary place in the generation, transformation and development of modes of existence, frameworks of reference, unique types of knowledge and even new forms of art. Of particular significance to the claim in this chapter about unique, singular types of knowledge, is the discovery made during research on the hip-hop and metal cultures' knowledge of how to handle conflict (*Currículo Silenciado. Una Propuesta Pedagógica sobre la Praxis Generacional de las Culturas Juveniles para Elaborar los Conflictos*). This research was carried out by Martha Marín and Adira Amaya and directed by Germán Muñoz in Bogotá in 2000.

Methodology

The accounts by young members of Colombian youth cultures which support the arguments and analyses in this chapter come from research projects carried out by the authors over the last 15 years, mainly in Bogotá. Although we have used a mixture of semiotic tools for analysis of cultural objects produced by youth cultures, all our research relies primarily on participant observation and oral history methods, both embodying approaches that have worked well for researchers of youth and popular culture in the past. Relevant accounts have all been translated into English by the authors, and edited to convey effectively the intention of the speaker. They are reinforced by quotes from other reports of similar research, and by secondary data from published research on global music icons.

Theorizing youth in Colombia

The aesthetic paradigm proposed by Félix Guattari (1994) helps us to understand better the importance of these creative processes since it shows the role played by aesthetics as a dimension of creation in the collective agency of discourses in our era. We will freely take some elements of this paradigm which Guattari conceived for the near future, but which we have seen functioning for some time in youth cultures.

First principle

> It thus becomes evident that art has no monopoly on creation but that it takes to an extreme the capacity of inventing mutant coordinates, of

engendering unknown qualities, never seen before, never thought of before.

(Guattari 1994: 193)

We are talking about the essence of a creative and sensitive (Spanish: *sensible*) order that relates to the artistic process, which in youth cultures leads young people towards self-creation, to the production of new subjectivities – to the search for, and generation of, *something else* in the domains of ethics, politics, art and forms of knowledge converted into praxis. One example of the functioning of this essence of a creative order is what we call 'motor forces of creation' within youth cultures such as punk and hip-hop.

Punk's motor forces of creation

In the case of punk, we have found 'do it yourself' (DIY), which punks call 'attitude', 'ethos', 'culture' and 'philosophy' related to self-management. In a Visual Arts graduate thesis on youth cultures written by a young female Bogotá punk and former skinhead, the following definition of DIY is made: 'don't work to enrich others and try to do things for yourselves' (Rojas Hernández 2001). In the history of punk, the 'do it yourself' slogan, to which is added; 'anyone can', was a response to the dominant belief that the act of musical creation required lots of money, education, influence and luck to distribute one's own creations through established corporate mechanisms. Nevertheless, the 'do it yourself' idea is not restricted to the area of music. In fact, it affects other areas of creation and of life. The DIY spirit inspired and motivated many young second-generation British punks to go against the commercialization of their culture, to create their own films and videos, to establish small independent, but significant, record labels, and to produce their own fanzines. At present, the anarchist wing of punk is no longer *against everything* but against that which means social and political oppression, and so considers DIY to be one of the most useful aspects of punk. It is a question of a type of thought that prefers action to apathy. DIY has remained in punk culture – in different moments and geographies – as a reminder of the fact that individual thinking does not seek the acquiescence of others to exist. It is a permanent urge to seek alternatives in different aspects of life, and functions as a spirit to recur to when this culture (or its descendants, such as hardcore and straight edge) reach a dead end. It has also been used as a way to expel all those who want to exploit punk commercially.

Hip-hop and the search for one's own style

In the case of hip-hop, in our research we also identified a motor force of creation: 'the search for one's own style'. There is a saying in the expressive practices of grafitti, rap, breaking (breakdancing), and DJing which is: 'fight with creativity and not with weapons'. This leitmotif indicates the extremely high value that hip-hop places on artistic experimentation – mainly on the creation of authentic individual style. Plagiarism has been despised from the very earliest stages of learning in any one of these forms of expression because it corrupts culture and attacks its most precious good, which is creativity.

When hip-hop demands that its participants create their own style, when it encourages the search for authentic cultural roots, it is laying the basis for hip-hoppers throughout the world to, first, develop local and autochthonous forms of expression; second, to use the raw materials of sound, images, rhythm and movement in processes of self-construction; and third, develop knowledge that is more in accordance with their immediate reality. So, although initially the search for a personal style seems to refer only to an artistic aspect (DJ rap, graffiti art and breaking), it affects the broader processes of subjectivity building and youth empowerment that take place within the culture, for example:

> We are volcanic beings but we are almost always inactive. Break, graffiti, rap and DJ come into one's life to liberate us and to allow the energy we have inside to come out.
> ('El Poeta', 18, rapper/graffiti artist from the *Localidad Cuarta*, Bogotá, 2001)

> To dance break is to demonstrate to life that one *can*.
> (Mario Cantor, young hip-hopper from Bogotá, 2001)

Without failing to recognize the incursions of marketing into youth cultures or their processes of expansion at the global level, we think that the discovery of motor forces of creation challenge those who understand global youth cultures as causing the loss of autochthonous values among youth in Latin American, African and Asian countries. The existence of 'do it yourself' and the 'search for one's own style' suggest that an adequate formulation of questions about the local/global relation of these youth cultures can no longer start with the simplistic own/others dichotomy and that it is important to seek other ways to understand this complex phenomenon.

In this sense, we have also observed that adults who work with young people are reluctant to value the wealth of youth cultures since the multiplicity of subjectivities that youth cultures propose is strongly related to music, and collide with the tranquillizing and easily assimilated idea of 'normal Colombian youths', even of 'Colombian youth' itself. This idea has begun to be debated by researchers of youth culture within the very same social dynamics. It is nothing more than a conceptual construct in which essentialism is mixed with patriotic yearnings and the ideals of the *good student*, of youth optimism, of *working youth*, of the *good citizen* and, finally, of youth undergoing *formation in values* who are imagined to *integrate into society*, and into some apparently neutral processes of social and economic development in order to *move ahead*.

Second principle

The second principle is the spread of creative processes into the domains of ethics, politics, knowledge converted into praxis, and art. That is to say, the work on 'what already exists and always on what could be is maintained as the focal point of resistance in the face of homogenesis (universes of unidimensional reference) and in favour of the creation of what is unique and irrepeatable' (Guattari 1994: 193), that is, in favour of singularization processes.

Struggle against homogenesis is palpable in the processes of constructing contemporary youth subjectivities: it is increasingly difficult to sustain that there is such a thing as 'a youth' or 'a way of being young'. At the beginning of the 1980s, youth cultures began to be detected on the streets of Latin America. When academicians realized years later that 'there were many ways of being young', the first trend of general thinking was to try to categorize heterogeneity. How? By identifying the names of the different cultures, enumerating and classifying their most obvious characteristics (appearance, jargon and musical tastes) and trying to understand them through the use of criteria such as identity and difference.

Challenging conventional understandings of youth cultures

At that time, the histories of these youth cultures were not well known in Colombia. Young people who began to explore them tried to find their way and to define tendencies following inspirational sounds. Academicians however, have tried to understand these so distant worlds by underlying the differences and by ignoring the dynamics of robbery, appropriation, divergence and momentaneous fusion that animate cultures. Nothing was therefore known about the almost musical procedures used by youth cultures to move in time and to produce something new. All of this has contributed to make these cultures seem unitary and impermeable compartments, identities or 'identity adscriptions' that occupied a separate place and that were differentiated from the others, that is to say, 'they were what the others were not'. For academicians, this logic of identity and difference, added to studies of youth tastes and consumer habits, proved useful. It encouraged the understanding of youth cultures as collectives in which youths enrol via processes of identification (definition of 'us') and of differentiation (definition of 'them').

Yet, with the passing of time, more information continued to arise regarding the history and real functioning of youth cultures. The crisis of the subject in the social sciences was simultaneously produced, and new orders began to appear in the contemporary world along with forms of power, economic models and other modalities in the construction of subjectivities. In the meantime, global youth cultures with a vocation for travel had found a niche in their new homes and extended the possibilities that their new surroundings offered them. All these factors contributed to the fact that the cultures were no longer perceived or thought of in the same way. We begin to understand now that youth culture investigation has been loaded with habits and taxonomies that lose their transparency and reveal their precarious position in the study of present youth cultures. In our experience, the study of the relationship that exists between youth cultures and music has produced a reconceptualization, not just of the cultures but of the music itself.

From the viewpoint of the aesthetic dimension it is possible to perceive hip-hop, metal, skinhead, punk and hardcore as huge laboratories for experimentation and creation that advance in time and in diverse geographies, organizing themselves around specific musical cores. Metal culture today is a world inhabited by visions of reality, life, death and music proposed by diverse genres: 'the paradigmatic *heavy metal* on the basis of which, later genres appear after numerous crossovers and pairings, such as *death metal, black metal, grind core, doom metal, gore, noise, industrial, death thrash, spatial, industrial rock and gothic rock*' (Serrano 1995), among others. The nucleus of skinhead culture consists of reggae, ska, street punk and oi. Punk culture gravitates around different facets of punk music. Hardcore culture, a descendant of punk, is organized around hardcore music that is a blend of metal and punk. Hip-hop, on the other hand, lives and is nourished by some sonic constructs in which diverse traditions and currents of black music converge.

The singularization process

Youth cultures associated with music stimulate 'singularization' processes (Guattari 1994) and the search for what is unique and irreplicable, since they contain within themselves a set of impulses that tend to carry out all of their potential. This is the reason for the constant defining of branches, sub-branches and fusions within and among these cultures. An example of singularization processes is that of the skinhead world. The origin of this culture born in England contains a multiplicity of elements including working-class pride, love of football and beer, valoration and defence of the right to work, fascination with music and the style of black Rude Boys, as well as concern about the loss of white homogeneity in working-class neighbourhoods with the arrival of immigrants in the 1960s. Each of these elements found its development in diverse cultural tendencies, and was also expressed and/or accompanied by a musical propulsion. We thus currently find skinheads who follow, in their distinctive music and cultural practice, the spirit of '69, Nazi skinheads or boneheads (who are not recognized as members of the culture by traditional and anti-Nazi skinheads), redskins (Communist skinheads), SHARP (skinheads against racial prejudice) and RASH (coalition of redskins and anarchists). In this way, music not only served as the means of expression for diverse ideas within the skinhead world, but also fomented multiplicity within the culture by favouring the development of offshoot branches. Thirty-five years after the birth of skinhead culture in England, expressions and representatives of each and every one of these branches are found in Colombia.

Youth cultures organized around music are not systems with a centre and a periphery. It is true that musical conventions, stylistic and linguistic synchronies, shared forms of body language, and generally similar forms of thought and sensitivities, are found in youth cultures wherever they manifest. It is also true that idols, musicians and emblematic figures play a fundamental role in the composition of something in common. Nevertheless, there is no one centre of production of meaning which participants in these cultures follow to the letter of the law. Although the welcome of a certain youth culture in another country implies some amount of imitation, the logic is not slavish imitation but that of creative, sensitive, musical and existential encounters within a 'rhizomatic' landscape (Deleuze and Guattari 1987).

Hierarchies in fact function because there will always be musicians or artists who will be considered 'gods' or 'models' to be followed. There will always be radicals who live their culture to the ultimate consequences. There will always be imposters despised by others who evolve to a more serious level. There will always be someone who has persisted in the quest for many years, and who is a living example of coherence between thought and action, which mobilizes great respect in these cultures. Nonetheless, one cannot deny that these are very heterogeneous, mobile and unstable hierarchies. Similarly, the cultural symbols and concepts produced, lack unequivocal or immutable meanings. Nor are they safe from robbery, reinterpretation or addition. It is no small thing that participants of these cultures may disperse today but later regroup. They may persist for a long time in their own thing or mutate. The panorama is definitely one of movement and instability. So one cannot speak of these cultures as centred, closed systems that are always identical to themselves everywhere and subject to central command.

Music is the connection

Contemporary popular music, like rock music, exists on different planes, in different relationships and has links to different contexts, within which it appears with different functions, linked to different meanings and values (Wicke 1995: 153). In reviewing the history of punk, more specifically the North American proto-punk scene in the late 1960s, we find a close relationship between music and the conservation of creative legacies for future punk. From the Velvet Underground to Iggy Pop, the rough, untutored quality of punk music carried and perhaps retransmitted a fundamental message for future punk garage bands which might be phrased as follows: 'It is possible to make good music without being a musician'. We can take the example from Iggy Pop, lead singer of The Stooges – considered to be the greatest true punk musical influence by many people. After he spent time with Sam Lay, famous black blues drummer, Iggy mused as follows on black music culture:

> I realized that they were far above me; that it was ridiculous to copy them as the majority of white blues groups did . . . I thought that what

you have to do is play your own blues, describe your own experience as these guys describe their own.
(Iggy Pop quoted in McNeil and McCain 1999: 33)

Other punk icons have expressed similar sentiments – stressing the DIY ethos, for example:

People who saw the Dolls said: 'anyone can do this.' I believe that the contribution of the Dolls was to demonstrate that any one could do it. When we were very young, rock 'n' roll stars used to presume 'I wear a satin suit, I'm great, I live in a golden cage and drive a pink cadillac.' With the Dolls we unmasked such myths . . . What we were doing was evident: returning music to the street.
(David Johansen of the New York Dolls quoted in McNeil and McCain 1999: 104)

The exciting, inspirational 'do it yourself' ethos of punk makes youth feel confident and allows band members to find their own rhythms and voices, the alignment of groups and themes. Punk and its ethos spread throughout America, Britain, Europe and the rest of the world, and eventually reached Colombia.

Punk culture in Colombia

Academic local knowledge of the history of punk in Colombia has been quite limited. Bands appeared and disappeared in the 'underground', and there were no early systematic studies of the subject, with the exception of one called 'Rock and punk. Punk is written with hate'. It is known that punk entered Colombia in a conflux of ideas, tides of disobedience, and visceral impulses that flowed through music, literature about punk and the images produced by the world press at that time. The nomadic circulation of local and world travellers, and the enthusiastic attitude of certain south-side youths who detected the appearance of a new sound in the air of Bogotá, also played a part in the evolution of punk culture in Colombia.

Those from the south side don't have many opportunities to travel but they realized [that punk had arrived] because they are the 'impassioned ones': they live with their '*antenas puestas*' [constantly on the alert].
(Gilles Charalambos, musician, videoartist and *Rock Premeditado* host, 2004)

Historical reviews of punk culture in Medellín point to Bogotá as the musical source. The HJCK radio programme *Rock Premeditado* in Bogotá has been identified as the first broadcaster of punk music and as the Bogotá–Medellín bridge in the late 1970s. The *Rock Premeditado* audience included the *apasionados* – 'impassioned ones' from the south side of Bogotá and some followers of heavy metal.

One band in particular – La Pestilencia – was iconic in the initial development of punk in Bogotá and provoked strong reactions. It garnered both strong adhesions and criticism among young fans and musicians who would later contribute to the development of a thriving punk culture in Bogotá, and go on to form part of the youth culture worlds of local skinhead and hardcore. The early years of punk in Bogotá were nourished by the coarseness of street life, crude sound and strange concerts in different environments that briefly included the presence of iconoclastic electronic experimenters and alternated, at other times, with the ultra-savage energy of heavy metal or 'asphalt' noise. The boundaries of what was punk music and what was not were ill-defined, and those were moments of discovery, definition – musical love affairs and visceral rejections.

In Medellín, a city that has been a landmark in the history of Colombian punk, the culture was born from rage and took shape through the crude sounds of under-resourced youth and musicians, as the following quotes show:

> New ideas were wanted and punk gave us the opportunity of autonomy, of freedom, of confronting our social reality head-on. Some of us began to do research, looking into some foreign books and magazines that talked about Punk . . . We also translated some Sex Pistols lyrics from a cassette that a friend in Bogotá had lent us. We realized that it was very applicable to our reality. We had found our own escape valve.
> (Freddy Rodas – 'El Chino', one of the first initiated into punk in Medellín, quoted in Medina 1997: 99)

> 'Medallo' [Medellín] punk fans were a legitimately bastard race, children of hate . . . Children without fathers or children of the first generation of peasants displaced by war, unemployed workers, slum dwellers . . . It was not surprising to find that street children from the inner city or from Moravia had adopted the new creed. Beings wretched from birth who simply had to incorporate nails and crest into their own maltreated ethos . . . The Mortigans, for example, whose name is derived from the word *mortecina* ('deathly'), lived in Moravia [the city's public garbage dump], a sector of Medellín that was then a methane-reeking mountain of waste produced by the entire population of Medellín.
> (Medina 1997: 99)

As the coded memory of a rebellious youth culture on the other side of the world, punk music brought DIY to Colombian punk fans:

> The instruments, if there were any, cost a fortune, so the slogan was 'do it yourself'. Tin cans, pots and pans, acoustic guitars, second-hand guitars

from pawn shops; anything and everything was used. They only lent us original guitars for a few minutes, enough time to make a makeshift sample. Loudspeakers and a tape recorder were enough.

(Freddy Rodas – 'El Chino', quoted in Medina 1997: 101)

Sandra Rojas Hernández, a member of the Bogotá punk band Polikarpa y sus Viciosas (Polikarpa's Vicious Girls) claims that

> With no pretensions of being musicians and obtaining their instruments with great effort, as well as a place to make noise, many of these urban-noise bands have been formed, in which the most important thing is often not the musical quality, but rather the quality of what is expressed in the lyrics and the music that flows from the heart, with the force of nonconformity.
>
> (Rojas Hernández 2001: 100)

For years, the survival of this youth culture in Colombia has been linked to the peculiar characteristics of creation and circulation of the music. That is, to the conditions of extreme poverty and self-management, to fury and rebellion regarding intolerable social conditions, to the flair for passing cassettes from hand to hand. By replacing selling with bartering, Colombian punks meant to preserve their own loud and crude music as a social good full of truth and meaning. In more recent times though, the animosity that many musicians feel for creative limits, and the incursion of some experimenters more interested in punk at the musical level than at the social one, have transformed the dynamics of musical creation. The original punks are also sharing symbolic creative space with university-educated punks, and with new punk fans and practitioners from the upper middle class. These changes are pushing the DIY principle to a 'more professional' level.

Punk lyrics and urban struggles

Lyrics of songs by some bands that appeared in Medellín between 1985 and 1989 are presented below. The late 1980s not only saw the rise of punk culture but also an expansion of drug trade that afflicted Medellín with waves of death, violence, bombs and corruption, creating all types of dead ends, misfortunes and lost opportunities for poor urban youth and young people from the communes.

Military Boots

(Los Podridos band)

Everyone against the wall!
Identification Cards!
One, two, three. Pigs.

This world is lost
the government is lost
lots of land for very few

Colombia is such a crazy place
and the people are dying of starvation

The government is ignorant
and in election time
innocent people in prison

And no, no
we can't protest
because the military boots
are gonna kill us right there.

(Urán 1997: 200)

Terrorist Attack

(IRA – Ideas de Revolución Adolescente band)

We wake up frightened
waiting for the tragedy
everyone sleeps convinced

that we will be their prey today.

Terrorists and bandits
thousands of bombs await them

Destroy
destroy
destroy.

Terrorist attack
only seeking to destroy
they spread panic and destroy

they spread hate and don't escape
only the rubble remains.

Destroy
destroy.

(Urán 1996: 200)

Analysing the ideological construction of punk culture in Medellín, Medina describes it as a 'patchwork' in which the only 'firm stitches were the words of the Punk groups that sang in Spanish'. He concludes that:

Latin American groups like Xenofobia and Narcosis, or Spanish groups like Siniestro Total, Ilegales, La Polla Records, Escorbuto, Parálisis Permanente, groups that defended militant anarchism in their lyrics . . . It is not surprising that groups of young amateurs in *punk* philosophy, with souls well-seasoned with hate, and functional illiterates (who had never signed their ID cards, and were much less likely to have consulted the classics of anarchist literature: Bakunin, Kropotzky, Goldman, Proudhon or, more recently, Robert Nozick), took anarchy, violence and destruction to be equivalents, celebrating the chaos in their most immediate surroundings.

(Medina 1997: 105)

Thoughts – what these youths call 'ideology' or 'philosophy' – also travel through the music and this causes distrust among those who are most accustomed to book-based knowledge. Some academicians have asked whether there is in fact a punk 'philosophy'. We have asked ourselves whether there is only one! The cultures have evolved in such a way that to begin to build up a body of knowledge about their creative processes of knowing and new frameworks of reference, it is necessary to formulate other questions. We need to forget questions like 'did the punks really understand Bakunin?' and enquire instead about how they have constructed, through music, some knowledge of their own about certain political concepts. That is to say, through a process bathed in music. Sonic knowledge – knowledge moulded by sound. Furthermore, there are various types of punks and, therefore, diverse forms of access to, and creation of, knowledge. In the present culture there are both the *podridos* (rotten ones) at the street level, and others interested in disseminating or consulting Noam Chomsky's articles about Plan Colombia on the internet.

Medina (1997) maintains that towards the end of the 1990s, many Medellín groups had abandoned their misogynous and sexist ideas and were updating the subject matter of their songs. There is no such detailed information regarding Bogotá, but it is worth noting that since the mid-1990s, the local punk culture has evolved in accordance with the crises imposed on Colombian society by growing corruption, poverty, war and violence. One example of this is DIY punk band Desarme, part of the Bogotá scene since 1993:

'Desarme' was born . . . as a feeling of nonconformity and reaction against the atrocities we see and suffer from day to day, supported by the authoritarian and repressive system that dominates the people of the world. Desarme is the ventilation of said feeling and the means of expressing what we think of all the injustices committed by those who wield power.

(Communiqué from the band published in Rojas Hernández 2001: 115)

The band manifests other aspects of DIY through its connections with other groups or collectives, through its cooperative work and international links. Desarme demonstrates the importance of music, of musicians in culture where music operates as both a creative and political impulse, as spiritual force for change.

Another example of punk critical artistry is Polikarpa y sus Viciosas, a female band that has well earned the place it occupies on the local music scene today. The Polikarpa y sus Viciosas repertoire includes songs strongly critical of paramilitaries and the ultra-right-wing. This is very timely political commentary just as the twenty-first century begins, when some sections of Colombian society, tired of war and inspired by the illusion of national security, call for a 'firm hand' and authority on the part of the government. Their lyrics demonstrate that in the face of 'no future', there are strong and courageous punk rallying cries, calls to action, to unite and to seek alternatives.

Third World People

(Polikarpa y sus Viciosas band)

We're marginalized
In third place for a location plan
They take control of the raw materials
For the good of the economy
We're the Third World
For capitalism to function
We have to kill and destroy ourselves
Not to create: we're forbidden to think
We have to eat shit
We have to live amid violence
We're Third World people
So that others can live off our lives.

Perhaps a point of encounter among punk, hardcore and rap youth cultures is that unwittingly, and via very different paths, they respond to what Henry Miller once said: 'there is nothing clean, nothing healthy, nothing promising in this age of prodigies; nothing, except continuing to tell what happens' (Miller, quoted in Kerouac 1995).

Music and free information

Rap lyrics have traditionally been considered unfoldings of an aggressive presence of youth in the cities, and a denunciation of the social injustices or inequalities experienced in ghettos and lower-class neighbourhoods. Music is often understood as a simple representation of the social and economic contradictions found in our societies, but expressions like 'let knowledge loose', or 'let wisdom fly', put us on the track of something more interesting and profound. When the rapper talks truly about knowledge obtained through life experiences, or through sharpening of the senses, it is a matter of high-quality information, as has been suggested by Chuck D, member of the legendary Public Enemy band:

> Once I realized that I'm a voice that people listen to, I realized I had to fill my voice with something of substance. Through rap music I've seen people all over the world magnetized to thoughts and ideas. My goal is to be used as a viaduct, as a dispatcher of information.
>
> (Chuck D and Yusuf 1997: 5)

The rapper disseminates information about and from the ghetto, that is to say, the rapper produces counter-information. When alterity is created through biased news reporting – for example 'the opportunistic, drug-trafficking Latin Americans', 'the juvenile delinquents from poor neighbourhoods' – which authorities use against youth, and which marginalizes people, then hip-hop creates its own news agency.

> Initially Rap was America's informal CNN because . . . it uses so many descriptive words [that people could] get a visual picture from what was being said . . . Every time we checked for ourselves on the news they were locking us up anyway, so the interpretation coming from Rap was a lot clearer. That's why I call Rap the Black CNN . . . Rap has become an unofficial [global] network of the young mentality.
>
> (Chuck D and Yusuf 1997: 256)

Similarly, the hip-hop group Alianza from Medellín informed us in 1989 that:

> People criticize us and call us 'bums'
> But nobody really wants to help young people
> Who are desperate to be on a street corner
> Standing there with nothing productive to do and thinking something bad
> The police arrive and want to manipulate us . . .
> This is the kids' proposal:
> We've got to respect the right to life
> Because there are some who violate and extirpate it every day
> Freedom of speech, but they'll kill you if you speak the truth
> Not even the government respects the law: they kill us and oppress us.
> We can't take this
> The right to educastration: to become just one more of the mass
> The right to health care: you land in a hospital, and what do you think?
> High taxes to pay
> It's better to die now of disease

> There's no longer any work because they say that young people will
>   always be killers . . .
> Could all of this be a warning?
>
> (Urán 1996: 206)

Given the fact that Colombian society is increasingly uninformed by the mass media, and torn apart by conflicts that most people don't really understand, some Bogotá punks of anarchistic inspiration take the lead from hip-hop and insist on the postulate of 'free information'. The previously limited musical ghetto of punk is opening up to other possibilities:

> The information is on the air [the net, life experiences and music]. We can't pull out of it just because of the radicalisms of Punk . . . Our goal is to create musical pieces that will also be communicative pieces. One example is 'Sin Dios' which produced its first self-made CD with a little book that contains the lyrics to their songs and writings about globalization . . . In the quest for a unique sound in the evolution of music, different genres are being mixed to reach more people.
>
> (Daniel, member of Desarme, 2004)

The music of Bogotá skinheads of the SHARP or RASH tendency also disseminates information. In their case, they wish to counteract the stereotypes of Nazi skinheads propagated by the mass media. These young people consider their creative musical work to be an evolution within the culture as a whole:

> The members of skinhead movements in Bogotá have wanted to advance as persons which is why the musical groups begin to create . . . It is an enormous evolution because there are all types of skinheads: those who do nothing but drink beer or watch football and others who are concerned about doing important, direct things on the informational, musical and cultural level . . . Our objective is information. To show our information so that people understand what a real skinhead is.
>
> (Freddy, Bogotá RASH skinhead, and Skandalo Oi, singer, 2004)

Both at global and Colombian level, music evolves along with the processes of the *Information Age* while still conserving the inspirational legacies and knowledge of the original youth cultures. On the other hand, if music displays such attraction and cohesion force it is, perhaps, because it contains sonic, visual, emotional, atmospheric and conceptual memories and devices that extend around the globe, eliciting complex echoes and adhesions among youth. As a young Bogotá hardcore music fan told us in 1993:

> Our connection with foreign hardcore groups is music. At least, we listen to *Hardcore* in Portuguese here. *Hardcore* is everywhere. It's that the music

is the ideology and the ideology can keep everyone united by a current . . . by a current of energy.
(group interview with Bogotá hardcore sympathizers, 1993)

That music should 'be the ideology' for members of these Colombian youth cultures is not surprising if we understand the especially agglutinating nature of these types of music, their extraordinary power to encompass elements of a very diverse nature. They operate powerfully at a number of perceptive, gestic, cognitive, linguistic and psychological levels.

Fundamental songs for skinhead culture, like the 4 Skin's *Kaos*, Sham 69's *Kids United*, and Cockney Rejects' *Oi, Oi, Oi* are condensed mnemotechnical and multisensorial pieces that show twenty-first century Bogotá skinheads what the clothes, gestures, ideas and energy of the young skinheads from the East End were like as they ran through the streets of London in the early years:

> Skinhead was lost, it went through a period of desolation in England and the skinheads were letting their hair grow. When *street punk* appeared, there was a revival of the original aggressiveness, the resurgence of a new breed and a new being that was eclipsed. Street Punk marked that moment in history that we continue to represent even today. When skinhead and punk youths unite in a single musical cause, when one sings Street Punk, one is experiencing that, the fundamental representation of having helped the skinhead to progress and of not having let him die.
> (Freddy, Bogotá RASH skinhead, and Skandalo Oi, singer 2004)

As a highly complex mechanism, music transports the symbolic, rhythmic and ethical nuclei of global youth cultures on their interoceanic voyages. For example, in Bogotá punk culture, when 'Nadie' and some other Bogotá punk youths discuss what happened at any given moment in the history of the culture, they must go back to the past, marking points of intersection, following signs along the way. Such historical landmarks are, naturally, the songs and the musical groups of the times.

Music also works as a force of mutation. With this term we refer to changes, transformations and 'becomings' of youth participating in the cultures that cannot always be classified according to known forms of natural, linear, progressive and foreseeable evolutions. This conceptual term has the potential to make visible phenomena present in youth cultures that in fact occur, but that have not been studied sufficiently, and that are not limited to the phenomena described by developmental psychology (Marín and Muñoz 2002). As a force of mutation, music impels young people in their transit from one culture to another. How is music related to the mutations? Do these mutations have to do with *only* changes in musical taste or is there *something deeper there*? And suddenly the question itself seems wrong since, as we have seen, the experience of the sound itself is very deep and very intense.

Marcia, a young Bogotá woman interviewed in 1998, underwent a profound experience of mutation. In her own words, she had gone 'from Punk to a Cyberpunk tendency, by way of Industrial'. She described how she first loved punk music:

> The people around me were into it. I listened to punk music, the content of the lyrics and it was something very real. That filled up my soul a lot. I listened to it and said: *it's good that someone is telling so many truths*. And it was also good to find a circle of people that shared all of that with me and to be able to talk about all of it and form groups in favour of one thing or another. Those people were moved by the music, by rebelliousness, a thirst for justice.
>
> (Marcia, 19 years, Bogotá youth, 1998)

Marcia began to tire of the relentless social criticism and 'ideology' of punk music and punk youth culture. She found it simplistic and unsatisfying on the individual level. Significant people she met introduced her to different kinds of sounds and conversations:

> [Punk] was a very easy structure that no longer interested me and then I began to listen to Industrial. I loved that because it's not so radical but there is plenty of punk in it. Industrial has a good basis for voices, it's more developed on the instrumental level, it's more experimental and it's like a sign of personal evolution. I then began to meet people with different types of character, who had other styles and ways of thinking and I also encountered others who were into Industrial because they were dissatisfied with Punk . . . It begins to seem useless to pose social questions to someone instead of talking about yourself. I think that this is also a key part of the music: to move from social criticism and pointing out every thing around you, to talking about yourself, your own being . . . My interest in the flow came out of the industrial stage because it was like affirming that the parameters that one experienced as a little punk stereotyped you and didn't let you flow. Now I have found Cyberpunk – very futuristic tendency: to set forth a vision of the mystery that exists regarding the future, and everything that human evolution is leading to; to focus all our energies on setting forth that concept of existence and to expound on future things . . . For me it would be ideal to reach a point of total fluidity in which the human body as such is obviated, to evolve to a point so high that it ceases to have physical and mental limitations, and becomes a point of light.
>
> (Marcia, 19 years, Bogotá youth, 1998)

No matter how complex the universes of meaning constructed in each youth culture may be, they concentrate on fragments and specific zones of existence. For this reason in some cases, they produce claustrophobia. When this happens, young people feel the call to leave a blind point of perception, and to abandon some elements characteristic of the type of subjectivity they had been constructing in their culture, in order to move on to another, or towards new co-ordinates, encounters and existential territories. We have also found a certain musical logic in the processes of mutation: punks that migrate to Industrial, metal fans that abandon the metal codes to freely submerge themselves in the blues, and also punks with a metal background who later become hardcore youths. Mutation is undoubtedly another facet of the creative impulse present in youth cultures.

Conclusion

Based on some elements taken from Guattari's aesthetic paradigm, from the aesthetics of existence and, above all, from findings made through years of research, we propose the aesthetic dimension as a tool that can be usefully applied to reconceptualize youth culture. This dimension of creation – of one's self, of other frameworks of reference, of new collective subjectivities and of other artistic forms, makes it possible to see youth cultures, especially the most creative among them, as having extraordinary powers of transformation, destruction and creation of Something Else. In this chapter we have signalled several new avenues of investigation: first, by studying the creative activity of youth by focusing upon life considered itself as a work of art, second, by focusing on the ways in which young individuals actively constitute their subjectivity through the mediums of music and some other forms of creation, and third, through understanding practices of self-styling.

Legacies that are not just concepts or ideologies converge in these cultures. It is not a question of philosophies dictated 'by poverty' or by any historic moment, or by temporary rebelliousness. They are, for the most part vital impulses present in the 'sonic' forces (Rose 1994), in dense flows of images, and in the deep, iridescent traces left by so many artists, thinkers, free spirits, *outsiders*, travellers, witches and warriors that have become mentors of, or sources of inspiration for, these cultures.

But how can this be so? Some will say – 'Isn't hip-hop sexist? Don't the anti-consumerists forget their ideals at times in their everyday lives, and don't they too become consumers in the alternative markets? Aren't we living in a stage of advanced capitalism and in a world in which imitation and imposture reign supreme?' This is true as we write these lines. But let's recall at this point what was said at the beginning of this chapter: youth cultures contain within themselves a set of impulses that tend to fulfil all of their potential. It's possible to encounter, either alternatively or simultaneously, libertarian gestures and microfascisms, solidarities and ghetto attitudes, mind openings and dilemmas, as well as all the shades of grey that exist between these polarities. In youth cultures, everything is possible (everything that is present in their initial set of impulses) and their forms of music work on those conditions of possibility.

The musical forms impel the cohesion, the singularization processes, the creation of multiplicities within the cultures and, as we have seen, the mutations of the participants as they move through them. Having opened the door to the aesthetic dimension, we sense the existence of *another* type of possible knowledge about youth cultures. Other panoramas spread out before us. New questions appear and it becomes possible to see the existing issues and questions from a new perspective. In our research experience, the study of some personal processes of mutation in relation to the music is leading us to see more clearly how the most contemporary concepts of the subject and subjectivity operate in youth cultures; and how the movement between fixity and fluidity that characterizes the processes of construction of subjectivity are produced. And, how young people's oscillations between attachment and freedom take place with respect to their cultures. It is worthwhile asking: what processes of self-creation, what alternative forms of existence can arise, and will arise, from cultures and forms of music like those described here?

Bibliography

Chuck D and Yusuf, J. (1997) *Fight the Power: rap, race and reality*, New York: Delacorte Press.

Deleuze, G. and Guattari, F. (1987) *A Thousand Plateaus: capitalism and schizophrenia*, trans. B. Massumi, Minneapolis, MN: University of Minnesota Press.

Foucault, M. (1987) *Hermenéutica del Sujeto*, Madrid: La Piqueta.

Guattari, F. (1994) 'El nuevo paradigma estético', in D.F. Schnitman (ed.) *Nuevos Paradigmas, Cultura y Subjetividad*, Buenos Aires: Paidós.

Kerouac, J. (1995) '*Los Subterráneos*', Barcelona: Anagrama.

McNeil, L. and McCain, G. (1999) *Por Favor, Mátame. Historia oral y no censurada del Punk*, Madrid: Celeste Ediciones y Música Cero.

Marín, M. and Muñoz, G. (2002) *Secretos de Mutantes. Música y creación en las culturas juveniles*, Bogotá: Universidad Central and Siglo del Hombre Editores.

Medina, G. (1997) 'Rock y punk. Punk se escribe con odio', in O. Urán (ed.) *Medellín en Vivo: la historia del rock*, 2nd edition, Medellín: Instituto Popular de Capacitación-Corporación Región-Viceministerio de la Juventud.

Rojas Hernández, S. (2001) *Gente de Oi*, Bogotá: Universidad Javeriana.

Rose, T. (1994) *Black Noise: rap music and black culture in contemporary America*, Hanover: University Press of New England.

Serrano, R. (1995) 'Texto complementario al árbol de géneros' in *Secretos de Mutantes*, internal document produced by a metal culture participant for the study on 'Rock y culturas juveniles', directed by Germán Muñoz. Bogotá: Departamento de Investigaciones de la Universidad Central.

Urán, O. (ed.) (1996) *Medellín en Vivo: la historia del rock 1*, Medellín: Instituto Popular de Capacitación-Corporación Región-Viceministerio de la Juventud.

—— (ed.) (1997) *Medellín en Vivo: la historia del rock 2*, Medellín: Instituto Popular de Capacitación-Corporación Región-Viceministerio de la Juventud.

Wicke, P. (1995) *Rock Music: culture, aesthetics and sociology*, Cambridge: Cambridge University Press.

8 *Tribus urbanas* and *chavos banda*[1]
Being a punk in Catalonia and Mexico

Carles Feixa

> There are *tribus urbanas* hanging around.
> (Quim, Lleida fieldwork informant, 1985)

> The relationships I had were always with pure *chavos banda*.
> (Diana, Mexico fieldwork informant, 1990)

A key purpose of this book is to examine the hybridity and plurality of youth worlds. This chapter describes youth cultures in two places on different continents – Catalonia in Spain, and Mexico. It examines how the transnational youth lifestyle known as punk, that arose in a concrete place and time – 1970s Britain – has been diffused and adapted in two other geographical and historical contexts – Spain in the 1980s and Mexico in the 1990s. Firstly, the presence of youth cultures in both national scenes is explained, then fieldwork experiences in Lleida and Mexico City are analysed. *Chavos banda* (youth gangs) in Mexico articulate a youth micro-culture of class, ethnic claims, territoriality and gender identity. Comparison with the more moderate *tribus urbanas* (urban tribes) in Catalonia offers us the possibility of reflecting on the globalization of youth styles, the emergence of new kinds of symbolic tensions, the context of urban growth/decay, and the cultural consequences of youth unemployment.

From local gangs to global tribes

> The punk adopted the rhetoric of crisis and translated it into tangible terms.
> (Hebdige 1979: 94)

It can be argued that urban youth gangs demonstrate a defining feature of contemporary social existence – mass culture (as lived experience) has fragmented into 'neo-tribalism' (Maffesoli 1996). Youth form localized networks of 'sociality' to survive and be powerful in uncertain economic and social times when mechanical solidarity has broken down. One of Maffesoli's insights is that aesthetics is the key to understanding urban youth 'tribes'.

The symbolic culture of urban youth gangs is organized around the street fashions, slang words, advertising logos and 'soundbites' of global popular culture appropriated into local contexts. It is only group membership that allows decoding of the symbolic signalling of the group. However, as tribal networks, youth gangs are far from static – multiple memberships may be possible and the groups themselves evolve in rapid succession. The emergence and evolution of ethnic youth gangs must be understood in the context of local, historical and often structural change. Even if the concept of 'urban tribe' has been introduced recently in youth studies under the influence of Maffesoli's seminal work, it has been used in Spain since the end of the 1970s as a metaphor for new youth transnational styles (Feixa 1988, 1998).

Since it was first mentioned by sociologists, the phenomenon of youth gangs has been at least partly associated with the cultural identity of second-generation emigrants in urban areas of North America (Whyte 1943) and Europe (Monod 1968). In a classic urban anthropology essay, William Foote Whyte analysed 'street corner society' – cornerville – local street gangs as a form of adaptation (although fraught with conflict) to the new urban context of Boston by the children of Italian immigrants. 'The younger generation have made up their own society, independent to some extent from the elderly people's influence' (Whyte 1943: 18–9). Through the creation of local gangs – 'street corner society' – their cultural expressions can be interpreted as attempts to magically recreate the lost cohesion of their original community. Apart from ethnicity, there are other factors that play a role in the formation of youth gangs, such as generation, gender, social class and territory. All these elements interact in the making up of generational styles that can be understood as 'symbolic solutions' to the unsolved problems of their 'parent' culture (Hall and Jefferson 1983). Ethnic youth gangs absorb different influences over time, and may even become rather antithetical to key defining features of the parent culture. These 'creolization' processes take place in multi-ethnic contexts; they are syncretic creations, the fruit of interaction between young people from diverse origins (Amit-Talai and Wulff 1995). And most importantly, as the global teenage market and 'countercultures' are consolidated, local gangs tend to be integrated in 'global tribes' that are present in different urban areas across the world.

This is the case of punk. From 1976 the new style emerged among young English working-class people, first in London suburbs and later in other cities in Britain and western countries. For Hebdige (1979) punk contained the distorted reflections of the most important post-war British subcultures, from teddy-boys to skinheads. The different style units adopted by the punks were an expression of a genuine aggressiveness and worry, and although they were created in a bizarre way, they adopted an accessible language. This explains the success of the metaphor – its flexible capacity to reflect on a whole set of contemporary problems – like the growth of youth unemployment. Like 1960s countercultures, punk followed a process of *fusion* that led, on the one hand, to the *diffusion* of some of its elements (including a tendency towards commercialization), and on the other hand, to its *fission* into different trends (punk-rock, hardcore, technopunk, cyberpunk and industrial). Some essayists have analysed punk as a symbolic synthesis of philosophic, aesthetic or musical trends, like *dandyism*, *flânêrie*, dada, surrealism, beat, pop, rastafarianism and so on. Every one of these analyses reveals some relevant aspects, but they all focus on the original British punk. To a certain extent they assume that there is a homogeneous universal code in which any new tendencies are merely slight variations of the same model. What is significant about punk, however, is that it has managed to take root in different, sometimes contradictory social and territorial contexts, and adapted efficiently to other national and local conditions. In the early 1980s, when punk was fading in its British birthplace, it was emerging from the ashes in other places like Spain and Mexico.

Youth cultures in Spain

As a European nation, Spain has an HDI ranking of 19, placing it well within the category of a high development country (UNDP 2003). Nevertheless, high urban unemployment and an increasingly large immigrant population constitute some uncertain conditions for Spanish youth:

> They grew in the big city's cement and are asphalt shipwrecked. Sonorous names, punky, heavy, mod, rocker, labels that shelter them in the warm security of their respective tribe. Occasionally the hatchet is dug up to stain with blood a world of music . . . Dominions, transit areas, territories contended for, another map of an unknown daily city, where other laws, other values prevail.
> ('Tribus '85. Morir con la chupa puesta', *Triunfo* magazine, 1984)

Los Golfos (*The Vagabonds*), one of the first films by Carlos Saura (1959) depicts the adventures of a youth gang in a Spanish suburb still in the middle of the post-war period, though on the threshold of modernization under the 'plans for development' being drawn up that year. This is the story of four young people in a Madrid suburb, progressively inclined towards more engaged confrontations. Inspired by Luis Buñuel's *Los Olvidados* (*The Forgotten Ones*), Saura details through a reportage-like style (reminiscent of *cinéma-verité*) the frustrations of youth in the beginning of these transformations. Another film, *La lenta agonía de los peces* (*The Slow Agony of the Fish*) portrays the doubts of a young Catalan man – played by the singer Joan Manuel Serrat – who falls in love with a Swedish girl in the Costa Brava, and discovers the countercultural movements beyond the Pyrénées. Each of these films depicts totally opposed youth cultures (proletarian *golfos* and upper-class *jipis*) that constitute both symbol and emblem of the process of accelerated cultural modernization taking place in the country at that time.

Internationally constituted youth lifestyles gained visibility in Spain only after the 1960s, a time of economic development and expansion. The tourist boom and mass media introduced new youth movements, mostly hippies and rockers – albeit with some peculiarities. They arrived some years after their European counterparts, they were censored by Francoist and Church authorities and they developed only in metropolitan areas like Barcelona and Madrid, and in some enclaves like the Balearic Islands (Cerdà and Rodríguez 2002). At a certain point in the process of transition into democracy (1975–81), youth styles burst upon the public scene in Spain in hybrid forms. They were promptly christened by the media *tribus urbanas*: urban tribes, a descriptive term which became very popular. The emergence of these distinctive youth groups in Europe leading up to the time of the formation of the European Union, seem to bear out Maffesoli's thesis of neo-tribalism in the late modern epoch. However, it has been argued in the Spanish context that the model of urban tribes was more of a media label or popular metaphor than an analytical tool for analysing youth cultures (Feixa 1998).

By the time Spain entered the European Union in 1986, 'urban tribes' were coming to be recognized in accounts of global youth culture. What was unique in Spain was the fact that youth styles which had emerged sequentially in English-speaking countries over three decades, emerged at the same time all mixed up together in the same urban places (punks with hippies, teddy boys with skinheads and so on). Another particularity was the way in which these styles developed differently across the country. Diversity was greatly influenced by the multicultural and multilingual diversity of Spain. In particular, the most dynamic territories for subcultures, besides Madrid, were Catalonia, the Basque country and Galicia. In their study of youth culture lifestyles around *la Movida* – a transgressive night-time cultural scene where artists like Pedro Almodóvar started their careers – Gil Calvo and Menéndez (1985) conclude that young people in the 1980s generally devoted more time and money to leisure activities. However, differential access to wealth, and variations in social class location, ensured that youth leisure behaviour was not homogeneous; social structure was found to determine an unequal leisure culture.

The hegemonic style during this time was punk. Not only did it represent the hope of freedom after the dictatorship, but it was also a perfect metaphor for the crisis (Fouce 2004). One famous study of Spanish youth cultures was by Costa, Pérez and Tropea (1996). Their account of *tribus urbanas* assumes that all youth movements are a neotribal phenomenon – 'asphalt indigenous'. It is presupposed that each separate group establishes a set of specific rules according to which members model their image. The tribe's development is presented like a minor mythology; their representative games are closed to 'normal' individuals; their differences from other young people are made evident, and their identification with the group is symbolized by wearing a kind of uniform. It is concluded that all *tribus urbanas* constitute potential factors of social agitation and disorder, and that their aesthetics show a desire for aggressive self-expression (Costa, Pérez and Tropea, 1996: 91). This conclusion is hardly surprising, given that a whole chapter of the book is devoted to the most belligerent of youth gangs – the Nazi skinheads – *pelaos* in Spain (see also Adán 1996).

In new millennium Spain we find evidence of the fading of boundaries between different subcultures, and an intensification of processes of social and symbolic syncretism around global youth cultures readily identified elsewhere. Three significant trends serve as examples. First, youth activism has been revived in the anti-globalization movement and its cultural effects, for example, the popularity of singer Manu Chao's hybrid music style, and the emergence of a neo-hippy aesthetic. Second, dance culture has fragmented so we see different expressions of the *fiestero* movement which attract lovers of electronic music and *fiestas* (Gamella and Álvarez 2001). The most intellectualized variant of *techno* happens around festivals like *Sonar*, but also manifests in digital publications and infinite embroidery upon *techno* style. The most ludic manifestations of *fiesteros* happen around the opening of new dance clubs, and in the fashion styles that go with them, arbitrated by the 'door police' who allow only those with the right clothes to enter (Gistain 2001). The most clandestine manifestation is around the 'rave' party phenomenon, with secrecy, SMS communication, specialized recreational drugs and so on. The third set of youth culture trends derives from the internet, which opens space in chatrooms and virtual communities to express different styles, like cyberpunks and hackers. This was crucial for the 'cell phone revolt' after the 11 March 2004 terrorist attack in Madrid that challenged the Spanish government (Feixa and Porzio 2005). In summary, distinctive elements of style and cultural practice are projected onto a regional, national and global stage. *Tribus urbanas* can be seen as prefiguring different political and cultural trends – from the transition into democracy to the transition into the information society.

'There are *tribus urbanas* hanging around'

> Well, the youngsters of the 80s were born in the 60s . . . and there was a great, an incredible demographic growth. So these youngsters found there were a lot of people going for only one job. This is why there are many *tribus urbanas* hanging around. Not having a job, they can't adapt to society and they create a group to belong to some sort of society, don't they?
>
> (Quim, Lleida fieldwork informant, 1985)

In 1984 I started to gather life stories of youth in Lleida, a small inland city in Catalonia, for a research thesis in anthropology. Catalonia in northeast Spain has six million inhabitants, most of them concentrated in the metropolitan area of Barcelona. Considered a nation without a state, prosperous Catalonia has its own language and self government. The prevailing image in the Lleida fieldwork data was that 'there are many *tribus urbanas* hanging around'. The phenomenon symbolically reflected political disenchantment that followed the end of Franco's regime, the lack of employment, and diminished expectations of young people for the future. In the beginning, *tribus urbanas* did not seem a relevant object of study. The term constituted an ideological construction, the real and the imaginary inextricably mingled. Furthermore, the phenomenon was far from involving the majority of youth. Nevertheless, during fieldwork, *tribus urbanas* as a descriptive category became increasingly appealing. Significantly, informants used different labels in interviews to define themselves and other groups of youths. For example, the term *pijos* was used to describe snobbish, middle-class youth obsessed with trends and consumption. This group contrasted with the *golfos* – layabouts – suburban (often immigrants), and usually unemployed. Other labels referred to more universal tropes of western youth culture – revivalist 'tribes' like hippies – *jipis* – and mods. However, it was noted that youth subculture models from, for example, the United Kingdom in the 1960s and 1970s, were not just imitated in Spain. Rather they were adapted to new functions and needs, and synthesized, even hybridized with indigenous influences, such as those of Gipsy culture or Catalan nationalism. In some cases, a process of symbolic inversion took place. For example, in 1984 Spain, 'mods' were no longer the working-class rivals of 'rockers' but middle-class young people attracted by the culture of the 1960s.

Close participant observation allowed me to confirm the importance of leisure spaces in the group structures of *tribus urbanas*. For the immediate post-war generation, walking along the main street of the city was the most common – and nearly the only – way to spend free time. It was called *fer la noria* (making the waterwheel) and consisted of walking up and down the same street under the close scrutiny of adults. In the 1950s the first private adolescent parties – *guateques* – started to take place. But it was only in the mid-1960s that young people found an alternative to *fer la noria* with *boîtes* or *discos* – though it was not until 1975 with Franco's death that young people developed their own leisure spaces in the city. These new leisure spaces constituted urban territories, where 'other laws, other values' prevailed. For example, in the old quarters of towns the *zona de vinos* – wine areas – emerged. In the beginning, *jipis* and punks congregated in old bars where the wine prices were cheap and they could listen to music, dress informally and smoke hashish in groups without being disturbed. As these venues became more popular with youth, other bars opened and thousands of young people would gather there at the weekend. *Zona de vinos* were dedicated youth space, like a sacred place, a neutral stage of social action where very different styles could co-exist.

But the youth leisure population reached a point where some sectors wanted to separate themselves and create their own meeting places out of the area. The first to leave were the *progres*, mainly left-wing students with counter-cultural influences who moved to bars in the downtown area, where they could hear jazz, progressive rock, and *nova cançó* – Catalan singer-songwriters. At the same time, new premises opened in the uptown area of Lleida – in so-called 'Dollar Street' – where prices were higher and a more commercial ethos prevailed. Venues included discos, pubs and open-air terraces. The middle-class *pijos* took up the style opportunities provided by these highly commercialized venues, in which brand-name clothing and disco music were *de moda* (fashionable). A new breed of venues appeared under the label of *posmodernos* – post-modern. These were large post-industrial spaces – often old warehouses – renovated with a 'tough' architectural style where people could drink and dance and be seen. 'Spectacular' looks, for example neo-punks and neo-rockers, were on display. Hard rock and vanguardist music was played. Subsequently, the original youth space in Lleida: *zona de vinos*, underwent a process of specialization. Other *zona* venues began to attract different sorts of customers – hardcores, heavies, rockabillies, *acratas* (anarchists), *pelaos* (skinheads), *okupas* (squatters), gays and feminists.

In summary, the historical emergence of *tribus urbanas* in Lleida was a cultural process with socio-political roots. Cultural differentiation was mainly through personal and vaguely-defined styles. Although some youth lived in working-class and marginal neighbourhoods, the meeting place for all was the urban centre, and the mass manifestation was *movida* (the night scene). It was true that every youth did identify with a particular *estilo* (style) to a greater or lesser extent. However, it is also the case that individuals could belong to various groups successively, could adopt only some of that group's external signs, could even just be friends with the group's members. In fact, my data indicated that the various *tribus* existed mainly as 'mental maps' to find one's way in daily interaction with other young people. In particular, members of *tribus* did not usually wear their 'style' clothes in their place of work or study; they were especially for the weekend and for the night, when the 'time of the tribes' began.

One morning in June 1985, walking along *Calle Mayor* in Lleida I met Félix. He had short hair, sunglasses and a big earring in one ear. He was unemployed and expecting some news from the civil service. I knew Félix was from La Terreta, one of the most popular neighbourhoods in the city, and that he was into alternative things, so I suggested interviewing him. I soon realized that the connecting thread in his whole life story was the influence of certain musical-aesthetic styles that marked different life-phases, an evolution that led him to his current identification as a punk. I didn't consider this to be a chance trajectory, but rather something linked to his social situation and ideological itinerary. Unlike some of his punk friends, like el Ruso, a singer in the group Drugstores Inc, Félix was apparently peace-loving and not too scandalous. But he wasn't revealing everything. Nowadays he is married and owns a disco bar in *la zona de vinos*, but is still influenced by the punk ideas of his teenage days.

Youth cultures in Mexico

Mexico has a large population and a massive number of urban and rural poor. The economic growth rate in 2003 was half that of Spain. Mexico has an

HDI ranking of 55. The dream of many young Mexicans is to migrate to America, and many have done so:

> It is well known that *pachucos* are youth gangs, usually of Mexican origin, living in southern cities of the United States. They deny themselves; they are full of contradictions, enigmas . . . Whether we want it or not, these beings are Mexican, to an extreme that Mexicans can grow to be.
>
> (Paz 1950: 13)

In his film *Zoot Suit* (1981), *chicano* director Luis Valdez tells the story of Henry Reyna, a young Mexican North American arrested and accused of murder in 1942, the same day he joined the Marines. The film starts in a Los Angeles dance club. Henry's friends madly dance the mambo, the boogie-woogie and the swing. They speak *caló* (a mixture of *Spanglish* and marginal slang). Their clothing is extravagant – the famous *zoot-suit*, similar to that worn by Harlem blacks. They are all *pachucos*, characteristic of the youth subculture of the 1940s, second-generation immigrants in California. After arguing with another gang, some Marines go to a party where the murder takes place. In spite of lack of evidence, Henry is arrested, tried and found guilty. Based on a true story, the film brought *pachucos* to public attention. The public prosecutor attributed their aggressiveness to 'the Indian element that has come to the United States in big numbers, and that for their cultural and biological background is prone to violence. All they know or feel is the desire to use a knife or any lethal arms' (Valenzuela 1988: 43).

The *pachuco* became a popular image of evil in Anglo-America, but a symbol of national identity for Mexicans. The Nobel Prize winner Octavio Paz dedicated the first chapter of one of his most famous essays to the *pachucos* (1950). The author describes his arrival in 1940s Los Angeles, where there were already over a million *chicanos*. He found a sort of 'Mexicanity' in the air, very clearly to be seen in the attitudes to life and 'disguises' worn by the street gangs of young *pachucos*. Between the culture of origin and the culture of destination, between the will to be different and the will to be equal, between infancy and adult life, the *pachuco* phenomenon seemed a 'hybrid solution' to social anomie. Paz's interpretation of them as 'an extreme that Mexicans can grow to be' is now classical. Their response is hostile and distorted in the face of a society that is rejecting them. This identity turns into a 'disguise that protects them and, at the same time, points them out and isolates them; hides them and shows them off' (Paz 1950: 15). At the same time, their image gained prestige, their stigma turned into an emblem, and their style quickly spread throughout the southern United States, Mexico's northern frontier cities, even to Mexico City itself (Vigil 1990).

From 1960s Mexican youth culture emerged *chavos de onda* (youth of the shadows) which included: local hippies – *jipitecas*, politically concerned students – who suffered in the 1968 carnage of *Plaza de las Tres Culturas*, and young *rocanroleros* (rock and rollers) from working-class neighbourhoods. The latter group emerged in the Avandaro Festival in 1973, which was their own particular Woodstock. Later on, after the Mexican rock-and-roll movement was repressed, *rocanroleros* took refuge in the *hoyos fonquis* – clandestine places – to hear live music. All this youth culture history was reflected in the characteristic 'jargon' of 1980s *chavos banda* – an evolution of *caló*. *Caló* – originally referring to the language of Gyspies – combines elements from different origins: 1940s *pachuco* slang, 1960s language of *chavos de onda*, Mexican indigenous languages, local and prison *argots*. When these are combined with expressions specially invented by *chavos banda*, *caló* becomes a sociolect impossible for a stranger to understand and a perfect example of hybrid youth cultures (Hernández 1999).

Chavos banda have been a presence in Mexico since the early 1980s. They became well known in 1981 when the *Panchitos* – a gang from Santa Fe – sent their famous manifesto to the press. This was a response to the labels they were given by the tabloid press, which called them layabouts and offenders. In the manifesto they declared their attitudes towards life at the tops of their voices. Their style became the emblem of a whole generation of working-class Mexican youth. Like *pachucos*, *chavos banda* turned the stigma of their social condition into an emblem of identity. It is mainly second-generation rural immigrants who make up this movement, and it is mainly the densely populated suburbs of Mexico City where they live. For the generation of the 1980s, punk style played a vanguardist role similar to hippy style in the 1960s. The rapid introduction of punk reveals the integration of Mexican youth culture into the global scene. Through commercial and underground circuits, products like fanzines, videos, music and fashion passed from the American teenage market to Mexican middle-class central city enclaves, and to the outlying working-class neighbourhoods (Urteaga 1998).

Chavos banda distance themselves from the middle-class *chavos fresa* in both social origin and style. The image of *chavos banda* is associated with a certain ecological context (the densely populated suburbs), way of dressing (jeans and leather jackets), type of music (rock and its different variants), economic structure (unemployment or the underground economy), way of having fun (gigs), meeting place (the corner), intense rivalry with the *tira* (police) and a critical appropriation of North American underground culture. *Chavos fresa* reference a different ecological context (residential or apartment areas), way of dressing (commercial trends), style of music (pop music and some Mexican music), primary activity (studying), way of having fun (the disco), meeting place (*zona rosa* and other trendy places) and imitation of North American consumer culture. While *chavos banda* have compact, permanent group structures, often organized on the basis of territory, *chavos fresa* organize themselves in less focused, more individualistic socio-cultural structures. They don't meet in the street but in bars or homes. *Chavos banda* are stigmatized by the dominant culture as rebels without a cause, violent, drug addicts; while *chavos fresa* are seen as conformist, passive, harmless and healthy (Feixa 2005).

During the 1990s and after the new millennium, a vast diversity of transnational youth lifestyles arrived in Mexico through the American border, thanks to the labour migrants – *espaldas mojadas* – and the internet. Most of them were global youth cultures from the American ghetto (hip-hop, rap, rave). But new hybrid trends also emerged like *raztecas* (a fusion of rastafarianism and pre-Hispanic revivalism), *nortec* (a fusion of northern Mexican popular music and *techno*) and *cholombianos* (a fusion of *cholos* gangs and Colombian tropical rhythms). At the same time, youth studies became a core for the renewal of Mexican cultural theory, moving from the periphery to the centre of the social sciences scene (Valenzuela 1988; Reguillo 1991; Urteaga and Feixa 2005).

'Always with pure *chavos banda*'

> The environment completely transforms ideas, people. It's not the same to get depressed here [at Nezahualcóyotl] as it is in *Distrito* [Federal]. To see the city with thousands of cars and people moving back and forth. This movement makes you think of other things. You don't see graffiti there like here, *signatures quién sabe qué banda?* [who knows what gang?] or *la banda de los locos* [gang of fools]. The relationships I had were always with pure *chavos banda* [gang youths]. In fact, I cannot relate to different people. It is impossible! I met many *bandas* because they liked rock. Nearly all of them belonged to a *banda* [gang].
>
> (Diana, Mexico fieldwork informant, 1990)

In September 1990 I arrived in Mexico City to conduct fieldwork research on Mexican youth. After studying young people in Lleida, I wanted to analyse ways of being young in a Latin American metropole. I thought Mexican youth would show very different characteristics to European youth. I certainly did not expect to find anything resembling *tribus urbanas*. I was surprised when I heard about *chavos banda* (youth gangs). According to my informants, they were young people from densely-populated urban environments. The media avidly described them in familiar terms of moral panic:

> About 20 thousand *bandas* (gangs) are sowing violence in Mexico city, at the indulgence of the police, who cannot eradicate it . . . Confused young people, hooked on drugs and alcohol, who carry out armed robberies on businesses or even dwellings, who commit rapes, and who cause terror to citizens. They are now the city's public enemy number one.
>
> (*Cuestión Policíaca* magazine, 2 September 1991)

Moving past the media moral panic I started to read more informed accounts. Street corners were their living space. They were passionate about rock 'n' roll. I found intellectuals who analysed the *banda* trend in positive terms, as expression of protest and omen of social change. The trend of marginal youth forming *bandas* had spread since the beginning of the 1980s among wide sectors of young people of both sexes, signifying the arrival of marginal urban style onto the public stage.

My first direct contact with *chavos banda* was in *el Chopo* – the *tianguis* (street market) of *chavos banda*. Every week thousands of extravagantly dressed youth from every corner of the city turn out religiously at *el Chopo* behind the railway station, not far from the regrettably well known *Plaza de las Tres Culturas*. *El Chopo* is a soulless place, surrounded by bleak factories and electricity pylons – noisy and crowded, but surprisingly well organized. Leaning on street walls leading to the place, old *jipitecas* offer their own handicrafts. Inside the market, punks stand out by virtue of clothing style and numbers. In the central aisle *metaleros* sell T-shirts, gadgets and recorded heavy metal music from their booths. In other booths various *bandas* – rockers, *nuevaoleros*, *progres*, *sicodélicos* – offer all sorts of fanzines, records, posters, pirate tapes, jewellery and clothing. About 2,000 young people browse the three rows of 150 booths. Some itinerant sellers offer a record exchange. There is a familiar atmosphere: many know each other and greet one another fondly, in a weekly complicity that contrasts with the big city's anonymity.

I meet a young punk at the *tianguis*. He tells me: '*El Chopo* is a source of infection in the city'. He is 26-year-old Ome Toxtli. He lives in Nezahualcóyotl (Neza), an enormous dormitory city of 4 million inhabitants on the outskirts of Mexico City. Through him I get to know the *mierdas punks* (shit punks). In *Neza York* (that's what they call it) *bandas* are a fact of life. In every street, or block, or suburb there is at least one. But few are as well known as the *mierdas*. Formed in 1982 from the alliance of three *bandas*, they were the first to overcome strict territorial boundaries and spread through nearly all Neza. In its glory days of 1985, the gang had about 600 members, grouped in sectors according to locality or ideological affinities. The history of this *banda* mirrors the path of many others. It began in self-destructive practice, confirming the constitution of the punk movement in a country undergoing extreme economic crisis. *Mierdas* ideology was expressed in aggressive looks and attitudes, quarrels with other *bandas*, drug consumption and a frenetic dance – the pogo. But a more 'political' ideology evolved through its attempts to generate alternative culture – music groups, co-operatives, fanzines and campaigns against torture. *Mierdas punks* went on to call themselves *movimiento punk* (MP). After the 1985 earthquake, the *banda* strove, in co-operation with the powerful urban popular movement, to make social improvements for youth. *Mierdas* were instrumental in the creation of *BUN* – *bandas unidas de Neza* (united gangs of Neza), an umbrella organization of co-operation between *bandas* that encouraged the focus of reform energies.

When I first met the *mierdas* the glory days had passed. The founders had grown up. Some had married, nearly all were working. However, a new generation had gathered at the street corner, identified themselves as 'punks' and offered meaningful identity structure to local youth as follows: first, the *banda* organizes local urban space by providing youth with a legitimate local identity which they can signal using *pintas* (graffiti). The *banda* also provides youth with *esquina* (a corner) where they can legitimately locate themselves. Membership of *mierdas* implicitly relates this new generation to other *bandas* in Neza. Different parts of the urban stage for their activities are made meaningful, for example, the graffiti wall. At the same time, they are invited into a universal, even global youth vision through rock 'n' roll fandom. Second, the project identity of the *banda* organizes the day by filling the hours with significant activities: meeting on the corner, making *cotorreo* (fun), strolling nomadically around the neighbourhood, working in the black economy, involvement in petty crime and drug consumption, especially cheap chemical inhalants. Every Saturday makes sense of the rest of the week. They go to *el Chopo* during daylight, and at night they go to the *tocada* – a spontaneous concert in the street or in some other urban public place. The *banda* organizes the life cycle by entry rituals, for example, *la novatada* (ragging) and *la pelea* or *carrilla* (quarrelling). They also recognize rituals of departure like marriage, steady work, emigration to the *gabacho* (America), going to prison or violent death. In short, membership of the *mierdas banda* provided local Neza youth in the early 1990s with a generational consciousness that places them in history (Mannheim 1928).

The *estilo* (style) of *chavos banda* was a syncretic product in which many traditions were mixed. On the one hand, traditions from outside like music and fashion trends, were disseminated through the *el Chopo* market. They were also available from fanzines, radio and some youth who went as *bracero* (illegal immigrants) to the *gabacho* (United States). On the other hand, some aspects of style signalled local conditions of generation, class, gender, ethnicity and territory. Generational identity challenged the parents' generation even though some had themselves been 'rebels without a cause' in 1968. Class identity signified expression of the harsh urban living conditions of heavily populated city sectors, challenging the comfortable conditions of middle-class residential areas. Gender identity expressed a certain trope of masculinity – the model of the 'macho' adult male Mexican. However, certain space was free for female style identity expressions. There were *puras chavas bandas* (female youth gangs) with names as provocative as Castradoras (Castrators) and iconoclastic feminist punk-rock bands like Virginidad Sacudida (Shaken Virginity). Ethnic identity expressed the cultural universe of the second generation of indigenous and peasant immigrants to Mexico city. Ethnicity was understood as an asset of Mexican multicultural collective identity in the face of the *gabacho* anglo culture. Pre-Hispanic symbols were incorporated into gang mythology, like the claim that 'Cuauhtémoc was the first punk'. Finally, territorial identity expressed hierarchies in the urban map (city centre *bandas* were distinguished from periphery *bandas*).

Ome Toxtli verified that the Mexican *banda* operates like a 'second family' and a 'school for life'. But this doesn't mean, as often claimed, that members come from broken homes or are illiterate. Most *chavos bandas* members were not in conflict with their parents. Most had attended educational institutions for as many years as their non-*banda* contemporaries. It was not true either that they were unproductive. Furthermore, community members did not appear troubled that *chavos* and *chavas* (male and female youth) gathered in the street. They even sometimes collaborated with the *bandas* in organizing *fiestas* and decorating the streets. They felt protected by the *bandas* from the *tiras* (police). In short, the *banda* formed part of the neighbourhood's daily landscape.

Contrasting *tribus urbanas* and *chavos banda*

You go through lots of different cultural and aesthetic things. You fancy some of them, others not. I've been through – don't know really: hippies, heavies, punks . . . In the end you find out that all styles, all philosophies are trying to break away from a really bent society. But all resistance to something turns out to be a mirror of that something in a way. So a society that produces really decadent groups, that must be for some reason. Maybe *tribus urbanas* mirror what society tries to bury.

(Félix, Lleida fieldwork informant, 1985)

The word *banda* has become too institutionalized, and I even dislike it now. I'd rather be just a *rocanrolear* [rock and roller], and that's all. Neza has a long rock-and-roll tradition. It's like a school. You never stop learning here. It's a shared experience, where we all contribute. For many it's more of a moral support being with the *banda* than being at home, it's like a second family.

(Ome Toxtli, Mexican fieldwork informant, 1990)

In comparing *tribus urbanas* and *chavos banda*, the first acknowledgement which must be made is that each is unique to the socio-cultural economic reality in which it is produced. There are, however, some obvious affinities between *tribus urbanas* and *chavos banda* which need to be teased out. What do Félix and Ome Toxtli have in common as youths? One of them is Catalan and the other one Mexican. However, both belong to gangs, both are punk rock music fans, both dress in an unusual way, both speak a jargon unintelligible to outsiders, and both formulated a counter-cultural argument in their fieldwork accounts. Despite living in different parts of the planet and existing in such completely different economic and social environments, what makes them both identify as 'punk'? It seems they share the same symbolic universe of cultural references which turn the stigma of marginalization and risk into markers of identity.

Turning first to points of similarity, for both *tribus urbanas* and *chavos banda*, the emergence of 'spectacular' youth cultural styles lay parallel to the economic and social crises of the 1980s in each country and to the side effects of these crises, such as juvenile unemployment, the rapid expansion of the black economy and the postmodern questioning of values. In both cases the most visible symbols of youth culture gangs were inextricably linked to particular music genres circulating at a global level, especially the different variations of rock, and its mutations: punk, hardcore and heavy metal. Furthermore, in both cases distinctive youth gangs emerged at a time of political crisis of hegemony – transition to democracy and the victory of PSOE – the Socialist Party – in Spain, challenges to the dominance of PRI – the Revolutionary Institutional Party – in Mexico. In both cases the media devoted great coverage to youth gang phenomena, ranging from sensationalistic 'satanizing' allegations to the opposite extreme of appropriating youth gang symbols and icons for advertising and similar commercial purposes. Both Félix and Ome Toxtli indicated that the deep generational conflicts of previous decades were to some extent resolved by the post-1980s flourishing of youth gangs and tribes. They implied that the family acts as a cushion for the young person, while the gang operates in a complementary way to that, rather than constituting an alternative to family life. In both cases gangs have found a plurality of ways to challenge authority, including self-destructive 'solutions' such as episodic vandalism and drug abuse, to constructive 'solutions' such as cultural creativity and political agitation for major reforms and changes. Both locations have seen the development of specific urban spaces for distinctive youth gang activities, such as *zona de vinos* in Lleida and *el Chopo* in Mexico City. These sites offer youth a place for gathering and cultural exchange. These places operate as a 'source of infection' for global and local styles. In both cases youth cultural communication circuits have been created, for example, music, fanzines, jargon and trends. Both cities have seen *tribus* and *banda* respectively involved in moments of convergence with larger group mobilizations, such as student strikes and anti-NATO protests in Spain in 1986, and the Mexican earthquake rescue and rebuilding in 1985. It is perhaps significant that in both locations, the most enduring style for youth gangs has remained that of punk. We may assume that punk style for these Hispanic youth groups signifies a true metaphor of crisis.

If we turn now to examination of differences, the first point of divergence is numerical. While *banda* is a massive phenomenon in densely-populated urban Mexico, *tribus urbanas* in Spain represent a relative minority of youth. Moreover, the original form of *tribus urbanas* proved a temporary social and cultural phenomenon which reached its peak in the mid-1980s. Conversely, the *banda* appears to be a much more chronologically continuous group structure with a steady and logical sequence of leaders and rituals. Furthermore, *banda* activities and ideology do not just refer to leisure and cultural style identity, they cover most of the details of daily life for *chavos* (youth) in the neighbourhoods. *Tribus urbanas* tend to be unstable, often unstructured, discontinuous groups to which members rarely make a total commitment. This is very different to the strong, tightly-organized loyalty shown by members of *banda*. Defence of urban territory is the main reason for endemic, often violent conflict between *bandas*. In contrast, *tribus urbanas* make the city centre their stage. Their rather infrequent and much milder conflicts are driven by

Figure 8.1 Punks in *el Chopo* street market, Mexico City, 1991. (Photo by Montserrat Iniesta)

style differences and football rivalry rather than territorial defence. While *chavos banda* gather around street corners in the suburban neighbourhood, *tribus urbanas* gather in and around leisure premises – bars, discos, disco-bars and *zona de vinos*. While *chavos banda* clothing style is appropriate for any time and place, the distinctive clothing of *tribus urbanas* is only worn during week-ends and in leisure spaces. *Chavos banda* members obtain their icons and accessories in primarily self-managed ways, through exchange, handicrafts, re-utilization, borrowing, or through the low-cost alternative economy of *el Chopo* market (see Figure 8.1). *Tribus urbanas* tend to buy clothes and accessories from shops and commercial outlets, even though they stamp individual style in the piecing and arranging of these. In that way *tribus urbanas* are much more firmly located within mainstream commercial channels. With regard to the culture industries, the connections of *chavos banda* to these institutions are episodic and occasional, even accidental at times. *Tribus urbanas* however, establish stable relations with the local cultural industries. Finally, considering relations with police, the response of authorities to the *banda* phenomenon has been mainly repressive in Mexico. In Catalonia police interventions were found to be more occasional, even though these did increase in the 1990s – examples included moving along squatters and skinheads.

Conclusion

> Power can and must deal with the management of life; puissance must assume the mantle of survival.
>
> (Maffesoli 1996: 63)

We can first conclude that although youth cultures always emerge from a distinctive national and socio-cultural economic context, there exist multiple means of transnational communication, so youth from far distant places come to identify themselves with similar styles. However, rather than signalling imitation and conformity, attachment to these styles is mainly symbolic – the deep meanings encode local tensions and resistances. For example, being a punk in 1990s Mexico City is not the same as being a punk in 1980s Lleida or 1970s London. Rather, local appropriations of a global youth style like punk produce different cultural expressions in different places at different times. The contrast in manifestations and meanings of punk style in *tribus urbanas* and *chavos banda* illustrates not global cultural homogenization, but its opposite.

This chapter implies a relationship between local gangs and global tribes in two senses: as social construction and as theoretical concept. As social construction, the diffusion of transnational youth lifestyles are connected with the global teenage market, but also with national and local historical situations in which urban tribes are used as metaphors for social change. This is particularly relevant for certain political and economic transition processes experienced by Spain in the 1980s and by Mexico in the 1990s. A similar phenomenon occurred in Iran after the Islamic Revolution of 1979 (see Shahabi's chapter in this book) and in Russia in 1989 during *perestroika* (when the term *neformalniye grupirovnik* – informal groups – was coined). As a theoretical concept, it is important to recognize that local use of the term *tribus urbanas* is not reducible to the diffusion of Maffesolian categories in recent academic literature. Semantically, 'urban tribe' is a verbal definition that is at the same time a *word* label, a *thing* (what the label defines) and a *concept* (that uses *words* to understand the nature of *things*). We must therefore locate the conceptual debate over 'urban tribes' in different national and intellectual contexts, and avoid confusing the denotative (descriptive) and connotative (metaphorical) uses of the term (Muggleton and Weinzierl 2003; Machado and Blass 2004). Urban tribes as a metaphor for the *glocalization* of youth cultures?

Youth from less privileged backgrounds in countries at the global periphery and at the centre, may be marginalized, but are not necessarily marginal when they take on the 'puissance' of tribal subcultures identified by Maffesoli. Through attachment to a particular iconoclastic youth culture style, such as punk, marginalization turns from stigma to a powerful symbol of solidarity, strength and resistance in the constitution of a distinctive youth gang. It is thanks to their membership of youth cultures that young men on the margins of the labour market like Félix and Ome Toxtli can assert their precarious identity in difficult times. The 'tribes' of urban youth culture become the 'distorting mirrors' that criticize the reality of the status quo through the play of metaphors which do not always have the metropoles of the north as source.

This claim is exemplified in my current research on 'global latin' gangs like the *Almighty Latin Kings* and *Queen Nation* (see the Postscript of this book). These kind of gangs recently emerged in Barcelona among second-generation immigrants from Latin America. After a certain murder took place, 'Latin gangs' were discovered by the media, producing campaigns of moral panic. At the same time they are an attractive locus of identification for youth of different ethnic origins, since they are hybrids of different subcultural traditions: North American Hispanic gangs, Latin American *pandillas* and *naciones*, European urban tribes and global virtual communities. The terms used by members to define themselves (tribe, nation, empire), their multinational composition (*latinos*, catalans, other migrants), their multi-level structures (crowns, chapters, rules), and the massive use of digital culture that serves to maintain transnational gang connections between New York, Guayaquil and Barcelona, illustrate the complexity of these new forms of youth socialization that erode geographical frontiers and transcend generational identities. These new 'global tribes' demonstrate that centre and periphery are not permanent places in youth cultures and that innovative trends can also come from the south.

Note

1 This chapter is dedicated to the memory of el Ruso and Ome Toxtli – Catalan and Mexican punk friends and informants. My thanks to Teresa López and Mary Skoblo for help in the translation.

Bibliography

Adán, T. (1996) *Ultras y Skinheads: la juventud visible*, Oviedo: Nobel.
Amit-Talai, V. and Wulff, H. (eds) (1995) *Youth Cultures: a cross-cultural perspective*, London: Routledge.
Cerdà, J. and Rodriguez, R. (2002) *La Repressio Franquista del Moviment Hippy a Formentera, 1968–1970*, Eivissa: Res Pública.
Costa, P.-O., Pérez, J.-M. and Tropea, F. (1996) *Tribus Urbanas*, Barcelona: Paidós.
Feixa, C. (1988) *La Tribu Juvenil: una aproximación transcultural a la juventud*, Torino: Occhiello.
—— (1998) *De Jóvenes, Bandas y Tribus*, Barcelona: Ariel. Foreword by M. Maffesoli.
—— (2005) 'The other side of violence: ethnicity and gender in a youth microculture', in L. Suurpää and T. Hoikkala (eds) *Masculinities and Violence in Youth Cultures*, Helsinki: Youth Research Society.

Feixa, C. and Porzio, L. (2005) 'Golfos, pijos, fiesteros: studies on youth cultures in Spain 1960–2004', *Young*, 13(1): 89–113.
Fouce, H. (2004) 'El Punk en el ojo del huracán. De la nueva ola a la movida', *Revista de Estudios de Juventud*, 64: 57–66.
Gamella, J. and Álvarez, A. (2001) *Las Rutas del Éxtasis*, Barcelona: Ariel.
Gil Calvo, E. and Menéndez, E. (1985) *Ocio y Practicas Culturales de los Jóvenes*, Madrid: Instituto de la Juventud.
Gistain, M. (2001) *Cultura de Clubs*, Zaragoza: Biblioteca Aragonesa de Cultura.
Hall, S. and Jefferson, T. (eds) (1983) *Resistance through Rituals: youth subcultures in post-war Britain*, London: Hutchinson.
Hebdige, D. (1979) *Subculture: the meaning of style*, London: Methuen.
Hernández, L. (1999) 'El argot de los jóvenes', *Jóvenes*, Mexico, 8: 96–107.
Machado, J. and Blass L.M. (2004) *Tribos Urbanas*, Lisbon: Imprensa Ciências Sociais.
Maffesoli, M. (1988) *Le Temps des Tribus*, Paris: Méridiens Klincksieck.
—— (1996) *The Time of the Tribes*, London: Sage.
Mannheim, K. (1952) 'The problem of generations', in *Essays in the Sociology of Knowledge*, London: Routledge and Kegan Paul.
Monod, J. (1968) *Les Barjots: Essai d'ethnologie des bandes de jeunes*, Paris: Juillard.
Muggleton, D. and Weinzierl, R. (eds) (2003) *The Post-Subcultures Reader*, London: Berg.
Paz, O. (1950) 'El pachuco y otros extremos', *El Laberinto de la Soledad*, Mexico: FCE.
Reguillo, R. (1991) *En la Calle otra Vez: las bandas: identidad urbana y usos de la comunicación*, Guadalajara, México: ITESO.
UNDP [United Nations Development Program] (2003) *Human Development Index*. Online. Available: <hdr.undp.org/reports/global/2003/pdf/presskit/HDR03> (accessed 23 November 2004).
Urteaga, M. (1998) *Por los Territorios del Rock*, Mexico: Causa Joven.
—— and Feixa, C. (2005) 'De jóvenes, músicas y las dificultades de Integrarse', in N. García Canclini (ed.) *La Antropología urbana en México*, Mexico: Fondo de Cultura Económica.
Valenzuela, J.M. (1988) *¡A la Brava Ése!: cholos, punks, chavos banda*, Tijuana: El Colegio de la Frontera Norte.
Vigil, J.D. (1990) *Barrio Gang: street life and identify in Southern California*, Austin, TX: University of Texas Press.
Whyte, W.F. (1943) *Street Corner Society*, Chicago, IL: University of Chicago Press.

9 Bboys

Hip-hop culture in Dakar, Sénégal[1]

Abdoulaye Niang

This chapter offers a considered analysis of hip-hop youth culture in Dakar, Sénégal, using research data collected around key questions of young people's creativity and commitment to social change. The discussion avoids suggesting a hierarchy of 'culture', 'subculture' and 'counter-culture'. 'Culture' here means every 'cultural system' that manifests itself by patterns, existence, code, knowledge and anthropo-cosmological sphere (Morin 1984: 348). So this definition includes the 'subculture' or the 'counter-culture' lived by *bboys*. The term 'bboy' comes from break boy, Bronx boy, bad boy . . . a bboy is a young man who practises hip-hop, while the term *fly-girl* is used specifically for young women. As the word bboys suggests, the hip-hop movement in this part of Francophone West Africa is a primarily masculine domain. Even while female MCs (Master of Ceremonies) and posses of fly-girls such as Alif, Black Sista, Sista Fa, Fatim strive to emerge, the presence of girls is still somehow marginalized in the Dakar hip-hop movement (Niang 2001: 79–80; Car-Rap-Id 2005: 1–6). In the discussion that follows, the aim is to allow the reader to grasp the complexity of the hip-hop phenomenon in Dakar. A major question examined below is whether hybrid hip-hop youth culture in Sénégal constitutes a social movement for change.

Despite frequent local claims by the older generation that hip-hop is a major threat to traditional values and practices, it would be wrong to consider that African societies embody cultural patterns absolutely opposed to progress, from which social change is virtually excluded (Shillington 1995). A society should not be regarded as a philharmonic orchestra where, under the uncontested leadership of the maestro (institutions, authority), the executants (actors) play their symphonic score (their roles) in perfect synchrony and harmony. Conversely, neither should a society be seen either as an eternal battlefield where the social actors do nothing but clash. Conflict and negotiation are co-dependent polarities in the construction of the social web. The special strength of any society in the handling of social disturbances lies in its capacity to reserve protected spaces for the expression of difference in any human community. For African societies it is a question of effectively transforming disorder into order. This is sometimes done positively in the form of dramatized protest – with an inversion of roles, or an inversion of the acts of disorder in acts of reinforcement. Disorder may also be handled more negatively in the form of victimization of a scapegoat within the framework of ritual practices. Many African societies have shown considerable skill in using disorder creatively to restore order (Balandier 1988). But in the late modernity of a rapidly globalizing world, these adaptive traditions have today rather lost their cultural force and authority.

African societies, in general, and Senegalese society in particular, encounter enormous difficulties in trying to revitalize these 'old tricks' of culture to deal with the disorderly challenges of modernization. Touraine defines historicity as the 'capacity [for a given society] to produce its social and cultural orientations from its activity and to give a direction to its practices' (1992: 56). Senegalese society seems increasingly to be unable to direct its own historicity, in the context of current ruptures and divisions. This loss of certainty may explain why certain adults take pleasure in providing reassuringly conservative explanations of youth disorder to the general public. Hip-hop fashions certainly arouse perceptible disquiet. The image of the urban rapper in Dakar strikes the ordinary passer-by as unusual. Hip-hop fashion features the style *check down* – where the trousers are worn very low by bringing the belt to semi-buttock – a reversed baseball cap, and large sport shoes. Hip-hop ideology preaches the violation of prohibitions as its creed. Members of the 'subculture' are readily catalogued as strays, fashion victims in ludicrous imitation of American black culture. However, as sociologists of youth we have to ask what is really the reason for this passion on the part of Senegalese youth for hip-hop culture, especially rap?

The phenomenon is much more complex than simple imitation. In fact, hip-hop touches on fundamental preoccupations of contemporary Senegalese society, particularly youth with their penetrating questions about meaning. The 'counter-culture' of hip-hop addresses deep questions about the orientation and organizing principles of Senegalese society in a rapidly globalizing world. The musical and cultural meaning of local rap is constituted in significant critical fields such as inadequate social policy, stultifying social practises, infuriating inequalities, and everyday harsh reality for Africans. There is every reason for African sociology to take an interest in this subject and there are multiple ways of understanding the phenomenon. In this chapter the hip-hop movement is understood as a cultural system in its own right, in which members gather in the first instance in a *posse* and sometimes in a *cartel* (several posses associated). These can be characterized as primary groups which organize to challenge inequalities in the existing social order. A significant locus of opposition lies in the creative proposal of a cultural alternative. Hip-hop in Sénégal is a complex social movement which combines a strong identity base, a limited recruitment pool and the ideal of representing the injured masses. It operates according to a logic of total commitment and according to an orthodoxy proclaimed in the form of this commitment. Naturally, such tight focus generates not only a lack of comprehension outside, but also a series of internal conflicts within the movement. In Dakar we commonly find a rejection by some other young people of the validity of bboys' practices, labelled as unreflective parodies of African-American urban fashion. We must ask, how can the Senegalese hip-hop movement that depends on a closed structure such as the posse yet claim to represent the masses?

Putting the bboys in a research context

The culture of hip-hop is truly international – 'rap can now surely be regarded as a universal musical language' (Mitchell 2002: 12). Yet the hip-hop movement in Sénégal has only recently aroused the interest of local researchers. It was ignored in the beginning. Knowledge about the phenomenon circulated only through 'unofficial' channels of diffusion. When Senegalese rap finally became a respectable research topic, many different kinds of analysis attempted to comprehend this youth culture.

For Mamadou Mbodj, rap music is a message but also a language, an opinion, a claim. He found rap to be an original and coded manner to say things differently, 'a communication of rupture' (Sarr 1997: 9), for people faced with under-employment, and suffering from a loss of credibility in the usual models of transmission of values. Mbodj notes three central principles of traditional values. The first is *doom topp baay* – the son obeys the father. The second is *ndaw topp mag* – the young person obeys the adult. The third is *jigéen topp goor* – the woman obeys the man (1993). At present these models, if not entirely absent, are severely disrupted. Yet at the same time the dynamic universe of global change in our time requires a great capacity on the part of the individual, especially a young person, who is called upon to function both in the hybrid local situation, and the high-speed marketplace of work and technology, corrupted by unemployment. The kinds of answers he or she seeks are not those given by the usual guides: parents and elders. This creates emptiness in the young person. The need is then for 'a new pedagogy of values' (Mbodj quoted in Sarr 1997: 9). This demand makes it possible for local rappers to pour out musical streams 'full of bitterness, aggression and violence in socially tolerated forms of expression: the songs and music of their own kind' (Sarr 1997: 9).

Lô agrees with the claim that the force of rap in Dakar lies in the message, and that 'the rappers shout mainly the rage of youth disoriented by the economic crisis'. Within this understanding, the young unemployed of Dakar 'throw themselves' on this art which offers a more suitable cultural framework to them, while also offering the possibility 'of making money' (Lô 1997: 17). In their analysis, ENDA (Environmental Development Action in the Third World) emphasizes the effectiveness of hip-hop youth culture in fostering integration, solidarity, unification and in relaying information. The artistic practice always encodes a perceptible social dimension. The production of hip-hop does not need expensive equipment or trained musicians. Given this kind of impetus, it seems perfectly natural to ENDA that rap music, which celebrates marginality and the culture of the dispossessed, should be popular. 'In a context of crisis and uncontrolled growth of slums of the rejected', rap succeeds by its permanent denunciation of social ills. In a country like Sénégal or Mali, where the unions, the press – the usual intermediaries between the individual and the authorities – have many difficulties correctly assuming the role normally reserved for them, it is claimed that rap constitutes 'a means of communicating . . ., thus a medium of claims and an instrument of development' in its own right (ENDA 1998: 1–2).

Other analysts also point out the capacity of hip-hop to increase young people's broad political awareness, leading to shifts in their attitudes, potential for activism (Dièye 1997: 7; Diop 2000: 8) and vision of social change. While generally sharing the concerns of these authors (Niang 2001: 130–5; Niang 2003: 18–32), this chapter emphasizes other aspects of the phenomenon to make hip-hop in Sénégal more comprehensible. The inquiry proceeds within the theoretical paradigm of sociology of action, or more precisely Actionalism (Touraine 1973), which places social actors at the centre of analysis of social phenomena, and borrows also from constructivist and complexity approaches (Morin 1994; Corcuff 1995). These approaches attempt to avoid the traditional dichotomies of structure/agency and macro/micro. The sociology of action expresses the idea that the structured set of human relations is not dependent on the weight of prior conditioning, but results from confrontations between divergent rationalities of actors. A frequent criticism of Actionalism is that it tends to over-estimate the freedom of the agent. This can however be countered by emphasizing the constructivist aspect of any human action. In a word, if we wish to grasp the complexity of the hip-hop movement in Dakar, it is a question of taking account, not only of the productive work of the social actor, but also of structures which constitute the constraining framework for the actor.

Methodology

This chapter is based primarily on research carried out between 1998 and 2001 on the Dakar hip-hop movement by the author (Niang 2001). Another study on the same topic was carried out between 2001 and 2003 (Niang 2003). A further project has been taking place since 2003. When the original project began in 1998, initial investigation of the phenomenon was carried out in three ways. I read articles, papers, magazines specializing in hip-hop and had exploratory discussions with key informants: rappers, DJs, writers, breakdancers and producers. I followed hip-hop on CDs, cassettes, radio and television and I surfed the web. When sufficient prior knowledge had been assembled, a survey was conducted at the beginning with 281 groups, but information was considered reliable from only 133. A sample of 117 bboys divided between 45 posses was recruited for interview and focus groups, from the total of 133 posses in the survey.

A combination of research methods was used – participant observation, semi-structured interviews, survey questionnaires and focus groups (Péladeau and Mercier 1993: 117), in order to allow the possibility of cross-checking information and to enable comparison of individual and group data. So, for example, the strong influence of the posse was evident in the standardization and the convergence of responses during focus groups. This contrasted sometimes with the particularity of individual interviews, allowing a useful comparison of data. In assembling the sample, four characteristics operated as criteria. First, the characteristic pattern of localization was categorized using the following initial geographical subsets for comparison: urban areas, peri-urban areas and mixed areas. Localization was also analysed according to more demographic district subsets: populous areas, semi-residential areas and residential areas. Second, seniority – old and new school rappers. Third, discography – posses with or without cassettes of their own. Finally, gender composition – whether posses were male, female or mixed.

Initial findings of the research with *bboys*

Interpretation of data so far has permitted the following tentative understandings:

- the posse is an identification and integration framework for the rapper
- rap generates new forms of musical, corporeal and textual expression
- rap causes disorder with a view to creating a new form of order
- the rapper constitutes himself as the voice of the whole community from which he comes
- Dakar rappers reappropriate received influences yet, in spite of some 'cultural standardization', local specificities remain.

At present it seems that hip-hop in Dakar is a complex phenomenon that functions somewhere between a social movement and a set of psychologically satisfying primary groups. This works against the possibility of realizing a full social movement (Melucci 1989). The remainder of the chapter is dedicated to an exposition of this understanding, but we must begin with some basic definitions.

Rap, hip-hop and the idea of a social movement

In Black American vernacular, 'rap' could mean conversation, debate, noise or rumour. On the purely technical level, to rap consists of outputting lyrics by stressing them in a poetic form, and a coded language, according to a variable flow. Rapping, in a variety of forms, was popular in African culture for thousands of years (Collins 1992) and the genre was modified further when African slaves were taken to the new world. When rap took off in the African-American ghettos in the 1970s, MCing in places like the south Bronx showed the influence of African *griots*, Jamaican 'toasting', and street poetry signalling the oral tradition in Black culture (DaveyD 2002). Politically, rap has expressed a profound sense of outrage at injustice and poverty (Ellison 1989). Very often rap is fast, aggressive and violent. It expresses experiences of injustice, marginalization, and censorship (Rose 1994; Mitchell 1996, 2002; Miller 2004). The practice of rap creates a space for reaction, a dialectical outpouring in which the rapper is constituted as spokesperson for the community.

An evocative term, rap encodes ideas of speed, force and energy – 'on the hop' – implying movement as a key concept in the lived practice of hip-hop. The bboy is never still, but moves all the time. Extraordinary energy is released by the break-dancer. Hip-hop as a set of cultural practices includes rapping, breakdancing, graffiti and DJing. Early breakdancing was called bboying. Graffiti first became popular in New York (George 1998). Youth gangs created identity 'tags' and put them wherever they could. Simple tags soon became artful and complex works in colour that covered large urban vertical surfaces (see Figure 9.1). Around the same time DJs such as Kool Herc, Africa Bambaataa, Grandmaster Flash and others mixed tracks so that the usual instrumental break in each song was extended (Fricke and Ahearn 2002: 26). During the 'break' part of a song the bboys danced. This all took place in the poorest of urban settings where most African-Americans and *latinos* lived. Hip-hop can be defined as a cultural protest system, an alternative identity affirmation. In Sénégal, it is dance that was first taken up by hip-hoppers (mid-1980s), then rap (end of the 1980s) then DJing and graffiti (mid-1990s). Hip-hop dance 'disappeared' for a while but came back. The bboy Rodrigue says for example, 'Dance gives you a certain freedom, a vision of the larger scheme of things, a stronger, more robust spirit, a readiness to fight and contest within oneself . . . Dance is the complement of rap . . . hip-hop, MCing, breakdancing, DJing – are like the five fingers of one's hand!'(Rodrigue, breakdancer, Dakar Plateau, 2005).

Graffiti also is now popular, and seems better accepted in Sénégal than in France or the United States. Docta, from Doxandem Squad, one of the pioneers of graffiti in Sénégal says, 'One must understand that graff, basically, is a way to communicate, to get your message out there . . . It is the visual communication of the Hip-Hop movement' (Docta, Médina, 2005).

Hip-hop youth culture in Dakar considered as a social movement certainly includes some basic principles: identity, opposition, totality (Touraine 1973). Hip-hop identity is affirmed both by posse cultural membership and the specific defining characteristics of the bboy. There is a tension for the bboy between his subjective identity; 'the individual aspects and the psychological components connected to the personality' (Fischer 1995: 167), and his objective identity – the 'face' allotted to him (Goffman 1974: 9). Turning to the posse as a primary group, three significant characteristics can be defined. The first is the existence of strong affinity relations within the framework of the commonplace and of everyday life. The second is the relatively restricted

Figure 9.1 Docta's graffiti at Maurice Delafosse High School. (Source: A. Niang)

number of interactive members who play a part in the posse, a real 'in-group'. The third is mobilization and adhesion around common purposes.

Hip-hop in Dakar

For greater convenience, I divided Dakar into survey areas (see Figure 9.2). Each survey area included a set of districts. The Plateau district concentrates essential administrative services, financial institutions and mercantile trade houses. This district also houses privileged expatriates and the upper-class Senegalese minority. Other exclusive residential districts, such as Fann Hock, Fann Residence and Point E, are also high-class security enclaves. Densely-populated inner-city districts such as Grand Dakar, Usine Ben Tally, Médina, like the suburbs of Pikine, Thiaroye, Guédiawaye, comprise the largest part of the city, accommodating populations with much more modest living standards. Dakar occupies only 0.3 per cent of the national territory but it is populated by 2,267,356 inhabitants, which represents 23 per cent of the total population (DPS 2004: 6).

Like other large African cities, Dakar is under tremendous population pressure, continuously absorbing new waves of internal immigrants. Political, administrative, economic and educational concentration, including 90 per cent of Senegal's industrial and manufacturing activity, seems to offer job opportunities to young people (DPS 1992; M'Bokolo, Gendreau-Massaloux, Le Callennec and Bah 1992: 508–12; Fall 1995: 257–75), resulting in great ethnic diversity. Multiculturalism makes Dakar a privileged place for exchanges and borrowings of all kinds. But Dakar is also afflicted by inequalities: ruptures

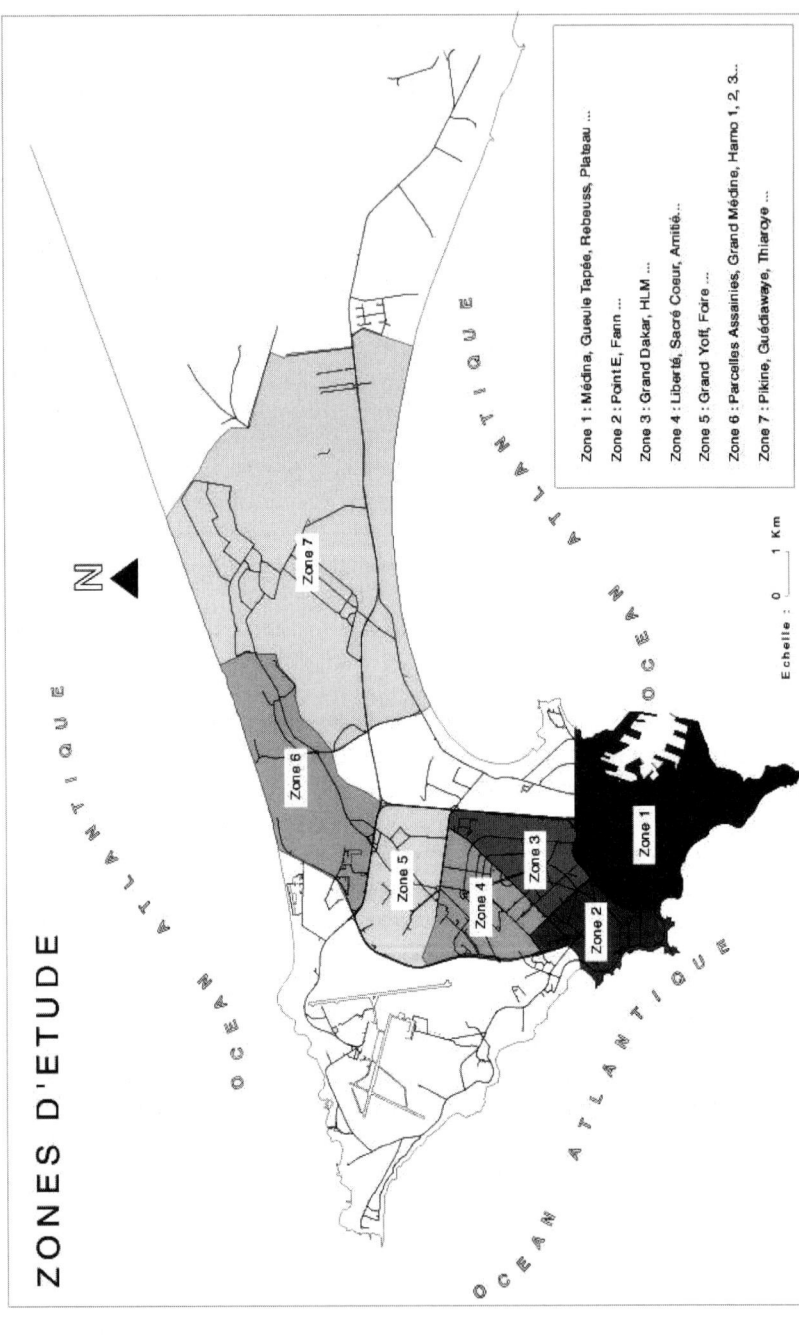

Figure 9.2 Map of Dakar showing zones of study (Source: Ly, I., Agence de Développement Municipial)

in urban solidarity. Vulnerable categories (such as young people) develop feelings of frustration which manifest in the formation of so-called 'deviant' social groups: gangs, bands and posses (Decker and Van Winkle 1996; McIntyre 2000; Thornberry, Krohn, Lizotte, Smith and Tobin 2003; Maclure and Sotelo 2004).

The hip-hop movement arrived in Dakar in the mid-1980s in this context of frustration and rupture, but took off first among the children of the privileged classes, who competed in imitating the latest American dance and music 'craze'. Hip-hop culture spread among youth, but the rap was mainly in French or English at first. According to the rapper Awadi, 'at the beginning it was really aped!' (quoted in Lô 1997: 13). Rap music in Dakar was created by a limited number of groups in the early days, 'In relation to rap, there were initially only a dozen groups: it was underground . . . There were just a few people who shared in this passion (Shadow Soundjata, VIB posse, Pikine, 2000).

As indicated above, hip-hop first attracted youths who had access to imported records and film clips. As the rapper Awadi says 'it was . . . buddies who were daddy's boy . . . and then it would be enough to be in a switched-on milieu' (quoted in Lô 1997: 13). But eventually 'a simple fashion mimed by the local middle-class became a true way of life' (Servant 2000). The coming of rap in Sénégal coincided with the first years of Structural Adjustment Programs,[2] which only contributed to an aggravation of the precariousness of urban life.

The crisis set off a series of social ruptures among young people. Mbodj (1993) recognized three levels of rupture in this crisis. He identified ruptures in the family and also in traditional practices of socialization and learning. The other – 'cultural rupture' – precipitated a 'process of interculturation' which brought together Senegalese and western culture. However, one can argue that western popular culture was a double-edged sword for young people. On the one hand it symbolized freedom, power and prestige. However, in a negative way, this foreign culture was often badly integrated individualism, a kind of monetarization of human relations. Urban Dakar was receptive to this kind of ideology and with it came hip-hop culture. On the positive side, as hip-hop culture grew, rappers became aware of the expressive possibilities. By the end of the 1980s and early 1990s, rap posses had replaced the initial dance groups. And gradually, what had appeared like a simple youth trend of cultural imitation became an 'interstitial culture' (Calvet 1994: 171). We should note though that the hip-hop cultural system of Dakar bboys is hybrid, distinct from those in the United States and in France, even if it shares with them certain characteristics. Distinctive identities that exist within this cultural system show this quite clearly.

For a movement like hip-hop, reviled from its very beginnings, the need to prove distinctiveness – difference from mainstream culture – was a major concern (Bourdieu 1979). Beyond this will to distinction from the mainstream cultural system, was added the desire to prove, in a challenging way, that bboys, as actors, existed: 'For us, Hip-Hop is something sacred; we carry it within ourselves. We feel it within ourselves. That is why we live Hip-Hop (Alpha, Fac Rap posse, Diamaguène, 2005).

Even in the United States where hip-hop often took the form of direct confrontation between bboys and forces of authority, the famous tough stance of hip-hop was developed much more around a sense of marginalization which the bboys felt victims of, rather than direct experiences of state violence. Maclure and Sotelo point out that in many developing countries 'gang membership represents a way for many adolescents to stand up to mainstream social institutions' (2004: 418).

In Sénégal also, it is a question of claims for legitimacy in two contradictory directions. On the one hand, bboys criticize inequalities. At the same time they are seeking integration into the same society they contest so strongly. Explanation of this apparent discursive loop must be sought within the symbolic system of local hip-hop. Members of hip-hop youth culture, while expressing the desire to be accepted by the majority, want at the same time to move within a cultural system more adapted to their specific cultural and social aspirations. This alternative model of identity is constructed within a pluralistic framework of hybridity, combining shaping principles of global hip-hop culture with bboys' traditional culture of origin, sometimes the new Islamic revivalism, and peer influences in the posse.

Bboys and hip-hop culture

Membership of hip-hop culture is signalled by Dakar bboys in many fields. These young people make use of distinctive identity signs in their clothing, their language, their gait, use of evocative nicknames and so on. For example, one of the young people surveyed is nicknamed SIAS which is also the name of a local organization disposing of household rubbish in Dakar. The nickname signals that he is there, as he says, in order to 'sweep up dirtiness', to *set settal* (purify) Senegalese society. The distinctive codes and signs of hip-hop arouse criticism from adults in particular. One rapper told the following story: 'One day as I walked in the city wearing my trousers in *check down*, a man and a woman called me insane, giving the reason that I was wearing my trousers in *check down* and shoes that were too big' (Seydina Alioune, 'style doff la' in Africa Mbolo 1997).

Some posse members expressed annoyance at the opinions of those who criticize hip-hop culture: 'It upsets me when someone does not respect the Double H movement that I love so much' (Mina, fly-girl of *ALIF* posse, Patte-d'Oie, 2000).

Senegalese hip-hop produces categories whose signifying codes are not easily understood by the uninitiated. Like many other youth cultures, language is a key symbol of the categorical establishment of identity, a 'we code' which differs from the 'they code' (Gumperz 1982: 53). The 'we code' is current in a delimited social milieu – which may include all hip-hop fans or a restricted local group. However, in either case the code expresses the will

Table 9.1 Language resources of posse members

Languages claimed	(n = 117)	%
Wolof	117	100
French	97	82.9
English	90	76.92
Other languages	22	18.8

to disassociate from high status official language codes. Simultaneously, the use of 'we code' constitutes a valorization of the hip-hop symbolic cultural system. These urban vernacular forms work like a kind of filter between the interior and the exterior of the group. It makes it possible for members to very quickly identify 'intruders' who do not belong to the neighbourhood (Cahill 2000), the movement, the cartel. Greetings in particular can be seen as passwords that have a security function for the protection of a sociability space reserved for the bboys.

Wolof is the majority language in Senegal, yet 'Wolof today is a linguistic stew of Wolof, French and English, and also contains some elements from the other 36 languages spoken in Senegal' (Mackintosh 1999).

The lexical sources of Wolof, French, English, Arabic and other slang give invaluable indication of the measure of hybridity which characterizes the construction of the Dakar bboys' identity frames (see Table 9.1). This differentiation and transgression can also be found in the redefinitions carried out by rappers in orthography. The bboy writes '1/2ground' for underground, '6T' for city. These forms are used for instance in the new forms of communication: emails and texting.

In Dakar, hip-hop is a 'counter-culture' organized in relatively closed communities, whose challenging practices are accepted only with difficulty by the wider society. However, the bboys do not necessarily constitute in their cultural practices a systematic rejection of the deep values of Senegalese society. Musicologists have noted the continuing presence of African musical and cultural forms in Senegalese rap (McIlvaine 2000: 21). Yet as a 'counter-culture' hip-hop appears to challenge traditional aesthetic categories, by promoting new scriptural and performance forms which go against local standards of beauty and respectability. Almost everything is redefined according to hip-hop cultural standards. These find frameworks of expression most eloquently in the posse.

The posse, place of sociability and identity formation

Almost half of the 117 rappers interviewed in the first stage of this project grew up together with other members of their respective groups (see Table 9.2). Their social ties in the posse are parallel to the ties woven through early neighbourhood play and games.

Table 9.2 Means by which posse members met each other

Way of meeting	Number	%
Grew up together	36	30.76
Met through a mutual acquaintance	23	19.65
Met during a hip-hop performance	16	13.67
Grew up together and met later through a mutual acquaintance	11	9.4
Grew up together and met later at a hip-hop performance	6	5.12
Member of the same family	6	5.12
Grew up together and met later by some other means	4	3.41
Met at a tea gathering in the late afternoon	4	3.41
Met at school	3	2.56
Met by chance	3	2.56
Other way of meeting	2	1.7
Met through a mutual acquaintance in some other way	2	1.7
Met during a hip-hop performance through a mutual acquaintance	1	0.85
Total	117	100

The posse is in part the childhood play group extended into adolescence and early adulthood, reinforcing identity formations through a lifetime of interactions. However, whether we are talking about those bboys for whom the posse constitutes a continuity of the neighbourhood peer group, or by other means – a meeting at a hip-hop event, introduction by a common acquaintance – the daily face to face interaction of posse members is a site for progressive emergence of norms, generating common norms which remain even if the individual is isolated later (Maisonneuve 1989: 70). The process is intensified in groups which transcend the simple collective situation. Dakar hip-hop *posses* fulfil a defined function (see above), so there is an allocation of identifying roles to the various members. Each rapper takes part: by production of texts, by developing sound expertise, getting knowledgeable about steps to obtain a contract of production, and so on – in the active constitution of the posse as a viable social entity.

Allocation to posse members of the various roles associated with producing texts seems a utilitarian principle of organization, but to understand it this way would be to somewhat miss the point. In fact, this actualization of functional identities around the collective art project of rap encodes a web of emotional relations which is a factor of cohesion for the posse. It is a kind of tacit bargain between the individual and the group. The bboy in his posse is constituted as a reliable person: his capacities are recognized and valued by the group as a whole. That in itself is a source of moral gratification and fortitude for a young person in the Dakar 'jungle'. To live and share experience and creativity with the other members of the posse is to be ensured of the fraternity of fellow 'real *niggas*' (true friends, brothers). Almost 100 per cent of the 117 posse members indicated that friendly and fraternal relations were a very important aspect of the posse for them. Before anything else, the posse is a family. The bboys identify permanently with their groups, even if they also represent broader communities. In the local rap lyrics there is a strong recurrence of terms which mark this attachment to the group, such as *sama crew* (my group). Attachment to the posse is always inextricably related to the omnipresent principle of commitment.

The commitment of the bboy

Commitment is directly connected to the production of iconoclastic texts as described above. In short, commitment is linked to bboy identity via the objective of the counter-project that the movement proposes. Apart from all the obvious differences in roles and even opinions about group strategies which may be noted, unanimity exists about the pressing need for the bboy to be committed to the sacrosanct principles of hip-hop culture. Bboys consider hip-hop more than simple artistic practice; it is a real mission for them. For example, according to MC Shiffaï from the Slam Revolution posse, rap has the capacity to 'lead [people] from shadow to light' (Slam Revolution 2000). So, according to over 90 per cent of hip-hop youth surveyed, a significant aspect of commitment must be to sensitize society. This task implies generating an acerbic criticism of the socio-political 'system': 'In this year 1-9-9-8, we'll pull out all the poisonous weeds. It is now that the big stuff starts to happen, in the most populous areas of town, it will explode like a nuclear bomb' (Rap'Adio, 'Xibaru underground, 1998).

The MC (master of ceremony), a title for the rapper which is universal in hip-hop cultures, is the pivotal figure in this task. According to the interviews, the Dakar MC is 'someone who represents with dignity' the hip-hop ideals, through 'real and positive lyrics'. 'As for me, what I can add is that the MC is like a cameraman who shoots what he sees happening in the street, and then shows it to you. Only then it's up to you to make the choice' (Yela, Sul Sully clan, Parcelles Assainies, 2005). Another MC confirms, 'If the MC sees something that people aren't able to talk about, he is the one who can do it, can take the *mike*, and put what he has to say on tape, so that the boys can hear it' (Momo, Slam Revolution, Liberté 5, 2005).

He must, as El Mag J of the Kemtaan Klan posse says, act as the 'spokesman of his generation' (interviewed in Parcelles Assainies, 2000). But the rapper does not limit the impact of his message to youth; he also tries to take into account adults, even if young people are the priority.

The form of the message and the coded language used, however, are more accessible to young people who decipher it more easily. Indeed, the idioms to which the bboys have recourse are often a mixture of several languages – Wolof, English, French, Spanish, Arabic – plus the use of Dakar youth culture slang. Moreover, the international focus of some posses requires them to use an even broader linguistic range. The kind of language used in Dakar rap depends on the targeted audience, the level of control of the language, and the nature of the topic. One of the contemporary trends identified in the research was that the bboys appear to be making more and more effort for the message to be comprehensible. This is a transformation compared with the former situation where the habitual over-use of 'subculturally' coded language made the message not very accessible at all to the general public. Such inaccessibility obviously limited the diffusion of the messages of hip-hop. Now, even if 'subcultural' coding is still present, the lyrics are more comprehensible; using better-understood terms, slower speed and clearer phrasing. The original highly-encoded language practices could be justified as long as the audience was just the restricted field of bboys.

But, looking at this trend from another angle, the confinement of hip-hop discourse to a specialized linguistic community has doubtful validity. If the goal is, for instance, to criticize political leaders or even globalization, then they need to fully grasp the nature of the critique before considering strategies and action. At present it would seem that the trend is to sensitize the public, make them understand hip-hop, be sympathetic to it, before advancing criticism. This implies that the major concern of contemporary Dakar hip-hop is to follow constructive steps and not be confined to the nihilistic standpoint of utter negation. 'I criticize! I criticize! I never give a solution. I have opinions like everyone else, but no one gives a damn about them' stated the rapper Awadi to those who accused rap of not being constructive in the 1990s (Awadi 1994). Proposing alternatives to the existing status quo is a test of credibility for the local Senegalese hip-hop movement as it moves from local: defined as encoded nihilistic youth vernacular – to local: defined as community-responsible.

In this way, Senegalese hip-hop attempts to prove its maturity and the legitimacy of its presence in the fields of political debate (for instance in the presidential elections, 2000) and models of behaviour, not only in Africa but beyond: 'African music is very, very rich . . . we try to bring that to the hip-hop music to show that apart from the basic roots of hip-hop there's another kind of behaviour, another way to act. That is the African *attitude*' (Faada Freddy from Daara J, quoted in Terrell, 2004).

In the survey, criticism was a priority in their membership of posses for only 14 per cent of respondents, although over 80 per cent of the rappers surveyed stated that they made criticisms. Any movement which advances critical claims in spheres as significant and crucial as politics and religion must justify the relevance of its remarks, while avoiding expressing negation only. Thereby, the society is invited to reflect on the amelioration of evils which undermine it. The evils most commonly evoked were poverty (92 per cent of respondents), unemployment (88 per cent) and social inequalities (85 per cent). It is notable that, either personally or through the experiences of many in their immediate circle – friends, parents – many bboys live the reality of the difficulties they evoke. The problems they identify are highly personal. For example, KT, from Rap'Adio posse, says, 'Why do some live in beautiful houses and others in straw huts? . . . I'll never forget all these things I wished to have without daring to say them' (Rap'Adio, 'dund gu dee geun', 1998).

Iba adds, 'Am I thus not a citizen of this country? Money is galore here, why don't I get my share?' (Rap'Adio, 'dund gu dee geun', 1998).

The fundamental reason behind this personalization of key problems is that in the hip-hip movement, social origin is frequently brandished like a proof of legitimacy of the bboy as approved spokesman, evidence that he shares the daily sufferings he denounces. Responsibility for the sufferings of the Senegalese people is often charged to politicians. For example, rappers reshape the word *politicien* (politician) as *politichien* by combining *politi* and *chien* (dog). Bboys display quite some audacity when they publicly criticize by name the political leaders, even the President of the Republic, in rap. We should note that the ex-President of the Republic Abdou Diouf was sufficiently impressed to give an audience to the PBS posse in February 1997.

Nevertheless, it would be incorrect to think that all hip-hop rappers adopt a radically critical attitude to the political scene. As a youth culture Senegalese hip-hop is far from uniform. Three categories can be schematically distinguished. The first is known as 'hardcore' – which describes the most radical posses. The second is known as 'cool' or 'soft' – this term describes posses which give greater emphasis to themes like love. The third, a composite category, lies halfway between the first two. Conflicts between these two opposite tendencies, which were frequent in the late 1990s, have greatly decreased today owing to the process described in part above. Senegalese hip-hop has become more professional, and this new impulse encourages posses to be more attentive to public expectations, 'We cannot afford to do what we like anymore; it is over . . . You can be hardcore, but should do things in such a way that the music that you make can be understood by the public'(Jougy, MC, Liberté 5, 2005).

Posses are generally less radical in their behaviour, although not necessarily in their political goals. Bboys share an awareness that rap from now on must be taken seriously, since it can enable a hip-hop artist to earn his living, and this alters the norms of commitment. But whatever the orientation of the posse, bboys are always committed to raising the political and social consciousness of Senegalese and, more widely, African people.

Conclusion

In summary, Senegalese rap has been categorized negatively by some people or it has been lionized as a radical and heroic form of 'common' art (Vuylsteke 2001). At either extreme of opinion, it has been exaggerated, or written off in simplistic terms as the local version of a global youth phenomenon. Either kind of account gives a deformed image of Senegalese hip-hop culture, with most studies not taking into account its great complexity. If some classify it in the category of ephemeral youth fashion – a 'fad' (König 1969) copied from American culture, others perceive it as an irresistible revolutionary movement. The reality is that hip-hop in Senegal, as in so many other parts of the developing world, has demonstrated once again its capacity to awaken young people to the creative and transformative possibilities of the music, the fashion and the art. Hip-hop everywhere offers a framework of expression for youth touched by a lack of identity references in a rapidly globalizing world. However, in contrast to French African and African-American rappers who articulate the voices of a demographic minority, the rappers of Dakar do not represent a minority voice, but belong to the category of local youth whose major unifying features are urban poverty, and the daily inequalities they endure.

The study reported in this chapter had as its main objective the task of generating knowledge about the phenomenon of hip-hop culture, especially rap, in the context of urban Dakar. Given this intention, one important question has been whether hip-hop constitutes a real social movement with the potential to assume the difficult pedagogic and spokesperson role for the dominated masses. On the one hand, hip-hop looks a lot like an urban social movement with the potential to bring about change. On the other hand, the basic unit of the posse can be readily identified as containing fundamental elements constitutive of the primary group. While these two views may not necessarily be irreconcilable, there is a larger question. How can hip-hop culture claim to represent the 'ordinary' Senegalese masses when the defining structure of this youth culture is the posse, a primary group with a tightly defined alternative identity, embracing a hybridized foreign cultural trend with which the aforesaid masses do not identify?

We can start by acknowledging that Senegalese hip-hop culture itself is not a homogenous entity. Even within the movement, oppositions exist. Furthermore, data from the research project indicates that existing internal oppositions have been altered by the professionalization of hip-hop. Old tensions are diminished in the redirection towards marketing the music and lifestyle, while new ones emerge. However, these kinds of residual differences within the 'subculture' are not entirely inhibiting to the potential effectiveness of hip-hop as a social movement. Moreover, it would be unrealistic to expect to find in hip-hop a social movement that represented, mobilized and united all social categories.

The major issue remains that, generally speaking, the masses do not identify with the alternative identity frame of the bboys, and the bboys do not identify with the conservative identity frame of ordinary Senegalese. Any social movement usually relies on a hardcore of activists who mobilize other actors desiring change. The hardcore of activists in the Senegalese hip-hop movement is made up by a minority of bboys deeply committed to producing a dynamic transformation in the society and culture. Yet these bboys are operating within a differentiated cultural system. There is thus a dissimilarity with the masses, based partly on a generational difference – the greater exposure to, and receptivity of, young people to external influences. This limits the impact of hip-hop as a social movement because it is seen as something external to Senegal. While its transformative potential to generate social alternatives is strongly realized by the bboys, for the rest of the population it has been at best a peripheral youth trend with some capacity to raise political and social consciousness.

Therefore there is absence of agreement from the rest of the population, even of some young people, about the form of the counter-project. Even if people agree with the bboys' analysis in principle, nevertheless any mainstream individual will probably reject the cultural forms and practices. Yet at the same time it is important to recognize that a renegotiation of the previously negative social relationship between the bboys and the rest of Senegalese society does appear to be taking place. It is possible to identify in the data two reasons for growing reciprocal concessions. The first is evidence that the population is coming to respect the bboys and their culture better. 'Mainstream' Senegalese society is calling more and more often on the rappers to raise public awareness of social problems such as HIV and AIDS, and to perform at charity fund-raising events. For instance, the charity event 'Festival Fouladou Rap' was organized in October 2004 to support the struggle against HIV and AIDS. Second, the bboys have gradually abandoned the amateurism and closed street-gang mentality of the early days of hip-hop in Senegal. It can be concluded that more and more young rappers intend not only to produce alternative music, art and lifestyle, but also to make of their hip-hop movement a tool of transformation towards professional cultural market insertion. They are in favour of social integration rather than continued marginality.

Notes

1. Thanks to Ousmane Ngom and France Bourgouin for their support in translation.
2. Structural Adjustment Programs (SAPs) are large IMF (International Monetary Fund) sequenced loans to developing countries that carry tight conditions – almost always involving radical cutting of public expenditure such as welfare programmes and housing assistance.

Bibliography

Africa Mbolo (1997) 'Style doff la', in *Petit Frère*, Dakar: Suñu Flavor.
Awadi, D. (1994) 'Le bourreau est noir', in *Boul Fale Bou Bess*, Dakar: PBS.
Balandier, G. (1988) *Le Désordre: éloge du mouvement*, Paris: Éditions Fayard.
Bourdieu, P. (1979) *La Distinction: critique sociale du jugement*, Paris: Éditions de Minuit.
Cahill, C. (2000) 'Street literacy: urban teenagers' strategies for negotiating their neighbourhood', *Journal of Youth Studies*, 3(3): 251–77.
Calvet, L.-J. (1994) *Les Voix de la Ville: introduction à la sociolinguistique urbaine*, Paris: Payot et Rivages.
Car-Rap-Id (2005) 'Les meufs dans le mouv', *Car-Rap-Id*, 3–10 May: 1–6.
Collins, J. (1992) *West African Pop Roots*, Philadelphia, PA: Temple University Press.
Corcuff, P. (1995) *Les Nouvelles Sociologies*, Paris: Nathan.
DaveyD (2002) 'DaveyD's historical version of hiphop culture'. Online. Available:

<www.hiphop-network.com/articles/general/daveydhhversion.asp> (accessed 24 October 2002).
Decker, S. and Van Winkle, B. (1996) *Life in the Gang: family, friends and violence*, Cambridge: Cambridge University Press.
Dièye, A.B. (1997) 'Réactions après la condamnation de SUDCOM. Les rappeurs montent au créneau', *Sud Quotidien*, 27 June: 7.
Diop, M. (2000) 'Mouvement hip hop: les rappeurs réclament la paternité de l'alternance', *Le Matin*, 25–6 March: 8.
DPS [Direction de la Prévision et de la Statistique] (1992) *Recensement Général de la Population et de l'Habitat de 1988: rapport national (résultats définitifs de Dakar)*, Dakar: DPS.
—— (2004) *Projections de Population du Sénégal Issues du Recensement de 2002*, Dakar: DPS.
Ellison, M. (1989) *Lyrical Protest: black music's struggle against discrimination*, New York: Praeger.
ENDA (1998) 'Participation populaire: Rap-Sahel', *Rencontres de Bamako*, 1: 1–2.
Fall, A.S. (1995) 'Relations à distance des migrants et réseaux d'insertion à Dakar', in P. Antoine and A.B. Diop (eds) *La Ville à Guichets Fermés: itinéraires, réseaux et insertions urbaines*, Dakar: IFAN/ORSTOM.
Fischer, G.-N. (1995) *Les Concepts Fondamentaux de la Psychologie Sociale*, Paris: Dunod/ PUM.
Fricke, J. and Ahearn, C. (2002) *Yes Yes Y'all: the experience music project oral history of hip-hop's first decade*, Cambridge, MA: De Capo Press.
George, N. (1998) *Hip Hop America*, New York: Penguin Books.
Goffman, E. (1974) *Les Rites d'Interaction*, Paris: Éditions de Minuit.
Gumperz, J. (1982) *Discourse Strategies*, Cambridge: Cambridge University Press.
König, R. (1969) *Sociologie de la Mode*, Paris: Payot.
Lô, M.E. (1997) *Le Rap à Dakar: rage d'une jeunesse, gage du business*, Dakar: CESTI.
McIlvaine, M. (2000) 'Hip Hop in the US and its manifestations in South Africa and Senegal'. Online. Available: <www.st2006.trincoll.edu/~mmcilvai/text/hip%20hop%20in%20senegal,%20US,%20south%20africa.doc> (accessed 11 January 2005).
McIntyre, A. (2000) *Inner-City Kids: adolescents confront life and violence in an urban community*, New York and London: New York University Press.
Mackintosh, M. (1999) 'South Central: Senegal's hip-hop scene', *Underdog Online*. Online. Available: <www.underdog-online.com/index.php/article/articleview/1999.html> (accessed 11 January 2005).
Maclure, R. and Sotelo, M. (2004) 'Youth gangs in Nicaragua: Gang membership as structured individualization', *Journal of Youth Studies*, 7(4): 417–32.
Maisonneuve, J. (1989) *Introduction à la Psychosociologie*, 6th edition, Paris: PUF.
Mbodj, G. (1993) 'Domaines et dimensions de la crise sociétale de la jeunesse', *Université, Recherche et Développement*, 2: 37–50.
M'Bokolo, E., Gendreau-Massaloux, M., Le Callennec, S. and Bah, T. (1992) *Afrique Noire: histoire et civilisation. Tome II. XIXème–XXème Siècle*, Paris: Hatier/AUPELF.
Melucci, A. (1989) *Nomads of the Present*, Philadelphia, PA: Temple University Press.
Miller, M. (2004) 'Rap's dirty South: from subculture to pop culture', *Journal of Popular Music Studies*, 16(2): 175–210.
Mitchell, T. (1996) *Popular Music and Local Identity: rock, pop and rap in Europe and Oceania*, London: Leicester University Press.

—— (2002) *Global Noise: rap and hip-hop outside the USA*, Middletown, CT: Wesleyan University Press.
Morin, E. (1984) *Sociologie*, Paris: Éditions Fayard.
—— (1994) *Introduction à la Pensée Complexe*, Paris: Éditions ESF.
Niang, A. (2001) *Étude Interdisciplinaire du Rap à Dakar à Travers une Approche de la Complexité: entre mouvement social et groupe primaire*, Saint-Louis: UGB.
—— (2003) *Les Jeunes Bboys de Dakar dans un Contexte de Redéfinition du Rapport Social: étude de la production du sens, des facteurs d'insertion/intégration selon une perspective constructiviste et une approche de la complexité*, Saint-Louis: UGB.
Péladeau, N. and Mercier, C. (1993) 'Approches qualitative et quantitative en évaluation de programmes', *Sociologie et Sociétés*, XXV(2): 111–24.
Rap'Adio (1998) 'Dund gu dee geun', in *Ku Weet Xam sa Bopp*, Dakar: Fitna Produk.
Rose, T. (1994) *Black Noise: rap music and black culture in contemporary America*, Hanover, NH: University of New England Press.
Sarr, I. (1997) 'Le rap Sénégalais est-il violent?', *Le Soleil*, 20–1 Septembre: 7–9.
Servant, J.-C. (2000) 'L'Afrique conteste en rap', *Site du Monde Diplomatique*. Online. Available: <www.mondediplomatique.fr/2000/12/servant/14583.html> (accessed 14 January 2001).
Shillington, K. (1995) *History of Africa*, New York: St Martin's Press.
Slam Revolution (2000) 'Intro', in *Jogge ci Jeundeum Jemm ci Leer*, Dakar: Slam Revolution.
Terrell, T. (2004) 'Hip-hop's round trip: Daara J's spirit-cosmic gestalt of the rhythm divine', *Rock, Paper, Scissors*. Online. Available: <www.rockpaperscissors.biz.index.cfm> (accessed 11 January 2005).
Thornberry, T., Krohn, M., Lizotte, A., Smith, C. and Tobin, K. (2003) *Gangs and Delinquency in a Developmental Perspective*, Cambridge: Cambridge University Press.
Touraine, A. (1973) *La Production de la Société*, Paris: Éditions Seuil.
—— (1992) *Critique de la Modernité*, Paris: Éditions Fayard.
Vuylsteke, C. (2001) 'The honorary revolutionaries', *Reportage*, January. Online. Available: <www.reportage.org/2001/RappersSenegal/PagesRappers.html> (accessed 11 January 2005).

10 Global? local?

Multi-level identifications among contemporary skinheads in France

Youra Petrova

France is undergoing some radical changes. Immigration, European union, loss of identifying symbols like currency, the hegemony of English, casualization and reskilling of the youth labour market, all contribute to the crisis of national identity. In this context, French skinheads are a minority subculture, but they constitute visible, active, well-structured groups attracting high levels of public concern. Skinhead youth culture is present in hybridized forms in almost every industrialized country in the world, each with locally-specific social, cultural and political features, and points of reference. At the same time, every skinhead group, even within a given country, is clearly distinct from other skinhead groups. Politically speaking they may occupy diametrically opposite positions – extreme-left or extreme-right – with group behaviours referenced to these positions. In France, skinhead youth culture presents as a variety of subgroups which span the political spectrum. Most often the political position concerns the question of racial identity and presence of immigrants in the country – for or against. At the same time, all manifestations of skinhead culture are characterized by the assumption of a radical attitude, and by acceptance of violence.

This chapter addresses contemporary dynamics in the formation of different identities in French skinhead subcultures, illustrating defining social and political characteristics in this process. It examines key aspects of the construction of multi-faceted skinhead identities using data from interviews and observations. The discussion below explains how social and political, collective and ontological identities are constructed through discursive meanings and dynamics.

Methodological points

This reported research relies on qualitative inquiry: observation, individual and collective interviews. The framework was a doctoral study commenced under the auspices of sociological research conducted by Wieviorka (1992) on racism in France, using the CADIS (Centre for Analyses and Sociological Intervention) 'sociological intervention method' derived from Alain Touraine. I also use data from analysis of the skinhead press and media –

fanzines/skinzines, web pages, special labels and discography to inform the discussion below. Lexical statistical analysis of the data was useful for bringing out the specific vocabulary of the people interviewed.

Looking at the 1990s, prior sociological research on French skinheads includes Peralva on violence and political skinhead identity (1994, 1996). In Germany, Groffmann (2001) studied German skinhead groups – cultural habits, attitudes and initiation rites. Farin (1997) and Heitmann (1997) studied skinheads as urban rebels, or mythical actors, while Pfahl-Traughber (1999) regards skinheads as part of new extreme-right conservatism and neo-Nazism. In Finland, Perho (2001) studied racist skinheads. In Norway, Fangen (1998) investigated ultra right-wing skinheads. In Australia, Moore (1994) considers skinheads as an urban youth subculture. Similarly, Young and Craig (1997) and Baron (1997) studied Canadian skinheads as subculture. In northern California, Knight (2002) claims the social construction of 'whiteness' as ethnic identity in the United States creates a racialized hierarchy where skinheads exist as an extreme expression of white supremacy. In Brazil, research on suburban skinheads (da Costa 1993) contrasts with a study by the same researcher on 'Christian skinheads' (da Costa 2004). Russian research on skinheads has commenced (Nesterov 2004).

From empirical studies of skinheads and skinhead culture across a number of countries we can draw certain conclusions about these extreme youth culture groups. First, they point to symbolic problems in contemporary society: some youth cannot find any sense in life, they search for new resistant configurations to triumph over modernity (Castells 1996, 1997). So, the rise and fall of extreme youth subcultures represents fluctuations in their quest for sense and meaning, and also signifies their attempts to find new reinterpretations of, or new adaptations to, the harsh realities of current urban life (Fornäs and Bolin 1995). Secondly, the enduring presence of parallel yet diverse skinhead subcultures in the major cities of the world indicates effects of globalization, in particular the softening of formal national–ethnic–religious boundaries, concomitant with a crisis in ideologies and the reinvention of some strong political or religious identities.

Some claim that the deep roots of the phenomenon lie in the withering away of Christianity in Europe in terms of practice. For example, Christian deconstruction has resulted in a plethora of alternative beliefs among young people and the progression of mystical-esoteric influence (Champion and Cohen 1999). It is suggested that this trend leads young people to a more personal faith, freer and more full of hope – the construction of a more relativist and autonomous belief framework (Lambert 1998). This trend has seen the domination of a lax morality – permissiveness, lack of direction, emphasis on personal autonomy – in fact a cultural Christianity. This has been described by Willaime (2005) as an ultra-modern reinvention of religion – forms of tradition radically reconfigured. In the case of 'Christian skinheads' we can see that this is no exaggeration.

Multi-level identifications and skinheads

I turn now to the ways in which skinhead subcultures interact during the construction process of multi-level identities. I look first at these processes in contemporary society in general, and secondly at the specific situation of the youth scene in France.

Skinheads and youth culture in France

In contemporary societies we are confronted with rising economic and cultural *globalization* and the development of pluri-cultural and pluri-ethnic societies, in which a variety of identities is constituted at the level of individual and collective subjectivity (Castells 1997). At the same time we have to deal with the problem of growing racism, violence and insecurity, as a result of the stigmatization of certain young people – especially young men – in the economic field. These young people react by opposition to processes of economic, commercial and computer globalization, aggressively rejecting and resisting these new challenges and changes. Skinhead culture as a collective identity today mobilizes a form of violent protest in relation to the globalization process. As Bauman (1998) points out, globalization provokes multi-faceted transformations, which others such as Harvey (1989) have referred to as space–time compression constituting new segregations, exclusions and hierarchies arising from transnational movements of labour and capital. The need for ontological security (Giddens 1991) triggers the trend towards 'localisation' (Hall 1991) and the reinvention of traditional identities (Bauman 1995).

So, first, while a global élite dominates relations within the space of flows (Castells 1996), there are sections of the population who still live on the extreme margins of this process, stigmatized and drawn towards a rigid 'us and them' mentality, to violence and rejection of societal norms. At the same time, as Bauman argues, the 'new middle class' between these two extreme poles endures and reacts with a significant identity crisis, reflecting insecurity, and fear of the future (Beck 1992; Bauman 1998). I argue that one of the main sources of skinhead racism in France is a personal sense of being excluded socially, economically and politically. For those young men embracing skinhead culture, finding a legitimate identity is a crucial search in the social, political and cultural field. The construction of their special skinhead identity is concerned with the effect of exclusion (Petrova 1998: 128–37).

According to recent theoretical debate on increasing social fragmentation and flexibility (Touraine 1992, 1994, 1997; Beck, Giddens and Lash 1994), there are new risks and new changes in relation to the destabilization of youth integration because modern urban social structure is broken up into micro-structures with many subdivisions, which either work together or separately. It is proposed that skinheads seek and find refuge in the do it yourself (DIY) micro-structures characteristic of many global contemporary youth cultures, yet are split into subgroups and branches where they represent a range of temporal resistant youth identifications. Thus, to be a skinhead in France is not just a matter of simple subcultural identification, but also designates the appearance of new aspirations among certain sectors of young people, pertinent to expedient socio-political issues and patterns.

Second, in France young people from both European and non-European backgrounds take a variety of positions with respect to racial integration and globalization of labour and financial markets. With regard to the new Europe – economic union – different skinhead groups resemble each other in the way they mutually refuse the existing status quo. Thus, from the data, extreme-right skinheads are opposed to commercial and banking Europe and aim at building a cultural Europe – racially exclusive. In contrast, red (left-wing) skinheads are for the construction of a social Europe. They are protesting against official European policy, which is still exclusive about the integration of extra-European Mediterranean countries, and rejects wider frontiers for Europe. So, for racist skinheads multiculturalism represents chaos, while for red skinheads, who idealize interbreeding in multiculturalism, the globalization process is the only postmodern solution with a future.

Therefore, as an *alternative* youth scene, skinhead culture in France is the site of a very real conflict between anti-racist youth and white race partisans. The defence of racial difference or its violent rejection is now a crucial point of attitudinal variation, and even skinheads are split into several branches on this issue. While racist skinhead attitudes are perhaps better known, there are also anti-racist skinhead groups, for example, SHARP (skinheads against racial prejudice) and red or Communist skinheads. These latter skinheads often join in solidarity with immigrant gangs and extreme-left students.

The social construction of skinhead identities

Skinhead youth culture is inspired by past class struggle and this represents the main similarity between all the different kinds of skinheads. In their characteristic nostalgia for traditional values in historical and social conflicts, as workers, as representatives of a working-class movement, contemporary skinheads are at the crossroads between industrial (early modern) and postmodern societies (Touraine 1969, 1992). Emulating workers in the past, they aim at rebuilding a mythical community based on solidarity, a recovery of the magical working-class community (Clarke 1976) in a modern tribe (Maffesoli 1988). Skinhead style originally grew out of a need to rediscover positive symbolic value as members of the working class (Fangen 1998). Their fundamental social identification is as a true proletarian.

Yet skinheads themselves are no longer usually the sons of traditional working-class men. Their social identity constitutes the unreal, mythical and nostalgic, referring to the mythologized past rather than the actual present, emphasizing particular symbols and issues. For example, skinheads often idolize the ancient European warrior tribes – Celts or Vikings. However, identities also develop through key static local ideas such as nation, ethnicity, region, city, even suburb. Through fear of having no identity (Bauman 1998) and faced with the dissolution of traditional collective identities in a more and more atomistic postmodern world, each individual in skinhead culture develops a diversity of memberships which he (more rarely she) applies according to the situation, in a logical progression from the general to the specific – from alternative youth culture in the broadest sense down to highly localized skinhead practices. Problems occur when skinheads develop a hierarchical attitude towards the range of diverse identities, and this fosters the emergence of chauvinistic and nationalistic identifications. In this case, local identity (especially whiteness) can be used to express anti-cosmopolitan feelings, and is associated with certain racist references. A similar identification and blaming process develops for members of some other male working-class youth groups such as bikers and trash-metal fans, and football hooligans (Mignon 1998). We can understand these identities as representing a set of concentric and overlapping spheres of identification. For example, at the local level they may own a city identity like Parisian skinheads, or Marseilles skinheads. Moving to a wider sphere of reference they may own urban or rural identities, for instance mobilizing against the destruction of traditional life styles in the country. Regional identities range northerners against southerners. Ethnic identity is paramount, especially being white in the face of the massive arrival in France of people of colour. There is also national identity – being French against the rest of the world. This segues into ownership of European identity – to be stridently European against people originating from Africa and elsewhere.

Most French skinheads own urban identities. They refuse the 'back to nature myth' of hippies and ferals, identifying with the urban landscape. They are the children of urban crisis expressing anomie and fear, as they themselves often say. Wherever skinheads are present in the countryside, traditional society in the local rural district or village is certain to be in a process of destabilization or transformation (Dubet and Lapeyronnie 1985), particularly through large-scale immigration combined with industrialization. French skinheads often define themselves as Breton, Norman, Corsican, Alsacian, Walloon, Flemish and so on, referring to their region of origin with pride. Furthermore, they will openly acknowledge if one of their parents or grand-parents comes from Poland, Russia, Italy, Portugal or even Turkey. In short, they are not usually against *European* multi-ethnic society, as such. In part because the French model of national integration has not been very efficient, skinheads idealize the idea of Europe as a union of European peoples, as a throwback to the Viking or Celtic era. According to the interviews, racist skinheads take this to the extreme, speaking of a 'white cultural Europe' or a 'white working-class Europe' stretching from the Atlantic to the Urals. They reject the postmodern order of non-European immigration and integration: 'Globalization? Inter-breeding? This is like trying to squash unstructured and rootless people into a huge world brothel! Instead of that shit, we are for a wide federal European State' (Mad, suburbs of Paris, 1995).

Red skinheads, in contrast, are generally anti-racist, they idealize multiculturalism and pluralism, ambivalence and alternative structures – a postmodern identity solution (Bauman 1995). Yet all skinhead identity formulation remains fuelled by unemployment, under-employment or the threat of those conditions. So for example, racist skinheads' anti-immigration position calls for the defence of a French working-class identity, but this is identified as a white working-class identity since they perceive the problem in terms of race. Racist skinheads take European white cultural identity as the benchmark for legitimate social identity, preaching not only racism but anti-Semitism, xenophobia and anti-Communism. Actual or threatened local unemployment may be only the starting point, but we should not lose sight of it.

The construction of racist skinhead identity

Racist skinhead ideology often represents a muddled syncretism of political, religious, aesthetic and biological references and myths. Skinheads try to construct a collective identity apart from other youth, driven by their subjective feelings of exclusion and cultural uprooting. A primary source of their violent behaviour is protest against being excluded socially, economically and politically. For racist skinheads, the main characteristics of their oppositional identity are identity hatred and jealousy (Sibony 1997). The anti-immigration position constitutes their solution to the improvement of living conditions for disenfranchized white working-class youth. Racist skinheads justify their violent racist attacks in these terms. Rejection of interbreeding is central. Racial purity is central to their ideology and explains everything for them. Moreover, taking their cue from Nazism, they propose a phantasmagorical anti-Semitism, where the Jew is seen as representative of a transnational mega-economic plot, a secret world conspiracy. Both the anti-Semitic Hammer Skins and 'Skins of the pagan god Thor' claim that the United States is blighted by a 'Zionist Occupation Government' (ZOG).

Historical sources and political identities of French skinheads

Political identities refer primarily to historical symbols and myths, for example, references to Communism by Communist skins (oriented to the extreme-left), and references to fascism or neo-Nazism by racist skinheads (oriented to the extreme-right). So while extreme-left skinheads wear the hammer and sickle on redskin jackets, extreme-right skinheads wear Nazi or neo-Nazi signs. Communism and fascism are historical references calling on European collective memory. Although both kinds of skinheads are opposed to civil democracy and want a strong state, there is often violent conflict between them since political identification is symbolically polarized.

Yet in fact most skinheads are not members of political parties or movements. Even racist skinheads usually refuse formal affiliation to extreme-right political organizations. If they have any unifying loyalty, it is to violence. So ironically their quest for political order is actually hindered by their violent attitude. According to my data, right-wing skinheads, the most numerous in France, try to represent themselves for the media and journalists as the iconic skinheads, defining extreme violence as their principal means of expression and action. We need to understand why these skinheads identify so strongly with violence.

Skinhead violence

Skinheads appeared in France in the late 1970s and are recognized as an enduring urban youth subculture. To this day their distinctive lifestyle and rebellious attitude continues to rely on their collective memory of the history of the 'movement' and its origins. Following the example of the original British skinheads, European skinheads initially looked for radical symbols of protest and forms of marginality, so as to shock and scandalize everyone – aspiring to outdo the punks. Late 1970s skinheads in England, France and Germany shaved their heads and proclaimed themselves extremists and *antisocial*; they wanted to be much rougher than the punks. They were also associated with football hooligans in violent civil disorder. In late 1970s France they claimed to be 'the last and only revolutionary representatives of young people', according to one informant.

In the early 1980s, certain ex-punks joined them, becoming 'skunks' – a hybrid subculture of skinheads and punks. But in contrast to punks, right-wing skinheads extolled extreme racist rhetoric and real violence. Punk violence was theatricalized to express anger, to show off in public, to call for public recognition, to exercise social or political influence. Politically they leaned to the left. Conversely, pushing radicalism, certain skinheads in France, England and Germany started to join extreme-right movements. According to informants, they saw this political rhetoric as the most radical – the extreme-right was seen to be more revolutionary. Fascist and Nazi symbols and gestures were celebrated as radical rebellious symbols – the swastika, the Celtic cross, the sunwheel – combined with provocative violent actions.

Since then, French skinheads have been divided into extreme-right skins (neo-Nazis) and extreme-left skins (Communist skins). Intergroup violence thus became a real and present factor in skinhead practice. However, we must remember that the construction of skinhead violence is intrinsically concerned with the effect of exclusion (Petrova 1998): 'We are skinheads because we are marginalized, uprooted in the big cities. We are totally lost in those fucking cities' (Jeff, Paris suburban area, 1991).

Feeling 'lost'; finding an identity in social, political and cultural fields (Bourdieu 1984) is a crucial question for them. Violence provides a pathway to this end. There are three main forms of skinhead violence identified in my data and discussed below. My findings confirm the research of Peralva (1994), who lists the following: anomic infra-political violence – haphazard and occasional (including sport riots); political participation in extreme-right action and racist attacks, and media or virtual reality violence – used especially in relation to journalists and television broadcasters. Generally, the intensity of skinhead violence depends on the way in which these three levels of violence are combined. As Peralva (1994: 151–3) points out, without extreme-right discourse, skinhead violence is 'blind violence' – a matter of fighting against all others.

Right skinheads' infra-political violence concerns their 'infra-racist attitudes', also xenophobia, sexism, anti-Communism (for infra-racism see Wieviorka 1991), although some violent action has to do with organized underworld crime connected with gangs like the *Hells Angels*. In principle, skinheads refuse drugs, instead drinking excessive amounts of beer, especially at events like football matches and rock concerts which often end, for them, in fights. They claim a particular territory as their own, and have some violent initiation rites such as 'beating-in'. Extreme violence is enacted against passers-by, high-school students ('middle-class kids'), alcoholics, drug addicts, homosexuals, but particularly against people of colour. Violence is used by racist skinheads especially to inspire fear and to force immigrants to move house. Some skinheads though are just petty criminals and thugs motivated by greed and/or lack of resources to carry out vehicle thefts, robbery in supermarkets, forgery of official papers or cheques, burglary, and so on. In this, their violent civil offences are close to those of other youngsters from under-privileged areas operating in the territorial groups of their peers:

> Why did I become a skinhead? When I was a kid, I was already in a gang, always out on the street . . . I was often beaten in the head, that was it . . . I wanted to be normal, but . . . I mean working, having a family of my own and all that stuff, you know . . . I almost got to have one, but after that I went to jail.
>
> (Frankky, Paris, 1992)

The leaders of skinhead groups operate a particularly strong discourse of resentment against exclusion. They just cannot stand to be smashed down (as they see it) and integrated into a multicultural society they did not choose: 'I totally hate integration. I don't want to integrate into an immigrant society just to please the government, because it loves immigrants and wishes to integrate all of them' (Jacques, Paris, 1991).

They believe that they constitute a national and pan-European 'movement', not simply 'gangs or groups of delinquents': 'The skinhead is seen as somebody who drinks, who is stupid, bad and hyper-aggressive, but behind that there is our whole political programme' (Olive, Paris, 1992).

However, in the eyes of the community, police and certain political or legal authorities they are seen as *bandes* (gangs) and juvenile delinquents. It is indeed difficult to accept their laissez-faire attitude to violence:

> As a skinhead, I like attacking anarchists and Communists. We beat punks, red-skins and Zulus. Or drug-dealers, homosexuals . . . but immigrants are victims just like we are. The immigrant is an oppressed person, just like we are. The true oppressors are the Jews, liberal capitalism and liberal socialism. I would accept being stabbed for my ideals, you know.
>
> (Paul, Paris, 1992)

Unusually, for this informant violence was not ostensibly about resentment of immigrants. Understanding how they construct masculinity is important for understanding skinhead groups' reaction to the threat of globalization. Their protest, masculinity exemplified in violence, constitutes a gendered rejection of the values of progress and modernity. Generally speaking, very few girls participate in skinhead groups, unlike punks, many of whom are young women. In the case of extreme-right skinheads where violence is used as a tool to gain recognition or to act in a special political sphere, hegemonic masculine identification refers to the normative or traditional identity of men, with values referenced to a largely imagined past in which male and female roles were strictly defined and divided.

> Concerning male–female identity, ask any skinhead – he'll answer the same way. We believe a woman can choose her job, she may ask for abortion or divorce; but if she is married, her man must rule at home, or else there is anarchy! Men have conquered women, as well as corn, horses, dogs and cows.
>
> (Jacques, Paris, 1992)

It is possible that this putative ownership of women is related to the perceived threat of interbreeding, that women must be controlled in order to keep racial purity. At any rate, such views are a significant aspect of French extreme-right skinhead discourse about the way the world should be for men.

Racial and political violence

In the French press one reads daily about racist attacks and other criminal behaviour by extreme-right skinheads, particularly violence directed towards immigrant suburban youth groups – *bandes* like Zulu-Nation, Red Foxes, Red Warriors and so on. While the press do not always recognize the political dimension of this racialized violence, for ultra right-wing skinheads, having a recognized political identity is a very important aspect of their legitimization strategies (see Olive's comments above). Like other youth, they seek to gain recognition in the public domain and escape from marginality (Dubet

1987). Racialized violence is their principal strategy in achieving this quest. Extreme-right skinhead political violence is the unofficial expression of a particular political discourse – that of extreme-right politics in France which says 'I have nothing against Blacks and Arabs, as long as they stay in their own countries and as long as they come here as tourists only!' Skinheads who are politically aligned with the typical *Le Pen* position make use of targeted violence: against immigrants, their homes and goods. But for many extreme-right skinheads, traditional nationalism seems to be 'too corny today, too reactionary and old-fashioned'. They prefer strong action. In the framework of a sense of crisis regarding national identity in France, anti-immigration violence constitutes their compelling solution to the improvement of conditions for 'ordinary' youth in the suburbs. They refer back to the imagined glory of working-class struggle in defence of this strategy. The following quote describes succinctly the narrative logic of this political position:

> My granddad was a Communist, a tough one, a real one. He fought for his ideas, for getting more paid holidays and all that stuff, but he would never understand the way those bloody foreigners profit from it now, bringing whole tribes here from Africa, all their wives that they declare as their cousins, etc. Then, they steal from us our social advantages, the few jobs we have, and we are the ones done over. And then we were harassed by blacks and Arabs at the school gates, and one day we were just fed up! Enough words, time for action.
>
> (Paul, Paris, 1992)

Extreme-right skinheads' anti-immigration position calls for the use of violence to aid protection of a white (male) working-class identity, or European white cultural identity. It contains other prejudicial elements: racism, xenophobia, neo-Nazism, neo-fascism, anti-Communism, ultra-militarism and sexism. The violence is real: verbal and physical attacks against non-whites, physical assaults, sexual offences, intimidation, petty theft, armed robbery, arson – against immigrant dwellings or vehicles, but also against the favoured fashion shops or goods of rival youth gangs – even homicide. In public space extreme-right skinheads engage in street fights for territorial power or for ideological reasons with knives, razor blades, bicycle chains, iron fists and other weapons like baseball bats and riot-guns. So can we even speak of any extreme-right skinhead ideology in the context of violence on this scale? The argument here is that there seems to be something there of an ideological nature, functioning as a justification for their racial violence. When all their comments are examined and their actions observed, we can perceive what appears to be a quasi-tribal syncretism of different political, religious and aesthetic references combined with a muddle of medieval myths. We hear the skinheads defining themselves as *neo-barbarians*, *neo-pagans* or *postmodern desperadoes*. Their greatest contempt is reserved for people of mixed race. Racial interbreeding is seen as a betrayal of one's own culture, and thus strictly forbidden:

> A half-breed person has no country, no culture. He lives in an empty space, like in a no-man's-land. Take the *Beurs*, for example [second or third generation children of Arab parents living in France]. They're a sub-race; neither French nor Arab. In France they're Arab shit, and back in Algeria they're also nothing. Islam is good for Arabs living happily in an Arab nation, but that's not here. They can't find any big Arab nation in France.
>
> (Jacques, Paris, 1992)

In the following set of quotes, we can see how the categories of those to be reviled are piled on each other in a random sequence indicating the muddled syncretism mentioned above. Jacques begins with a statement against transnational commodified symbols of youth culture, then shifts to a denigration of American racism, implying a lack of social capital. 'We are against the hamburger and Coca-Cola culture. In the United States people are totally segregationist; they don't have any contact with each other. Blacks are killing each other inside their ghettos.' He then mentions Jews. Borrowing from Nazi anti-Semitism, the Jew is seen by extreme-right skinheads as the representative of an economic mega-plot and secret world conspiracy:

> It's the whites and Jews who rule, but they are completely degenerate. The United States, world capitalism and economic globalization want to make us mere consumers of their fucking products. We are for people power, like the *Sans-Culottes*. We are for eradicating unemployment.

Having expressed the political position of defending the interests of the ordinary working man, he then moves to talking about immigrants:

> We don't really have anything against the immigrant. We don't like him, but the real enemy is the one who opened up unlimited access to immigration – the liberal capitalist. The immigrant is just as done in as we are. He is an outcast just like us. The one who oppresses, the only guilty one, is the Semite – the mercantile Jew.
>
> (Jacques, Paris, 1992)

This last set of statements mixes racism, anti-Semitism and anti-capitalism, laced with populist references. In itself it stands as fairly typical of the ideological position of extreme-right skinheads.

Broadcast media and skinhead violence

Skinheads not only use actual physical violence, they also rely on the broadcast media to represent their violence in 'virtual' reality. This form of violence is employed to increase their popular support and win them a place in the public sphere through media attention. As Peralva pointed out (1994: 152) it is clear enough that skinheads are to a great extent a media phenomenon. They have open access to a mass audience through staged violence, specially arranged to be filmed, which corresponds to a journalistic demand. Skinhead violence is often exaggerated for broadcast media. It is systematically theatricalized and in a sense, even commercialized, as the following quote shows:

> When we hit somebody, it is a staged event. Society understands, through us, that there is a real problem with immigration. If we hadn't swung at the immigrants, people would have never realized that there is a race problem in France with an 'everyday racist' attitude behind it. If there weren't any real racist issues in France, no one would talk about us, we would not be filmed for TV and there would be no public debate about the point.
>
> (Blondy, Brest, 1995)

He implies that skinheads 'reveal' the race problem through their acts of violence, not create it. Skinheads use the broadcast media in a highly instrumental way to put race issues on the public agenda. They also take part in extreme-right meetings which get lots of media coverage. They appear in the stands during media-saturated football matches. As the most spectacular and vivid supporters they are immediately caught on camera. One informant claimed that 'stadiums are the only space of freedom for us. They're our true public scene'. Data confirms that skinheads like being interviewed on television and by press journalists, and they readily agreed to participate in television documentaries on violence, youth cultures and extreme-right movements. Ironically, although the media condemn skinheads and call for restrictions on their activities, intense media coverage only encourages the violence, making it more extreme. Skinheads claim that broadcast media coverage of their violence increases popular support for their tactics, for example:

> I see more and more people yelling 'bravo' when we beat an immigrant in the street. They are just normal people: men and women, old people, nice looking people like you, not like me, no, but like you . . . and they say, 'Bravo boys, go get 'em! We're fed up with those immigrants!

This informant then switched the discourse to anti-capitalism:

> I'd rather beat up some big boss with a Mercedes, who gets those wagonloads of immigrants into France to work for 1,000 francs per month, but I can't find him! So, I'm doing what I can with what I've got. And actually, we are doing a far better job for the citizens than the police are!
>
> (Big Mike, Paris suburbs, 1995)

Skinheads regard themselves as urban vigilantes. It seems as though the approval of 'ordinary' French people legitimizes their violent tactics.

As this implies, there are various forms of skinhead violence, from the general to the specific, from the physical to the virtual. Furthermore, there are different stages of identification with violence in skinhead youth culture. In theory, each skinhead is able to pass sequentially through the various stages, moving from anomic violence to targeted violence, to staged violence for the media. Many of the informants quoted above are skinhead gang leaders, who speak on behalf of their members, many of whom may be far less articulate and focused about the meaning of their subcultural practices. So at a greater level of distinction between young right-wing skinheads within their groups, it can argued that leading figures tend to identify themselves with infra-political, racist and media/virtual forms of violence as they try to lead the group in political participation and ideology. But the majority of their ordinary skinhead followers usually identify themselves with just infra-political violence – fighting other youth gangs and political constituencies, only occasionally dabbling in the other forms of violence. Although we must note that for some, their level of identification with violence tends towards the criminal, and towards forms of lucrative intimidation. Finally, there are singers and/or musicians in skinhead rock bands (making so-called 'oi' music) who are usually linked only peripherally to skinhead gangs. They tend to identify only with media/virtual violence, in a theatrical and symbolic way.

Skinhead collective identity in relation to other youth groups

It is important to recognize skinheads as belonging to a specific youth culture, even if a spectacular and confronting one. Skinheads as a youth group also operate a cultural model of references, as Lagree (1982) wrote about beatniks, hippies and punks from the 1960s to the 1970s. They do not exist in a generational vacuum and we must examine skinheads' collective identity related to other youth groups. And skinhead youth culture is first of all culturally defined. The music is distinctive, as is the look, the dance, justifications and ideology – the collective lifestyle shared by members of a group. Skinhead collective identity also refers to a certain collective memory – a movement with its own history. This is based on some common social characteristics and personal biographies.

Although they have very varied family backgrounds – some of the leading figures are well educated, from upper middle-class families – most skinheads are unemployed young adult men, with experiences of family dislocation, violence and substance abuse. As indicated previously, skinheads constitute a masculinist cultural group. Skinhead collective identities are usually constructed in alternative or marginal ways, apart from legitimate institutions, and in connection with other youth subcultures (in relation to rejection or acceptance). The break with society begins in the teenage years at school and then becomes exacerbated by troubles with the police and the law when they gather to form gangs. Skinheads define themselves as existing in a world of strict 'us' and 'them' boundaries, and their cultural identity develops in relation to other types of subcultures, to other young people and to other generations.

With regard to other types of subcultures the question of differentiation often rests on political participation: to be or not to be politically active. Skinheads tend to participate in alternative politics, looking for new forms of participating in politics, 'every day life politics', although this often looks a lot like urban vigilantism. For extreme-right skinheads having a distinctive, even shocking political identity is a very important part of their legitimization strategies; gaining recognition in the public domain and escaping from marginality. They achieve this by gang warfare and street battles with other politically-defined youth cultural gangs. But for yet other skinhead groups, politics is not so attractive and they refuse all kinds of official political participation. They proclaim themselves culturally and politically independent, even neutral, not-belonging, for example French Trojan skinheads. Leaning to the left, although not in a formal political sense, these skinheads are nostalgic for an original working class, they refer to social justice and equality, to anti-capitalist struggles. They are more open to multi-ethnic society and to globalization. Their cultural identity as skinheads is more ambiguous and they are more nomadic, mixing and fraternizing with other youth cultures. Just like the first skinheads, they have black friends, but in principle they don't like the Arabs – *les Beurs*. Similarly, their British antecedents were in agreement with the Jamaican Rudies or Rude Boys but not with the 'Pakis' – Pakistani and Indian youth (Hebdige 1979).

Skinhead youth in France really are very different – more extreme – than other French youth in their practices, appearance, ideology and lifestyle. It is really only in skinheads' plans for the future that they were found to be not too much different from other young people. The research found that like most youth, they aspired to find interesting jobs with elements of creativity and responsibility. Like other French youth they seemed to be very active in the use of the internet, English language words and phrases, and music fandom. For leisure they said they wanted international concerts and travel. At this level of identity, then, despite their celebration of past warlike tribes, they seemed typically postmodern and globalized (Castells 1997; Ruano-Borbalan 1998).

Concerning relationships with other generations, they claim to feel closer to their grandparents' generation, and desire to maintain their forebears' cultural traditions, festivities and values. What they hope to pass on to their own children is pictured primarily through the affirmation of this cultural identity, strongly linked to the idealized past.

Conceptualizing skinhead identity in France

Skinheads' individual autonomous identification (self-identity) appears during the phase of adhesion to an alternative set of values, and rejection of a mainstream legitimate identity. In the making of skinhead identity, despite the diversity of groups and political orientations, there is the crucial point of definition of self and of other. We can identify some general tendencies involved in this 'us' and 'them' process – the expression of which is violence.

First, in contemporary societies, civil, national, religious and political identities are transmitted less and less through the family and traditional institutions owing to the global transformation of different major institutional structures. This is linked to political democratization and the rise of individualistic behaviour. Young people do not have simple lives any more. Their lives are complex and full of risks. They are encouraged towards individualistic – atomistic – solutions (see Furlong and Cartmel 1997). Secondly, an ontological identity like that of the skinhead is not a static thing. It is a process, constructed over time, from early adolescence well into adulthood. Its starting point is in the family but it is sustained and shaped through contacts with others (Dubar 2000). Affirmation of difference from mainstream culture is the most distinctive youth subcultural element. For most youth subcultures, the definition of 'insiders' and 'outsiders' is crucial for group membership and solidarity. Members operate their social and cultural practices according to ingroup–outgroup boundaries and define their own style in opposition – us and them – to other subcultures. In skinhead culture this oppositional formation in relation to the other is radical and violent.

In skinhead subculture it is always a matter of violence and opposition towards imaginary 'enemies'. This is the rationale for skinhead group formation – to fight the enemy group. Yet at the same time a skinhead will behave as a solitary individual who hardly belongs to any collective group identification – if they cannot find any enemy, they will fight with each other. They often fight with other skinhead groups coming from different towns or districts, even if they share a political ideology. Thus, the feeling of skinhead group allegiance is primarily constituted in confrontational behaviour towards others, in rough and aggressive opposition to almost everyone else in the society. However, it should also be emphasized that because individual identity is always stronger than skinheads' collective identity, the dynamics between collective and individual identity contain some possibilities for change or reversal of the situation; possibly moving either towards collective assimilation into other youth groups or towards an individual break with the subculture and reintegration with other young people, even replacing the group identity eventually with a professional or family identity.

Conclusion

Being a 'skinhead' seems a temporary youth identification, but the age frontiers stretch out further and further. The model skinhead, according to references and identification, is on average 35 years old in England, with some dating from the first generation of skinheads there. Like other youth cultures, skinhead subculture illuminates important processes and dynamics in the formation of different identities of global youth in contemporary France, illustrating in a very radical and spectacular way certain characteristics of the wider global/cultural process. Hybridized French skinhead culture builds on international skinhead subcultural models, but these are referenced locally, in terms of job loss, immigration and urban alienation. From the beginning, the range of French skinhead identities was formed in relation to three main processes of change in contemporary Europe: the collapse of Communism in Eastern Europe and the lack of strong ideologies; the crisis in the working class, and the effects of globalization.

The rolling out of these changes has reformulated traditional skinhead identity for French youth. In the variety of (sub)urban skinhead groups we can glimpse new kinds of citizenship claims. In the case of red-skinheads we can see the emergence of pluri-ethnic-multicultural identities which look towards a genuinely multicultural world. In the case of extreme-right skinheads we can see the disturbing emergence of ethno-national-community identities and cultural resistance to the globalization processes, which look toward authoritarian forms of governance and cultural boundary maintenance – perhaps even ethnic cleansing. In the case of Hammer Skins and Internet Skins as a generational trend, we can see the re-emergence of strong anti-Semitic feelings and nostalgic pro-Aryan white race sentiments.

Most contemporary skinheads, living in the French metropolis or the suburbs, claim to be anti-postmodern. They are protesting against consumerism, the free market system, and especially marketing, which they see as unfair mental manipulation of human beings. They reject 'computer imperialism', and the formation of what they imagine to be a world police conspiracy in America directed by a new powerful transnational élite – acting against all kind of rebels, differences, and spontaneous or individualistic activism. Accordingly, around the end of the 1990s and the beginning of the new century, some alternative skinhead formations appeared that mixed up extreme-right and extreme-left orientations. So, they became more invisible for the establishment and simultaneously affirmed themselves as alternative, living in parallel. Others reacted by forming very small groups, radical or very conservative, but all claiming to work 'for saving the spirituality of the world'. At present, many skinheads represent intensely hybrid identity formations – complex meaning-making at the group level. They combine proto-Asiatic myths, European legends from primitive or medieval tribes with their pagan gods and beliefs, with Darwinist theories of evolution, or with Christian ideals of equality and justice. All use historical figures of what is for them the representation of the warrior, hero or the martyr. So they identify themselves with Samurais, with Viking or Celtic leaders, with Trojans or gladiators. Using French history, they take themselves to be *Chouan* (historically situated in the past French pro-monarchic movement), or *Charlemagne* skins, or *Sans-Culottes* revolutionary skins. And then, like many other countries there are Christian skinheads.

And from the data it seems that when all these identifications are not enough, they invent extra-terrestrial life, or science-fiction versions (*Matrix*-style) of identity. All this imagery implies a claim for a completely free imagination, living in the past or in the future, mixing social and political beliefs with childish dreams, going beyond limitations. It can be seen as an argument for eternal youthfulness, in the face of cold rationality, Middle East wars and European mercantilism. At the same time, their myth-making symbolizes the ideal of becoming a fully integrated person, of identity practices that stand in for ontological lack, that reflect the loss of strong primordial identities. It is a profound statement of finally taking part in the adult world.

However, this is largely achieved through the free expression of violence, seen as natural self-defence against other groups and gang attacks in contemporary insecure society. The racism is provocative but deeply felt, the nationalism is chauvinistic and locally referenced. Everywhere, French skinheads claim to be from the same white nation, integrating a few coloured associates, some of whom identify themselves 'as more or less white', like some skinheads in Brazil. Central is the fraternity principle during fighting. Their values are constituted as universal, glorious, tragic: courage, blood and honour. They define themselves as members of a supremacist nation – like skinheads in Japan – according to their speeches. They prefer imagining the past or the future, affirming their rupture with present society.

In short, French skinheads are always altering identities, and shifting space dimensions in relation to the expression of violence, yet they still want a New Order. They want their demands for individual liberty to be heard. They say: let's keep our youthful, rebellious attitude as long as possible – let's destroy to rebuild. In this we may glimpse a kind of residual 'punk' heritage in contemporary French skinhead subculture.

Bibliography

Baron, S.W. (1997) 'Canadian male street skinheads: street gang or street terrorists?', *Canadian Revue of Sociology and Anthropology*, 43(2): 125–54.
Bauman, Z. (1995) *Life in Fragments: essays in postmodern morality*, Oxford: Blackwell.
—— (1998) *Le Goût Humain de la Mondialisation*, Paris: Hachette Littératures.
Beck, U. (1992) *Risk Society: towards a new modernity*, London: Sage.
——, Giddens, A. and Lash, S. (1994) *Reflexive Modernisation: politics, tradition and aesthetics in the modern social order*, Cambridge: Polity Press.
Bourdieu, P. (1984) [1979] *Distinction: a social critique of the judgement of taste*, trans. R. Nice, Cambridge, MA: Harvard University Press.

Castells, M. (1996) *The Rise of the Network Society, The Information Age: economy, society and culture*, vol. 1, Oxford: Blackwell.
—— (1997) *The Power of Identity, The Information Age: economy, society and culture*, vol. 2, Oxford: Blackwell.
Champion, F. and Cohen, M. (1999) *Sectes et Démocratie*, Paris: Éditions Seuil.
Clarke, J. (1976) 'Skinheads and the magical recovery of community', in S. Hall and T. Jefferson (eds) *Resistance through Rituals*, London: Hutchinson.
da Costa, M.R. (1993) *Carecasos do Subirbio: os caminhos de um nomadismo moderno*, Petropolis: Vozes.
—— (2004) 'Tribos urbanas, communidade Zadoque e os carecas de Cristo', in J. Machado and L.M. Blass (eds) *Tribos Urbanas*, Lisbon: ICS (Institute of Social Sciences).
Dubar, C. (2000) *La Crise des Identités: l'interprétation d'une mutation*, Paris: Presses Universitaires de France
Dubet, F. (1987) *La Galère: jeunes en survie*, Paris: Éditions Fayard.
—— and Lapeyronnie, D. (1985) *L'État et les Jeunes*, Paris: Éditions Ouvrière.
Fangen, K. (1998) 'Right-wing skinheads – nostalgia and binary oppositions', *Young*, 6(2): 33–49.
Farin, K. (1997) 'Urban rebels: die Geschichte der Skinhead bewegung', in K. Farin (ed.) *Die Skins: mythos und realität*, Berlin: Verlag.
Fornäs, J. and Bolin, G. (1995) *Youth Culture in Late Modernity*, London: Sage.
Furlong, A. and Cartmel, F. (1997) *Young People and Social Change: individualization and risk in late modernity*, Buckingham: Open University Press.
Giddens, A. (1991) *Modernity and Self-identity: self and society in the late modern age*, Cambridge: Polity Press.
Groffman, A.C. (2001) *Das Unvollendete Drama: Jugend und Skinheadgruppen im Vereinigungsprozess*, Opladen: Leske and Budrich.
Hall, S. (1991) 'The local and the global', in A. King (ed.) *Culture, Globalization and the World-System*, London: Macmillan Press.
Harvey, D. (1989) *The Condition of Postmodernity*, Oxford: Blackwell.
Hebdige, D. (1979) *Subculture: the meaning of style*, New York: Methuen.
Heitmann, H. (1997) 'Die skinhead-studie', in K. Farin (ed.) *Die Skins: mythos und realität*, Berlin: Verlag.
Knight, S.A. (2002) 'On the margins of whiteness: skinhead subculture in northern California', Research Thesis in Anthropology, Sacramento: California State University.
Lagree, J.-C. (1982) *Les Jeunes Chantent leurs Cultures*, Paris: Éditions L'Harmattan.
Lambert, Y. (1998) 'Les jeunes et la religion: un cadrage général', *Agora /Débats Jeunesses Revue*, 9(3): 23–32.
Maffesoli, M. (1988) *Le Temps des Tribus: le déclin de l'individualisme dans les sociétés de masse*, Paris: Éditions Méridiens-Klinksieck.
Mignon, P. (1998) *La Passion du Football*, Paris: O. Jacob.
Moore, D. (1994) *The Lads in Action: social process in an urban youth subculture*, Aldershot: Arena.
Nesterov, D. (2004) *Skiny: Rus' Probuzdaetsya*, Moscow: UltraKultura.
Peralva, A. (1994) 'La violence skinhead', in P. Perrineau (ed.) *L'Engagement Politique: déclin ou mutation?* Paris: Presses de la Fondation Nationale des Sciences Politiques.
—— (1996) 'Être skinhead, une identité politique?' in J. Chevallier (ed.) *L'Identité Politique*, Paris: Presses Universitaires de France.

Perho, S. (2001) 'Features of racist sub(culture) among youth in Joensuu', in V. Puuronen (ed.) *Youth on the Threshold of the 3rd Millennium*, Joensuu: University of Joensuu/Karelian Institute Publications.

Petrova Y. (1998) 'Skinheads ou le racisme des jeunes exclus', *Ville-Ecole-Intégration Revue*, Montrouge: National Centre for Pedagogical Documentation, 115 (December): 123–47.

Pfahl-Traughber, A. (1999) *Rechtsextremismus in Der Bundesrepublik*, Munich: C.H. Beck.

Ruano-Borbalan, J.-C. (ed.) (1998) *L'Identité*, Paris: Human Science Editions.

Sibony, D. (1997) *Le 'Racisme' ou la Haine Identitaire*, Paris: Christian Bourgeois.

Touraine, A. (1969) *La Société Post-industrielle*, Paris: Denoël.

—— (1992) *Critique de la Modernité*, Paris: Éditions Fayard.

—— (1994) *Qu'est-ce que c'est la Démocratie?* Paris: Éditions Fayard.

—— (1997) *Pourrons-nous Vivre Ensemble?* Paris: Éditions Fayard.

Young, K. and Craig, L. (1997) 'Beyond white pride: identity, meaning and contradiction in the Canadian skinhead subculture', *Canadian Revue of Sociology and Anthropology*, 43(2): 175–206.

Wieviorka, M. (1991) *Espaces du Racisme*, Paris: Éditions Seuil.

—— (1992) *La France Raciste*, Paris: Éditions Seuil.

Willaime, J.-P. (2005) *Sociologie du Protestantisme*, Paris: Que Sais-je?

Postscript
Global youth and transnationalism: the next generation

Carles Feixa and Pam Nilan

As we were busy putting the finishing touches to this book on 7 July 2005, four bombs were detonated on the London transport system with high casualty rates. The British nation was shocked to find that the suspected terrorists – linked to Al Qaeda – were not outsiders, but young second-generation immigrant men born and brought up in England with no history of defined terrorist links. A week later, after a second (failed) terrorist attack in London, a young dark-skinned man in the underground was shot eight times by police as a suspected extremist Muslim terrorist, but was later revealed to be a Brazilian electrician. Such events, like the Madrid train bombings on 11 March 2004 or the 11 September 2001 attacks in the United States, defy simple explanation, but they do make our theorizing of global youth transnationalism more urgent. There is great danger of descending into platitudes when writing any kind of analysis of dire events 'under fire' of a book deadline, but we feel that in a postscript on youth transnationalism, we should comment.

We feel it is appropriate that the youthful second generation of global terrorists has been compared with cast members of the science fiction television series *Star Trek*. In this cult saga, there is a periodic replacement of old actors by new protagonists – 'the next generation' – but the script remains immutable – the eternal war between 'good' and the 'evil' – *us* and *them*. The structure of the global *jihadist* movement and the composition of its members change as quickly as inter-galactic travellers do, yet the fundamentalist logic remains. What was perhaps most striking about the London terror attacks was the youth and suburban obscurity of the perpetrators:

> it was most likely the brainchild of young, unknown members of an . . . obscure group which calls itself 'the Secret al Qaeda Organization in Europe' . . . It is likely that the newest generation of jihadists does not have direct links with Osama bin Laden . . . their indoctrination has taken place inside informal European mosques, inside private houses, in university prayer rooms; it has been conducted among groups of friends and family members.
>
> (Napoleoni 2005)

It is in this way that the profiles of the recent London terrorists are related, first: to interpretations of ethnographic material on Muslim youth (of all persuasions) and their opponents (for example white supremacist skinheads) in some of the chapters in this book, especially those by Nilan, Shahabi, Petrova, Butcher and Thomas, and Huq, and second: to our commentary below on youth transnationalism. The jihadic 'battle' by the relatively young extremists and suicide bombers against the West is inspired by a global Islamist ideology, expressed in outrages that are emphatically *transnational* despite local origins. The terrorist 'groups' are organized in intergenerational knowledge and skill networks who rely on a sense of shared counter-cultural history, and are connected through *digital* technologies not only to each other, but to a global *social movement* with a massive *youth*ful following. This is a global social movement performed by a 'diasporic youth generation', as Huq terms similarly located young actors in a very different 'social drama'.

The tragic examples above also strikingly illustrate how youth transnationalism is a double-edged sword. Behind spectacular events such as those just mentioned, there is a worrying presence, a spectre: new forms of mediated youth sociability that cross geographical and time borders to reconstruct *exclusive* global identities. One of the best known examples of hybrid youth culture is the emergence of new transnational movements of persons and symbols (Appadurai 2001). Young cosmopolitans have often been prophets of transnational connections (Hannerz 1996). If the antecedent of this book referred to young Swedish artists in Manhattan (Amit-Talai and Wulff 1995), this volume focuses on young cosmopolitans in places like Tehran and Bogotá. The prime movers of youth transnationalism are social actors in the new migration fluxes that connect different continents. In their diaspora, the Lebanese in Australia, Algerians in France and Pakistanis in Britain, for example, find their cultural roots easier to maintain in the digital era thanks to sophisticated cell phones, internet sites and satellite television networks. As youth move, so do their social networks and symbolic universes.

We may take the example of how once-local Latino gangs have become *global gangs* – an emblematic example of this phenomenon. Their cultural identities emerge in a border area where, on top of the hegemonic host culture and the traditional parent culture, various other subcultural traditions meet (Matza 1973; Brotherton and Barrios 2004) in both virtual and real time and space. In this kind of evolution, we can outline four basic matrices. The first matrix begins with the North American tradition, represented by the original *gang* model theory. Youth gangs were tightly tied to the process of urbanization in the United States, and to the process of 'magic recovery' of the original ethnic identity by second and third generations of young people whose parents or grandparents were immigrants. This was translated into the model of a territorial gang, well organized and basically composed of males – the classic object of urban ethnography (Thrasher 1926; Whyte 1943). However, in the last decade or so there has been an evolution of gangs towards more complex and less territorial forms of socializing (Hagedorn 2001; Vigil 2002).

The Latin Kings – now considered one of the major North American gang networks – appeared in Chicago at the end of World War II when different Hispanic/ Latino petty gangs amalgamated. By the 1980s the Latin Kings had evolved from criminal to political organization, and focused on the claiming of Latin identity and the condemnation of police brutality. The gang network – a complex confederation of local groups – was renamed the Almighty Latin King Nation, and a female version was added – the Latin Queens. A series of cultural productions were created – manifestos, magazines, websites. International expansion followed national diffusion – Latin America and then Europe. The original Latin Kings had become a sort of transnational franchisee with multiple 'glocal' connections (Kontos 2003; Brotherton and Barrios 2004).

The Latin Kings' presence in Spain is strongly linked to recent immigration – thousands of young men and women of Latin and South American origin who arrived in Barcelona and Madrid after the new millennium, thanks in part to family reunion legislation. They were effectively exiled from their original homes and social environments at one of the most critical times in their lives – the currently fragmented transition into adult life. On the 28 October 2003 a Colombian adolescent was murdered by a group of youngsters in Barcelona as he left his secondary school. According to a subsequent investigation, the murder was an act of revenge by members of another American-origin Latino gang – the Ñetas – who allegedly mistook the victim for a member of the Latin Kings with whom they had fought a few days before. This case 'unveiled' the phenomenon of 'Latino street gangs' to the Spanish media and awoke a wave of 'moral panic' that has not stopped yet. In a perhaps ironic twist, it has motivated the creation of new Latino gangs in Barcelona and other European cities, like Vatos Locos – inspired by 1950s Mexican-American Crazy Boys, Panteras Negras – inspired by 1960s Afro-American Black Panthers, and Maras Salvatruchas – inspired by Central-American 1990s gangs.

This example demonstrates the new forms of mediated youth sociability that cross geographical and time borders to reconstruct exclusive global identities, and how important postcolonial migration fluxes are in the phenomenon. In a moment of further global hybridity another gang has recently emerged – the Moro Kings – the North African reply to the Latin Kings. There is evidence that young Pakistanis and Filipinos are also attempting entry to some of these semi-clandestine groups, or trying to create their own globally-oriented gangs. In all this there are some interesting implications for ethnographies of youth in habitually focusing on bounded sites of research. In the global gang phenomenon, contact with local leaders of global gangs can only take place after contact has been made with the leaders and mentors at their transnational headquarters. So research in Barcelona and Genoa is only possible after connections have been established with New York and Guayaquil. 'Global' youth implies global multi-sited research.

The second matrix of global gang evolution is exemplified by the difference in scale between Latin-American gang formations: *pandillas* and *naciones*.

A *pandilla* is a social street group organized under neighbourhoods with precise geographical boundaries. *Pandillas* produce two types of behaviour on a regular basis: aggressive confrontation, and material and/or symbolic solutions. Even though their external appearance borrows some features of hip-hop culture, they create a distinctive and rich lifestyle that solves conflict through street music and dance defiance. *Naciones* represent a higher level of gang organization. In Ecuador they are a sort of brotherhood or tribe, mainly pacifist, devoted to music and graffiti. They are bigger organizational units than *pandilla*, with many hundreds of members – sometimes involved in illicit activities. *Naciones* have evolved further towards the creation of *empires*, an even more elevated level of organization, which not only provides for widespread mobilization of youth, but also may connect with organized transnational crime or mass social movements opposed to corporate globalization (Reguillo 2001; Cerbino 2004).

The third trope of youth transnationalism is represented by the subcultural lifestyles that young migrants meet when they arrive, for example, in Europe. Although these young people might have had access in their places of origin to some of these styles already internationally diffused (like punk or hip-hop), it is after arriving in Barcelona or Genoa or Manchester that they get in touch with the globally-mediated youth scene. They meet the local tradition, represented by existing neighbourhood gangs and more or less traditional youth associations. However, the European tradition is also present as a sounding board for styles born in certain cities of the old continent in the 1960s, such as skinheads. At the same time they can connect to subcultural lifestyles such as hip-hop and rastafari that, in spite of having appeared first in the Caribbean or America, have evolved as more or less underground trends in the big immigrant-receiving cities of Europe. As nomadic social actors, immigrant youth are mediated by global networks to pass (metaphorically or actually) through local gangs to global tribes. Yet on the connections and disconnections between migrant youth cultures from different origins, so far we have news from conflict interactions only, not from creative exchanges (Queirolo and Torre 2005).

As the fourth and last matrix we have the virtual tradition represented by youth identity models that circulate through the net. In this case, rather than subcultural (or cybercultural) traditions, they are new communication spaces. They are the means and the message at the same time. The internet is a place for consumption and information that spreads and amplifies new rhetorics of identity. For example, Latin American immigrant youth in Spain can access the internet through the local cybercafés which they share with adult immigrants and autochthonous young people. Here they can access web pages about the gangs, develop weblogs about their complex lives and get involved in forums. In the months following the death of Ronny Tapias in Barcelona, Latin Kings and Ñetas exchanged insults and defied each other freely in internet discussion group forums. They provided links to pages where youthful supporters could find products related to the gang, like clothes, music and other things. Some of these forums showed very high rates of participation. Significantly, all sorts of people could participate: gang members from Barcelona and Madrid, young people in Latin American cities, Spanish youths sympathetic with gangs, xenophobes, and even members of the North American chapters of those gangs who, in their typical Spanglish, were wondering why the Latin Kings and Netas were still at war in Barcelona when they had made it up in New York. The internet has effectively 'globalized' the gangs. These new 'global gangs' are not strictly territorial any more, nor do they have a compact structure. They are nomadic identity clusters that mix cultural elements from their respective countries of origin, from their host countries and from many other transnational styles that circulate through the net (Feixa and Muñoz 2004).

Virtual communities not only offer social infrastructure for global youth networks like the antiglobalization movement and nazi skinheads. The internet has generated several youth trends, from hackers to cyberkids (Himanen 2002; Holloway and Valentine 2003). Holden's chapter in this book illustrates how new technologies like internet-connected cell phones can be at the same time an instrument of isolation and an icon of communication. Some adolechnics may be pathological loners but they are also 'inventors of worlds' – later adopted by youths and adults across the globe. One important difference from previous technological change is that for the first time young people are not, by definition, in a subaltern position. As Castells (1996) points out, cyberculture itself was the creation of hippies and cyberpunks and other youth subjects active in the diffusion of the network society. And significantly for our topic here: this occurs not only in San Francisco and Tokyo, but also in Dakar and Quito – in high-tech home networks, but also in low-tech cybercafés and on rented cell phones. To be connected or disconnected is now perhaps more a question of cultural hybridity choice than of technological resources. The Next Generation could be the Net Generation (Tapscott 1998).

Another example of youth digital transnationalism was the so-called 'mobile phone revolt' that occurred in Spain after the terrorist attack on 11 March 2004 (Feixa and Porzio 2005). Most of the perpetrators of the train attack were young males from North African countries, some of them with university degrees, members of a fanatical *jihadist* terrorist cell – most of them committed suicide some days after the bombings, when discovered by police. The biographical notes published in the newspapers in the following days revealed the social and ideological origins of their victims. More than 40 per cent of the nearly 200 victims were under 30 years of age. Thirty per cent were immigrants from nearly 20 countries in four continents. Many of them were secondary school or university students (nearly 10 per cent of the dead). Others were the children of workers or immigrants with precarious jobs (mechanics, porters, maids, babysitters, etc). Ironically, many of them had taken part in the demonstrations against the war in Iraq – in which millions of people had gathered exactly one year before. People from all ages participated in the demonstrations, but young people were the most numerous and active.

Despite evidence of Al Qaeda responsibility, the Spanish government initially kept pointing to ETA (the Basque terrorist group). In the massive unrest in all Spanish cities that took place immediately after the bombing, some young people asked the following question: 'Who did it?' Messages in the succinct SMS language used by adolescents circulated very quickly. By the afternoon, hundreds of people started to gather in a peaceful but protesting mood. Most of them knew the truth, because they had watched cable television. *Indymedia* and *weblogs* also played a key role. Mobile phone companies registered a sudden rise in the number of SMS messages and internet connections during that weekend. On 14 March – general election day – the voter participation rate went up by ten percentage points and most of them were young new voters. The conservative party was beaten by the socialist opposition. In a television documentary, Manuel Castells said that it was the first 'digital' revolt in history (although actually there had been a precedent in the Philippines during mobilization against the former president). Nevertheless, other young people, the terrorists themselves, also used those same digital networks to be in contact, and to prepare the attacks. The bombs were activated by mobile phones. So the last word on 'Global Youth?' – for the best and for the worst.

In *Star Trek* there is a room in the starship *Enterprise* called Holosection, where crew members play virtual reality games based on holograms that reproduce scenes of past or imaginary spaces and times. In some episodes they threaten to become real. Some members of the next generation of global youth cultures will be touched by 'heaven' holosections that become real 'hell'(s) in the minds of a second generation of *jihadists*. Nevertheless, this book reminds us that there are other holosections of young nomads of the present, like the British *bhangra* and French rap fans who build their diasporic memories through music, the French Canadian Games participants speaking franglais, the Australian *ingenious* migrants in between two cultures, the Japanese adolechnic who invents social worlds through *keitai*, the Islamist Indonesian *anak baru gede* who manage a balance between tradition and modernity, the Iranian post-revolution *rap-iha* and *hevi-ha* who live out their subcultures in a time of re-Islamization, the Colombian *raperos* who believe that music is the connection, the Mexican and Catalan punks who express crisis through safety pins, the Senegalese bboy who becomes the spokesman of his generation, and the French skinheads who consider themselves modern *sans-culottes*.

All these young people in the five continents are inventing new 'holosections' that connect their transnational plural worlds to renewed hybrid cultures. They are the hybrid cultures of the next generation.

Post-Postscript

In November 2005, before correcting the final proofs of this book, two further events involving youth protagonism and global implications took place. In

Paris, there was extensive rioting by second- and third-generation migrant youth in the suburbs. This spread through France and Belgium, shocking the masses and outraging political institutions. We note that despite some media coverage, what those young people had in common was not religion but rap. Conversely, at the same time in Barcelona, during the presentation of Feixa's collaborative research about Latin American youth migrants in Spain, representatives of the two major gangs mentioned above – Latin Kings and Ñetas – made a public appearance in hip-hop style. In front of a surprised audience, they proclaimed their condemnation of violence, explained their aspirations as young migrants and asserted their will to make legal associations. In fact this process is now transpiring, and positively affecting the situation of those groups in cities like Madrid, New York, Quito and Genoa. We conclude that youth cultures have the potential to lead the way in thinking about global conflicts and strategies for resolving them.

Bibliography

Amit-Talai, V. and Wulff, H. (eds) (1995) *Youth Cultures: a cross-cultural perspective*, London: Routledge.
Appadurai, A. (ed.) (2001) *Globalization*, Durham and London: Duke University Press.
Brotherton, D. and Barrios, L. (2004) *The Almighty Latin King and Queen Nation*, New York: Columbia University Press.
Castells, M. (1996) *The Rise of the Network Society, The Information Age: economy, society and culture*, vol. 1, Oxford: Blackwell.
Cerbino, M. (2004) *Pandillas Juveniles: cultura y conficto de la calle*, Quito: Abya-Yala.
Feixa, C. and Muñoz, G. (2004) 'Reyes Latinos? Pistas para Superar los Estereotipos', *El País*, 12 December. Online. Available: <www.elpais.es> (accessed 15 July 2005).
—— and Porzio, L. (2005) 'Golfos, pijos, fiesteros: studies on youth cultures in Spain 1960–2004', *Young* 13(1): 89–113.
Hagedorn, J.M. (2001) 'Globalization, gangs and collaborative research', in M.W. Klein, H.-J. Kerner, C.L. Maxson and E. Weitekamp (eds) *The Eurogang Paradox: street gangs and youth groups in the U.S. and Europe*, London: Kluwer.
Hannerz, U. (1996) *Transnational Connections*, London: Routledge.
Himanen, P. (2002) *The Hacker Ethic and the Spirit of the Information Age*, Berkeley, CA: University of California Press.
Holloway, S.L. and Valentine, G. (2003) *Cyberkids: children in the information age*, London: Routledge.
Kontos, L. (2003) 'Between criminal and political deviance: a sociological analysis of the New York chapter of the Almighty Latin King and Queen Nation', in D. Muggleton and R. Weinzierl (eds) *The Post-subcultures Reader*, London: Berg.
Matza, D. (1973) 'Subterranean traditions of youth', in H. Silverstein (ed.) *The Sociology of Youth: evolution and revolution*, New York: Macmillan.
Napoleoni. L. (2005) 'The Next Generation', *BuzzFlash*, 15 July. Online. Available: <www.buzzflash.com/contributors/05/07/con05232.html> (accessed 20 July 2005).

Queirolo, L. and Torre, A. (eds) (2005) *Il Fantasma delle Bande: Giovani dall'America Latina a Genova*, Genova: Fratelli Frilli Editore.

Reguillo, R. (2001) *Emergencia de Culturas Juveniles*, Buenos Aires: Norma.

Tapscott, D. (1998) *Growing Up Digital: the rise of the net generation*, New York, McGraw-Hill.

Thrasher, F.M. (1926) *The Gang: a study of 1313 gangs in Chicago*, Chicago, IL: University of Chicago Press.

Vigil, J.D. (2002) *A Rainbow of Gangs: street cultures in the mega-city*, Austin, TX: University of Texas Press.

Whyte, W. (1943) *Street Corner Society*, Chicago, IL: University of Chicago Press.

Index

Acadia 33, 38, 40–1, 46–8
Acadian Games 32, 35–6, 40–1, 42, 45, 46–8, 50
actionalism 170; *see also under* Touraine's theories
activism 9, 153, 162, 170, 201; *see also* radical youth
adaptive strategies 66–8
ADF 24, 27
adolechnics 4, 72–88, 209, 210
aesthetics 131–2, 135, 147, 149, 152, 161, 177, 191, 195
Alberta 33, 34, 38, 43–6, 48–9
Alberta Francophone Games 32, 35–6, 43–6, 48–9
alcohol 94, 158, 193
Alianza 143–4
Allain, G. 35
Alliance Ethnik 18
amae 88
ancestry 20, 34, 38–41, 44, 50
anti-Semitism 191, 196, 201
Arian 116
art 130; life as 130, 147
Asian youth 15, 206; *see also* British Asian underground
assimilation 14, 19, 35, 53; crisis of 35; *see also* integration
Australia 53–69, 206
Australianness 54, 55, 57, 59–60, 68, 69
avant-garde 8, 18, 22
Awadi 175, 180

banlieues 18, 20–2, 25
Bannerji, H. 2
basiji 116, 117–18, 122, 126, 127
Bauman, Zygmunt 27, 188
Bazin, H. 18

bboys 167–83, 210
Behnia, B. 118–19
belonging 56–7, 59–66, 68
Bhabha, Homi, K. 1, 54, 93, 108
bhangra 17, 19, 21, 25, 69, 210; *see also* British Asian underground
bilingualism 37–40
Birmingham Centre for Contemporary Cultural Studies (CCCS) 9, 15, 24, 28
Björk 21
body, the 58, 94
Bourdieu, Pierre 2, 6, 92
Bowie, David 21
Brake, M. 15
breakdance 18, 132–3, 172
bricolage 111, 118, 120, 123–5, 127
British Asian underground 14–29
Britpop 15
Butler, Judith 33

caló 156, 157
Canada 32–51
cars 56, 59
cartels 168, 177
cartoons 98–9
Castells, Manuel 6, 84, 209, 210
Cathus, O. 21
cell phones *see* mobile phones
Chao, Manu 153
chavos banda 149, 157–64
chavos fresa 157
check down 168, 176
Chisholm, Lynne 6
Christianity 187, 201
class 3, 5, 28, 114, 117, 150, 154, 157, 160, 175, 188, 189–90, 198, 201; theory 15
clothes *see* fashion
clubcultures 6

214 Index

Colombia 130–48, 206, 210
commitment 168, 179–81
communication 59, 77–8, 208; forms 79; theory 79–82; types 79–80; *see also* technology
conformists 114, 157
consumerism 8–9, 105, 118, 121, 147, 201
consumption 84, 87, 92–4, 101, 103; cultural, 1, 14, 118; moment 124
conventional youth 114
cool-hunters 3, 8
cosmetics 121; *halal* 92, 93, 104
cosmopolitan youth 111, 114–117, 120–2, 126, 206
Costa, P.-O. 152
creativity 1, 9, 130–3, 147, 162, 178, 182, 199; *see also* motor forces of creation
creolization 1, 66, 150
cultural entrepreneurs 123
culture industries 8, 14, 93, 121, 124, 125, 163
cybercultures 6, 59, 68, 208, 209

Dakar 167, 169, 172, 173–6, 178
dance 21, 153, 175, 208; *see also* breakdance
de Certeau, Michel 119
Desarme 141–2
diasporic experience 16, 53, 206, 210
difference 1, 2, 53, 63, 64, 134, 167, 200; ethnic 14
Dimitriadis, G. 91
discourse 32, 33–5, 40–5, 50, 76, 87
DJ Maryam 116
DJs 132–3, 172
'do it yourself' (DIY) 132, 133, 137, 138, 141, 188
Doi, T. 88
double consciousness 16, 29
downloading 16, 73, 76, 77, 80, 82
Driscoll, C. 104
drugs 96, 97, 115, 139, 153, 154, 158, 160, 162, 193

E17 21
Ecuador 208
email 59, 73, 76–7, 78, 177
ENDA (Environmental Development Action in the Third World) 169–70
ethnic minorities 54; second generation 14–29, 55–69, 206
ethnicity 34, 41, 57, 58, 68–9, 120, 150, 160, 190

exclusion 64, 69, 188, 191, 192, 193
exteriorization 82

family 56, 60–2, 68, 200
fanzines 16, 22, 132, 157, 159, 160, 162, 187
fascism 191, 192, 195
fashion 9, 14, 55, 58–9, 67, 68, 92, 94, 96, 98, 100, 103, 107, 116, 118, 123, 150, 157, 160, 168, 176, 209
feminism 118, 160
filtering 91, 101–2, 107
fly-girls 167
folklore 40, 44
food 44, 55, 62, 63, 64, 68, 69
football 115–16, 163, 192, 197
Foucault, Michel 33, 130–1
fragmentation: social 88, 188
France 14–29, 172, 175, 186–202, 206, 210
Franco-Ontarian Games 32, 36, 41–3, 45, 49–50
francophoneness 32–51; discursive construction of 33–5
Frankfurt School 118
French Canadian 33, 34, 38, 41, 43–4, 46, 48, 50
French hip-hop 14–29
Friedman, J. 56
friends 56, 63, 66–7, 68–9
Frith, Simon 14
Front Nationale 20, 22–3, 195
Fun-Da-Mental 17, 23

games 32, 35–7, 40–51, 210
gangs 8, 54, 62, 149–50, 163–4, 175, 176, 193–4, 206–9; global 206, 207, 209; *see also chavos banda; naciones; pachucos; pandillas; tribus urbanas*
García Canclini, Néstor 1–2, 124
gay youth 15
gender 5, 29, 62, 66, 68, 75, 113, 127, 150, 160, 194
Gérin-Lajoie D. 37
German Turkish rap 28
Gil Calvo, Enrique 152
Gilroy, Paul 16
Giroux, H. 93
global: definition of 3; -local 87; micro 86, 87–8; macro 86–7
globalization 1, 2, 3, 7, 8, 15, 16, 27, 28, 29, 86, 94, 123–4, 125, 168, 180, 187–90, 194, 199, 200, 208; anti- 153, 209; *see also* transnationalism

golfos 151, 154
graffiti 2, 14, 18, 21, 22, 132–3, 160, 172–3, 208
Gramsci, Antonio 9
Grossberg, L. 128
Guattari, Félix 131–2, 147
Guerra, C. 57

habitus 2, 3, 8; reflexive 2–3, 92–3, 101
hacktivists 10
hair 58, 96, 104, 114, 116
halal products 92, 93, 104, 105
Hall, Stuart 2, 15
Hannerz, Ulf 124, 126
hardcore 130, 135, 138, 142, 144–5, 147, 162
Harvey, David 188
heavy metal 115, 116, 123, 124, 135, 138, 147, 162
Hebdige, Dick 15, 150
hegemony 2, 9, 122
hejab 115, 117, 119, 120; *bad-* 113, 117, 118
heritage: cultural 57, 63, 68–9
Hewitt, R. 26
hijab 69
hip-hop 4, 21, 64, 121, 130, 132–3, 135, 143, 144, 147, 208; *see also* French hip-hop, rap, Senegalese hip-hop
hippies 152, 156, 157, 190, 198, 209; neo-153, 154; *see also jipis*
historicity 168
Holden, Todd Joseph Miles 209
holosections 210
homogenesis: struggle against 134
humour 25
Huq, Rupa 206
Hutnyk, J. 24–5
hybridity: asymmetrical 46–50; complex 91–5; definition of 1–2; francophone 32–51; of musical forms 20–1, 25, 26, 28, 29, 124

IAM 18, 24, 25
ideal types 113
identity 2, 134; adscriptions 134; collective 198–9, 200; construction of 1, 6–9, 29, 33, 36, 56–8, 68, 76–7, 84–5, 91, 92, 95, 103, 108, 114, 125, 172, 176, 189–94; crisis 65; discourses 4, 33–5, 76, 93; display 68; ethnic 14, 24; frames 85, 177, 182; global 206, 207; markers 108, 116; mediated 84–6; multi-level 188–94; national 20, 28, 200; politics 6; rhetorics of 208
imagined communities 54
immigration 15, 17, 19, 23, 28, 34, 135, 151, 156, 157, 160, 165, 186, 191, 193–4, 195, 201, 207, 208
'in-betweenness' 53, 56, 59, 63–6, 68
individualization 7, 84; *see also* interiority
Indonesia 91–108
ingenuity 53, 68–9, 210
institutionalization 46, 48–9
integration 14, 19, 28, 53, 190, 193
interiority 82
internet 16, 80, 82, 94, 114, 115, 118, 126, 141, 153, 158, 199, 206, 208–10; *see also* websites
IRA (Ideas de Revolución Adolescente) 140
Iran 111–27, 164, 206, 210
Islam 92–108, 125, 127, 176, 206, 209, 210
Islamization 112–13, 114, 117–18, 125, 210
Italian rap 28
Ito, Y. 78, 88

Japan 72–88
Jefferson, T. 15
jilbab 104, 107
jipis 151, 154
Johansson, T. 122
Jones, S. 15

Kalra, V. 26
Kaur, R. 26
keitai see mobile phones

La Pestilencia 138
Lagree, J.-C. 198
language 55, 57, 59, 61, 64, 67, 68, 157, 169, 176–7, 179–80, 187; *see also* francophoneness; slang
Lapassade, G. 18
Latin Kings 207
Leichty, M. 95
lifestyles 6, 7, 67, 92, 95, 103, 111, 113–18, 199
linguistic: heritage 39, 50; practice 26
Lô, M.E. 169
local, the 2, 3, 86–7, 190; cultures 1, 67, 92, 108; micro- 88
localism 111, 114, 123
locality 56, 68
London 39; bombings 205–6

Los Podridos 139–40
Lull, J. 124

McDonaldization 8, 111
McLuhan, Marshall 83
Maclure, R. 176
McRobbie, Angela 6
McVeigh, B. 82
Madrid: bombings 205
Maffesoli, Michel 6, 9, 149–50, 152, 164
magazines 207; teen 91, 104–7
Mali 170
marketing 201; global 93, 133
Marx, Karl 7
Marxism 16
masculinity 194, 198
mass culture reading 111, 118, 122
Mbodj, Mamadou 169, 175
MC Solaar 18, 19, 25, 27
MC-ing 171–2, 179
media 54, 62, 93–4, 95, 103, 106–7, 114, 124, 126, 130, 144, 152, 158; consumption 55, 68; skinheads and broadcast 196–8
Medina, G. 140–1
megacities 8
Menéndez, E. 152
Merton, Robert 114
Mexico 149, 155–64, 210
Miegel, F. 122
migrants 53, 55, 65, 67, 69, 206; stereotyping of 54–5; *see also* immigration
Miller, Henry 142
Ministère AMER 18, 21
Moaveni, A. 120
mobile phones 58, 59, 68, 72–88, 92, 94, 103, 206, 209, 210; history of 73; personalizing 75–7; routinizing 77–8; *see also* SMS
modernity 91–3, 101–3, 107, 113, 124, 126–7, 168, 187, 194
modernization 112–13, 151, 168
Mohammadi, A. 111, 120, 124
Monica, Agnes 100
Morley, D. 83
motor forces of creation 132–3
Muggleton, David 9
multiculturalism 14, 19–20, 28, 34, 41, 53, 54, 55, 69, 173, 191, 193, 201
music 2, 8, 14, 44, 55, 56, 59, 67, 68, 69, 94, 95, 98, 100–1, 104, 113, 115–16, 124, 130–48, 134–7, 147, 155, 157, 160, 162, 182, 198, 199, 208, 209, 210; free information and 142–7; innovation in 15–16; popular 4, 14–29, 103, 116; *see also* hardcore; heavy metal; hip-hop; *nasyid*; punk; rap; techno music
Muslim youth culture 91–108
Muslimah 91, 104–7
mutual support 81
myth 34, 54, 152, 160, 189–90, 191, 195, 201–2

naciones 207
Nagamine, Y. 83
nasyid 92, 93, 104–5, 107
national policies 14, 19, 26, 28
Nazism 191, 192, 195, 209
neo-tribes 6, 149, 152
networking 6, 59, 82–4, 149, 209
New York Dolls, the 137
Nique Ta Mère (NTM) 18, 19, 22–3
nomination groups 116

official culture 111, 113–15, 125, 126, 127
Okabe, D. 80
Ontario 33, 34, 38, 41–3, 49–50
otherness 68, 114
Owen, C. 52

pachucos 156–7
pandillas 207
Papastergiadis, N. 34–5
parallel worlds 91, 103–7
Paris 9, 18, 211
parties 105–6, 115–16
Paz, Octavio 156
pedagogy: cultural, 93
Peralva, A. 193, 197
Pérez, J.-M. 152
performance 1, 2, 32, 33, 35, 44, 50, 62, 68
Phoenix, A. 39
Pieterse, N. 124
plural worlds 2–3, 210
Polikarpa y sus Viciosas 139, 142
politicized readings 111, 118–22
Pop Idol competitions 96, 98
Pop, Iggy 136–7
popular culture 56–9, 68, 119, 126; global trends of 91, 94, 107–8, 126
population size 46, 48, 49
posses 168, 170–3, 175, 176, 177–81
post-colonial: culture 14, 18–20, 26, 207; theory 3, 16

Postman, Neil 118
postmodern 1–2, 25, 66, 88, 101, 125, 155, 161, 189–90, 191, 199; anti- 201; bricolage 111, 118, 120, 123–5, 127; readings 111
Poulet, G. 20
power 134, 163–4; social 46, 50; structures 2, 9, 69
production moment 124
Public Enemy 4, 143
Punjabi MC 21, 25
punk 4, 114–20, 123, 124, 130, 132, 135–42, 144–7, 149–52, 155, 157, 159–64, 192, 194, 198, 202, 210; lyrics 139–42; *mierdas* 159

racism 23–6, 121, 186, 188–92, 194–6, 202; infra- 193
radical youth 117–18; *see also basiji*
Raghav 25
rap 14, 18, 28, 114, 115, 116, 121, 123, 124, 132–3, 142–3, 168, 169, 171–3, 175, 177, 179, 210; *see also* hip-hop
raves 153
record companies 18–19, 27, 132
reflexivity 3, 4, 7, 8, 57, 91, 92, 93, 102, 107, 108
religion 9, 66, 68, 91, 92, 93, 96, 102–3, 107–8, 124, 187, 191, 195; *see also* Christianity; Islam
resistance 9–10
Rich, Rishi 25
risk 6–7, 188
ritual exchanges 80–81
Ritzer, G. 8
Robins, K. 83
Rojek, C. 16
role-playing games (RPG) 74, 76
Rosengren, K. 114
Russia 164

Sagoo, Bally 25
Sawhney, Nitin 17
scenes 6
Scott, J. 118, 119
Sean, Jay 25
selection 91, 101–2, 107, 120
self-styling 130–1, 147
Senegalese hip-hop 167–83, 210
sex 93–4, 97, 105, 107
Sex Pistols, the 138
sexuality 80, 107
Sharma, A. 24–5
Sharma, S. 24–5

Sheila on 7 100
shopping 58, 94, 104–5
sinetron see soap operas
Singh, Talvin 18–19, 20, 25
singularization 135–6
skinheads 130, 135, 138, 144–5, 153, 164, 206, 208, 209; Christian 187; in France 186–202, 210; red 189, 191, 200
slang 14, 106, 116, 150, 157, 162
Slank 100
SMS 59, 98, 153, 177, 210
soap operas 98–9, 105
social construction 1, 189–94
social movements 1, 168, 170, 171–3, 176, 179–83, 206
socialization 80, 86, 114, 125
Sotelo, M. 184
space 57, 59, 64, 68, 83–4, 105; non- 83–4, 86, 88; public 67, 115, 160, 163; third 93, 108; virtual 206, 210
Spain 149, 151–5, 162–4, 205, 207, 208, 209–10
sport 98; *see also* games
Sreberny-Mohammadi, A. 111, 120, 124
style: search for one's own 132–3
subaltern 1–3, 209
subcultures 5, 8–9, 15, 24, 57, 58, 87–8, 111–27, 150, 153, 167, 168, 189, 208; post- 6
subjectivity 188; construction of 4, 6–7, 9, 132–3, 134, 147, 148; multiple 133; nomadic 10; *see also* identity
surveillance 92, 107, 108
Sweetman, P. 2–3, 92
Syal, Meera 19
Sydney; western 54–69
symbolism 150, 153, 192, 206
syncretism 1, 111, 153, 160, 191, 195–6
Sztompka, P. 123

techno music 116, 153
technology 16, 28, 55, 59, 67–8, 72–88, 92, 97, 101, 103, 114, 124, 165, 169, 206, 209–10; *see also* internet; mobile phones
television 97–9, 114; satellite 114–18, 124–5, 126, 206
terrorism 92, 153, 205–6, 209–10
Toop, D. 18
Touraine, Alain 6, 168, 186; theories 6, 13, 168, 185, 186, 188, 189, 204
tradition 61, 92, 102–3, 107, 125, 167, 169, 189, 190, 199; virtual 208

traditional cultures 14, 67, 108, 176, 177; post- 92
transactions: cultural 2
transition 7
translating 57
transnationalism 2, 6, 16, 29, 56–7, 149, 150, 158, 163–4, 188, 205–10
tribes 6, 149–50, 164; global 150, 164, 208; *see also* neo-tribes; *tribus urbanas*
tribus urbanas 149, 152–5, 158, 161–4
Tropea, F. 152
typologies 113–18

underground 22, 115, 126, 137, 157, 157; *see also* British Asian underground
United Kingdom 14–29, 120, 121, 206
United States of America 97, 98, 120, 121, 172, 175, 176
Université du Hip Hop 21–2

Vasta, E. 62
veiling 119

Velvet Underground, the 136
violence 15, 54, 122, 141, 156, 162, 186, 188, 192–8, 199, 200, 202
virtual cultures 2, 208–9
visual cultures 2

Wallerstein, Immanuel 4
Weber, Max 113
websites 104–5, 187, 207
western culture: Muslim youth and 97–101, 107
westernization 112, 118, 124
White, R. 57
Whyte, William Foote 150
Wieviorka, M. 186
Willis, Paul 56, 86
Windahl, S. 114
'wogs' 56, 58, 59, 64
women 15
Wulff, Helena 61

youth: challenging understandings of 134–5; definition of 1

eBooks – at www.eBookstore.tandf.co.uk

A library at your fingertips!

eBooks are electronic versions of printed books. You can store them on your PC/laptop or browse them online.

They have advantages for anyone needing rapid access to a wide variety of published, copyright information.

eBooks can help your research by enabling you to bookmark chapters, annotate text and use instant searches to find specific words or phrases. Several eBook files would fit on even a small laptop or PDA.

NEW: Save money by eSubscribing: cheap, online access to any eBook for as long as you need it.

Annual subscription packages

We now offer special low-cost bulk subscriptions to packages of eBooks in certain subject areas. These are available to libraries or to individuals.

For more information please contact webmaster.ebooks@tandf.co.uk

We're continually developing the eBook concept, so keep up to date by visiting the website.

www.eBookstore.tandf.co.uk